Explore
WILDERNESS
AUSTRALIA

NEIL HERMES

NEW HOLLAND

First published in 1997 by
New Holland (Publishers) Ltd
London • Cape Town • Sydney • Singapore

3/2 Aquatic Drive
Frenchs Forest, NSW 2086
Australia

80 McKenzie Street
Cape Town 8001
South Africa

24 Nutford Place
London W1H 6DQ
United Kingdom

Every effort has been made by the Publisher to ensure that telephone numbers are correct at the time of publishing.

ISBN 1 86436 224 3

Publishing manager: Mariëlle Renssen
Commissioning editor: Averill Chase
Editors: Joanne Holliman, Anouska Good
Designer: Laurence Lemmon-Warde
DTP cartographer: John Loubser
Picture researchers: Bronwyn Rennex, Karen Adler

Reproduction by cmyk prepress
Printed and bound in Singapore by Tien Wah Press (Pte) Ltd

TITLE PAGE *Twisted, exhausted trees stand firm in Australia's inland wilderness.*
THIS PAGE *Plum Pudding Island, looking like its namesake, lies just offshore from Hamilton Island.*

PHOTOGRAPHIC CREDITS

Copyright © in photographs **NHIL** (Shaen Adey) with the exception of the following:
Kelvin Aitken: pp48, 66; **John P Cooper**/Nature Focus: p112; **Tom & Pam Gardner**/Nature Focus: pp40, 72,
144, 170; **Robert Garvey**/Terra Australis PhotoAgency: p115; with compliments of **Pete Griffiths** (Peregrine Tours): pp37, 187;
C Andrew Henley/Nature Focus: p138; **Neil Hermes:** pp10, 15, 16 (top), 21 (bottom), 60, 129, 149, 156; **Geoff Higgins:** pp11 (left & right),
13 (bottom), 16 (bottom), 32, 33, 35, 36, 41, 43, 54, 79, 114, 135, 140, 165 (bottom), 172; **Wayne Lawler**/ECOPIX: pp55, 56, 57;
NHIL: pp12, 13 (top), 14, 18, 25 (bottom), 47, 52, 91, 94, 106, 111, 126 (right), 162, 163, 169, 173, 174, 176, 177 (top), 178, 185, 186;
NHIL (Bruce Elder): p81; **NHIL** (Vicki Hastrich): p34; **NHIL** (Anthony Johnson): pp2–3, 45, 64, 68 (left), 78, 90, 157, 182;
NHIL (Nick Rains): pp7, 8, 9; with compliments of **NSW National Parks and Wildlife Services**: p23; **Frank Park**/Nature Focus: p130;
Lynn Pedler/Nature Focus: p164; **R L Smith**/Nature Focus: p124; **Dave Watts**/Nature Focus: p184; **Flavio Zampieri**: p21 (top).

NHIL = New Holland Image Library

CONTENTS

INTRODUCTION

Australia is a vast country, and discovering its many diverse wilderness regions should entail not only a physical journey but also a journey of understanding. This book has been written so that it may contribute to a better understanding of the interdependency between the complex landscapes and intertwined environments that make up this ancient continent and, thereby, help us to become better custodians of the land. This can only happen if we appreciate and interact with the precious natural heritage through which we travel.

Explore Wilderness Australia is designed to introduce you to the best wilderness areas on the continent by briefly describing many of the national parks, nature reserves and forests; all of Australia's mainland World Heritage sites are included. The information provided should enable you to easily identify the regions you wish to explore, and explains the amount of time you will need and the type of transportation necessary in order to get to and travel through the area. Opportunities for experiencing wilderness walks and canoe trips are described in many of the areas covered along with park facilities.

What is wilderness?

The concept of wilderness has traditionally focused on such characteristics as inaccessibility, remoteness, lack of habitation, and savage wildness. Many purists would exclude, by definition, any kind of human activity from an area so identified. At its most extreme, that view would make a book on visiting the wilderness quite brief!

I consider 'wilderness' to be an experience, rather than a condition of the land. The reality is that for the last 40 000 years or more no place on the continent of Australia has been excluded from human activity. Kakadu, for example, is a place where Aboriginal people still live, and it is also, for me, a stimulating wilderness. Human activities cannot, therefore, be entirely excluded from the landscape.

How to plan your trip

Throughout the book there are a number of maps to help you find your way to the wilderness regions. Each chapter contains the phone numbers of the parks discussed. At the end of the book there is an extended listing of contact numbers for travel centres, map providers, tour operators, road assistance, and accommodation. For those with limited time, taking daytrips or extended tours with any of the many excellent ecotour operators is recommended. These tours vary in the range and level of physical activities undertaken, so a trip suitable to your taste can be selected.

LEFT *While many of the original trees on Fraser Island were felled to make way for farmland, verdant forests of native candlebark, stringybark, peppermint, red box, and silver wattle have regenerated on the world's largest sand island.*

highways should only be undertaken by well-equipped groups. Basic precautions include having a reliable well-maintained vehicle, travelling in convoy, carrying extra fuel, water and food, and using the best maps available. For very remote tracks, such as the Canning Stock Route, vehicle spare parts, a winch and a Royal Flying Doctor radio are essential items of equipment. Before travelling in this type of area seek advice from the relevant state automobile club. In remote locations always seek local advice from police, rangers or roadhouses.

Camping

Most national parks have camp sites for car-based campers. Basic facilities generally include pit toilets, picnic tables, fireplaces and shelter sheds. Some camp sites are more comprehensively equipped. There is usually a fee for camping and sometimes advance booking or advance payment is required. If in doubt, it is wise to ring ahead. Fees are mostly paid at the park visitor centre. Camping for wilderness walkers is usually permitted except in small, urban or particularly sensitive parks. Sometimes permits are required. It is always best to notify rangers before setting out on cross-country treks.

Local tour operators know the best spots and deal with the logistics of what routes to take and which equipment to bring. The best ecotour operators have excellent, accurate local knowledge and are experts at helping visitors gain the most enjoyment and insight from any trip.

For those with more time, further information about each area you visit is widely available. The state capitals provide a variety of information centres for their region. At least half a day could usefully be spent visiting the offices of the state's tourism authority, national parks service, automobile association and forestry service. In addition most capital cities have at least one good map shop.

Once you are on your travels, regional visitor centres are extremely useful places for extra information, particularly details on local organised tours. A local phone call may be all that is needed to get the best and latest information. Most Australian national parks have a ranger station or visitor centre and a brief stop for up-to-date local details about roads, camping grounds, availability of water, etc., should become part of your routine.

Remote area travel

Travelling by vehicle in the well-populated areas of Australia's east coast and south-west corner should present no logistical problems. However, much of the north and inland is remote and any travel off the main sealed

Precautions

For visitors from the northern hemisphere one of the most serious threats when exploring remote locations is heat stress. International visitors from cold climates find the sudden onslaught of the Australian heat too overwhelming. Hats and appropriate clothing to protect you from the sun will help maintain body fluids.

There are many animals on the continent that can inflict bites and stings. Some injuries can be fatal. In northern Australia take particular care to avoid saltwater crocodiles which are much more aggressive than their freshwater cousins. With bans imposed in the 1970s on hunting these animals, they are now spreading further south and further inland. Take local advice and err towards caution.

There are several species of venomous snake in Australia, but bites are generally rare and fatalities are even more unlikely if correct treatment is received promptly. When walking in the bush always wear boots and long trousers. Avoid insect bites by using repellents and wearing clothes that cover the limbs.

One last word

The enormity of the Australian continent makes travelling between places time-consuming. To fully appreciate all that is on offer, plan your trip wisely and allow yourself plenty of time to enjoy each location.

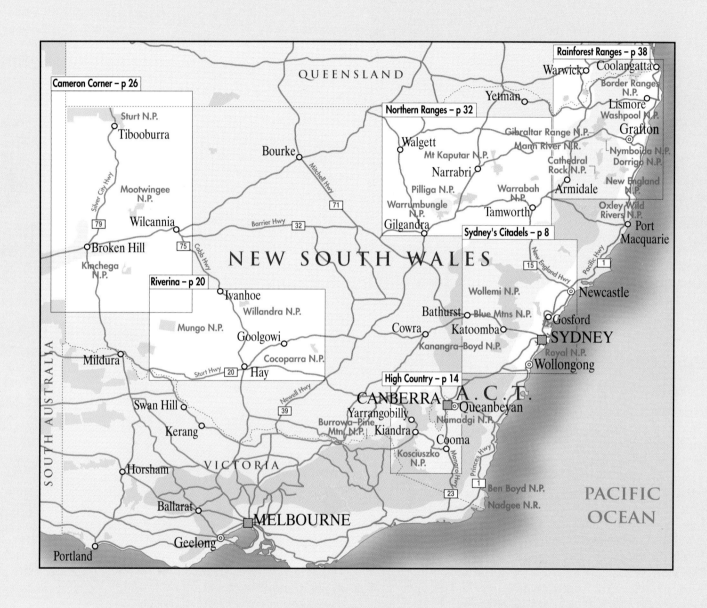

Cameron Corner – p 26

Rainforest Ranges – p 38

Northern Ranges – p 32

Sydney's Citadels – p 8

Riverina – p 20

High Country – p 14

QUEENSLAND

NEW SOUTH WALES

SOUTH AUSTRALIA

VICTORIA

A.C.T.

PACIFIC OCEAN

Warwick
Coolangatta
Border Ranges N.P.
Yetman
Lismore
Washpool N.P.
Grafton
Sturt N.P.
Tibooburra
Walgett
Gibraltar Range N.P.
Mann River N.R.
Nymboida N.P.
Dorrigo N.P.
Bourke
Mt Kaputar N.P.
Narrabri
Cathedral Rock N.P.
New England N.P.
Mootwingee N.P.
Pilliga N.P.
Warrabah N.P.
Armidale
Wilcannia
Warrumbungle N.P.
Tamworth
Oxley Wild Rivers N.P.
Broken Hill
Gilgandra
Port Macquarie
Kinchega N.P.
Ivanhoe
Wollemi N.P.
Newcastle
Willandra N.P.
Bathurst
Blue Mtns N.P.
Gosford
Mungo N.P.
Cowra
Katoomba
SYDNEY
Goolgowi
Kanangra-Boyd N.P.
Royal N.P.
Mildura
Cocoparra N.P.
Wollongong
Hay
CANBERRA
Queanbeyan
Swan Hill
Yarrangobilly
Namadgi N.P.
Burrowa–Pine Mtn. N.P.
Kiandra
Kerang
Cooma
Kosciuszko N.P.
Horsham
Ben Boyd N.P.
Ballarat
Nadgee N.R.
MELBOURNE
Geelong
Portland

Silver City Hwy
Barrier Hwy
Cobb Hwy
Sturt Hwy
Newell Hwy
Mitchell Hwy
New England Hwy
Pacific Hwy
Princes Hwy
Monaro Hwy

79
75
32
71
20
39
15
1
23
1

New South Wales and Australian Capital Territory

SYDNEY'S CITADELS

Blue Mountains • Wollemi •

Kanangra Boyd

A vast tract of bushland in the form of a series of national parks surrounds Sydney. The best way to explore these regions is on foot but in some areas water access and small aircraft provide an exciting alternative. The national parks offer well-marked walking trails and, to make the most of what can be seen and explored, overnight trips are recommended. A number of parks have camping facilities, and nearby towns, particularly in the Blue Mountains, have small, cosy guesthouses.

Travel Tips

The nearest airport to these regions is Sydney's Mascot Airport. As all of the areas are close to Sydney, Australia's largest metropolis, it is perhaps wise to avoid the peak travel periods of school holidays and long weekends. There are many organised bus and safari tours heading to the mountains, regular train access and well-serviced roads – the Pacific and New England highways head north from the city, the Hume and Princes south, and the Great Western west – so a four-wheel-drive vehicle is not necessary. Take care while driving since some of the roads become narrow and winding as they make their way up the sandstone plateau. Also take care in the parks after heavy rains, which can make the walking tracks around the narrow gorges slippery and dangerous.

PREVIOUS PAGE *Near Blackheath in the Blue Mountains, the Valley of the Waters Creek creates cascades that fall off the escarpment lined with blackash and peppermint into the Jamison Valley.*

ABOVE *The majestic sandstone towers of the Three Sisters rise like sentinels from the Jamison Valley and can be best seen near Katoomba.*

OPPOSITE *Over millions of years the Grose River has carved through sandstone and shale to create the towering vertical cliffs of the wide and deep Grose Valley.*

BLUE MOUNTAINS NATIONAL PARK

Although one of the most visited national parks in the country, this need not be a deterrent for those looking for a true wilderness experience. The main attractions, such as the lookouts at Grose Valley and Echo Point, where the Three Sisters dominate the landscape, do draw many thousands of visitors each year, but there are also many large, rarely frequented areas accessible on foot. The park is so large that once away from the popular sights, you could almost be on your own.

The sheer sandstone canyons and cliffs of the Blue Mountains plateau were a huge barrier to early European settlers. The crossing was made possible in 1813 by the explorers immortalised in the town names of Blaxland, Wentworth and Lawson; today the road and railway line follow the very narrow corridor discovered by these entrepid men with the help of Aboriginal guides.

Rich in flora and fauna

Despite the shallow and often infertile soil that covers the plateau, gum forests and heathlands are rich in plants – pockets of rainforest can even be found. The floral highlights are the spring-flowering heathlands where a rich profusion of banksias, grevilleas and waratahs, so characteristic of the Australian bush, flourish. The region is also rich in wildlife but, other than birds, most animals are either nocturnal, cryptic or both, and consequently difficult to observe. Honeyeaters, lorikeets and whistlers are abundant and noisy residents.

Walking trails

The Blue Mountains form part of the Great Dividing Range which runs down the east coast of Australia. When planning a visit you will find it helpful to consider the park in three separate sections: the Nepean, the Three Sisters, and the Grose Valley. Walking tracks within these regions are clearly marked and maps are available from the visitor centres.

The Nepean, south of Glenbrook, contains spectacular scenery, gorges, swimming holes, and easy walking trails. This area is close to Sydney so it can be very busy, especially on weekends. Many tracks are from 1 to 6km, and the Red Hand Cave trail is an ideal walk. A fire trail leads to the Oaks picnic area and the Nepean Lookout. Camping is permitted at Euroka Clearing but advance booking is essential.

The famous and very popular Three Sisters rise out of the Jamison Valley near Katoomba. The best views are from Echo Point where there are also great wilderness walking areas with well-marked trails of 1 to 10km. The return walk to the Ruined Castle is a good way to sample the highlights of this sandstone landscape.

The beauty and majesty of Grose Valley has impressed many, including Charles Darwin who visited the region in 1836. Among the valley's highlights are Perrys Lookdown and Govetts Leap. To truly appreciate the gorges, the walk to Blue Gum Forest is an enjoyable round trip from Blackheath, while the Grand Canyon walk from Evans Lookout is about 5km long and takes about three hours to complete. Overnight camping is permissible at many spots, including Acacia Flat and Burra Korain Flat in Grose Valley, and at Perrys Lookout on the plateau.

Adventurous pursuits

Rock climbing and canyoning are popular with the more adventurous outdoor enthusiasts. Some of the climbs are regarded as among the best in the country. There are a number of four-wheel-drive access roads, especially from the west. Detailed, up-to-date maps and local advice on road conditions should be sought from the park authorities, automobile clubs or police. Kings Tableland Road south of Wentworth Falls will take you to some of the prime spots, while access to the far southern sections of park is from Yerranderie.

Overnight walks

For the overnight wilderness walker the park provides dozens of options, but be aware that the terrain is labyrinthine and cold wet weather can descend quickly in the mountains, so preparations need to be thorough. Before setting off consult the park staff. The best areas are the Wallengambe Wilderness north of Mount Wilson and the areas south of Lake Burragorang. Some walks connect to public transport for the return journey. Bush camping is permitted anywhere in the park away from tracks and roads, except in Grose Valley, where camping is restricted, and at Lake Burragorang, where camping is not permitted within 3km of the water's edge.

How to get there

The Blue Mountains is well serviced by train, bus and car. By car, head west along the Great Western Highway and follow the signs. For a great round trip, take the Bells Line of Road back to Sydney through the historic towns of Richmond and Windsor. There are visitor centres as well as the Blue Mountains Heritage Centre at Blackheath where maps and advice can be obtained.

Blue Mountains Heritage Centre tel: (02) 4787–8877

WOLLEMI NATIONAL PARK

Wollemi is the second-largest national park in New South Wales (Kosciuszko is the largest). Wild walks and rivers, caves, minimal facilities and a few rough four-wheel-drive tracks make this a wilderness paradise. The sandstone plateau is bisected by fast-flowing streams heading east and west, and most of the park is heavily wooded gum forest. It is incredible to think that all of this is within easy reach of Australia's largest city. Wollemi was only declared a national park in 1979.

Wilderness tracks

There is no doubt that the best way to explore Wollemi is on foot or by canoe. It is possible to spend a week traversing the park on one remote walk, like the 30- to 40-km hikes across the park from Glen Davis to Putty taking in sections of the Wollemi Range, or from Newnes to Colo Heights exploring parts of the Colo River Gorge. Access to these longer walks is from the Bells Line of Road in the south, which has a number of small townships in handy spots, such as Mount Wilson and Kurrajong Heights. In the east Colo Heights, Putty and Bulga have track starting-points, and in the north the best track starts are at the end of Martindale Road south of Denman or from Baerami Creek Road.

River sports

The west-flowing Cudgegong River at Olinda, east of Rylstone, is an excellent canoeing location. Stretches of the stream above Kandos Weir are suitable for swimming

WARATAH

The shallow and infertile soil of the sandstone plateaux of the south-east is where one of the country's most exquisite flowering plant, the waratah, is found. It is a small bush, which grows up to 4m high, and its blooms are the nation's best-known native flower; during the spring and summer the bushes are adorned with dense, giant heads of blood-red flowers.

The name waratah is derived from the Aboriginal word for the plant, *warata*. The genus scientific name, *Telopea*, is taken from the Greek word meaning 'seeing far off', and refers to the large size of the flowers.

There are only four species within the waratah genus; the most brilliant of these is the New South Wales waratah (*Telopea speciosissima*) (pictured), the floral emblem of that state. Near the coast the flowers of this shrub begin to open in early spring, but in cooler mountainous areas they may continue to bloom until Christmas. A second species, the Braidwood waratah (*T. mongaensis*), is found only in one small patch of forest near Batemans Bay on the south coast. This species is very rare and endangered. The tree waratah (*T. oreades*) is found in the forests of East Gippsland in Victoria, and the Tasmanian waratah (*T. truncata*) is found in the mountains of Tasmania.

Waratahs belong to a diverse group of Australian heathland plants, the protea family. Other common members of this large plant family – hakeas, grevilleas and banksias – are often found growing together, and many of these species favour the same shallow and well-drained soil as the waratahs.

Like their international relatives, the South African proteas, their flower heads create highly decorative displays. Now cultivated for these blooms, the dazzling heads are often seen displayed either in freshly cut or dried-flower arrangements.

ABOVE *Quiet and serene in places, a rugged torrent in others, the Colo River is a major feature of Wollemi National Park.*

ABOVE RIGHT *Eroded sandstone with dramatic overhangs, cliffs and caves are a feature of the Sydney hinterland.*

and liloing – a sport where an inflated airbed is used to float down the calmer water – while a camping area with basic facilities is provided at Dunns Swamp. For those looking to explore the remote wilderness this is a good central location from which to commence a cross-park walk.

Glen Davis on the Capertee River is also a good spot to canoe as well as gain access to one of the best whitewater rafting trips in the country, down the Colo River Gorge. You can exit from this river system at Colo on The Putty Road.

Bushwalks

Glen Davis and Newnes on the western side of the park are convenient starting points for bushwalks, with excellent bush camping areas as well. Both towns are steeped in mining and industrial history. Although little evidence remains of those early days, the two old mine sites were once connected by a pipeline which today makes an interesting 10-km one-way walk. Major shale oil mines operated on these sites from the turn of the century but fell into disuse with changing economic conditions in the 1950s.

One remaining feature of interest is on the old railway line. A disused 400-m-long railway tunnel, 7km south of Newnes, is home to a colony of glow worms. These insect larvae hang suspended from the roof of the tunnel with their luminescent abdomens exposed. The 8-km-return track is along the railway line with a nice level gradient. Don't forget a torch.

Picnics and camping areas

Colo and the surrounding villages on The Putty Road and Mountain Lagoon Road provide the most easily accessible picnic and camping areas in the park. There are basic camping facilities at Colo, Ward Park and on Comleroy Road near Mount Butler. To bush camp in the Colo Gorge, take the Bob Turners Walk, which starts on The Putty Road 7km past Colo Heights.

Four-wheel-drive tracks

There are some tracks across the park that are open for four-wheel-drive access depending on the road conditions at the time of setting out. For example, there is a four-wheel-drive track from Rylestone to Olinda, across the park along the Hunter Range, through the Putty State Forest and then on to The Putty Road. This road is sometimes closed if the surface condition is unstable. Unsealed roads that are open change from time to time and most are not marked on maps. If remote tracks are marked on maps, the information is often out of date. It is best to check with the park staff on current road conditions.

How to get there

Access to Wollemi is from The Putty Road, marking the eastern border of the park. Enter around the towns of Colo and Colo Heights. The Bells Line of Road from Windsor skirts the southern border. At Lithgow turn north along Mudgee Road to the turn-off to Newnes and Glen Davis. At Mudgee in the north turn onto the Rylstone Road and enter via Olinda. Rylstone Road connects with Muswellbrook via Denman.

Wollemi National Park tel: (02) 6543–3533

KANANGRA BOYD NATIONAL PARK

The granite peaks and gorges of the Kanangra Boyd wilderness stand in stark contrast to the sandstone mesas of the adjacent Blue Mountains. The change in geological formation leads to a more rugged landscape dominated by Mount Cloudmaker. Grass grows on the deeper soils of this plateau, and kangaroos and wombats inhabit the forests. To the south the limestone formations of the Kowmung River Gorge provide a further contrast.

Kanangra Boyd National Park has an interesting history since it was protected as a small tourist reserve as early as 1891. Other small reserves dotted the region, including a travelling stock and camping reserve at Boyd Crossing and the Colong Caves Reserve on the Kowmung River, which was declared in 1899. A controversy in the 1960s over mining the limestone along the Kowmung River Gorge culminated in the consolidation of all the reserves into a national park in 1969.

Trekking and night walks

Kanangra Walls Road, the only road into the park, leads to the park's dominant landform, sheer sandstone cliffs known as the Kanangra Walls. The power of the landscape and its relative isolation is daunting. There are a number of short tracks in the area and at least a few hours should be spent exploring the plateau. From the Walls it is possible to see across to Mount Cloudmaker, the park's largest peak, in the north.

The entry road passes the camp ground adjacent to Boyd Creek about 6km short of the Walls. Basic camping facilities are set amongst a forest of snow gums and bush camping is allowed away from roads and tracks. There is a range of walks, including trekking across to the southern sections of the Blue Mountains National Park. There are about five different night-walking routes to the Kanangra Walls, all starting at Katoomba in the Blue Mountains. These are true wilderness experiences and walkers need to be well prepared.

Limestone caves

The region is rich in limestone caves, although none of the caves in the south of Kanangra Boyd are open to the public. Adjacent to the park is one of the best known cave systems in the world, the Jenolan Caves. The beauty of these structures is derived from the purity of the limestone and the extent of the dripstone formations.

The caves are located beside the Jenolan River, which cuts a 450-m-deep valley into the thick, 150-km-wide limestone belt. They were discovered by a bushranger in 1838, and in 1866 were among the earliest areas reserved for conservation purposes in Australia. The caves opened for public viewing in 1867 and today eight are on display with regular guided tours. Features include the Carlotta Arch and the 85-m-high Devils Coach House.

Extensive accommodation is available at the Jenolan Caves, ranging from five-star luxury rooms to bunkhouses or camping grounds that are delightful. Several excellent walks offer visitors the chance to see the wild and rare brush-tailed rock wallaby.

Limestone belts containing a further number of caves dot the southern highland south and west of the Jenolan Caves. Abercrombie Caves, south of Trunkey Creek, and Wombeyan Caves on the road between Taralga and Mittagong have impressive caves that are open for public viewing with guided tours. At Wombeyan Caves a self-guided tour through the Fig Tree Cave is also on offer. Camping and on-site caravans are available at both sites. Several marked bushwalks explore the surrounding bushland reserves.

Jenolan, Abercrombie and Wombeyan caves also provide adventure caving for those who really want to experience true underground exploring. Booking ahead is essential.

Adventure seeking

Bungonia is a public recreation area located beside the Bungonia Gorge on the Shoalhaven River. Its dramatic scenery is a great location for canyoning, canoeing and caving. There are no public cave tours but the 170 or so known caves are popular among explorers. The park has a large number of bush camping sites with modern facilities such as hot showers and communal kitchens. Bushwalks are popular and the visitor centre provides details of the trails available. The steep five-hour walk to the floor of Bungonia Gorge is recommended for agile bushwalkers.

ABOVE *Three streams cutting deep into grey limestone have created the series of caves at Jenolan.*

OPPOSITE TOP *Kanangra Boyd, dominated by plateaus and valleys, provides wonderful wilderness walks.*

How to get there

To get to Kanangra Boyd National Park from the north, head to Oberon, off the Great Western Highway, and then travel via the Jenolan Caves. Abercrombie Caves is south of Trunkey Creek, Wombeyan Caves between Taralga and Mittagong. Bungonia is 26km east of Goulburn.

Kanangra Boyd National Park tel: (02) 6336–1972
Jenolan Caves tel: (02) 6359–3311
Abercrombie and Wombeyan caves tel: (02) 4843–5976

Don't Miss...

Adventure Experiences

Canoeing the Colo River Gorge in Wollemi National Park is a must for the adventurous. The river stretches for about 70km and contains 150 rapids. Normal difficulty grading is moderate but after heavy rain, rises to grade six.

Adventure caving, as opposed to cave tours, is available at Jenolan, Abercrombie, Bungonia and Wombeyan caves.

In the Blue Mountains rock climbing and canyoning are popular but are best done with experienced local groups. Among the best canyons are the Claustral and Jamison.

Sydney's Other National Parks

Ku-ring-gai Chase National Park forms the northern boundary of suburban Sydney. There are many scenic points, short, clearly marked walks and accessible Aboriginal rock-art sites. Ku-ring-gai's waterways are good for boating and houseboats can be hired.

Royal National Park lies south of the city and is the oldest national park in Australia, declared in 1879, and the second-oldest in the world. Access is by road or by train, which stops at Engadine, Heathcote or Waterfall. There are many short walks, and camping is permitted in the park.

The Colo River provides an ideal environment for canoeing.

Sydney Harbour National Park comprises approximately ten separate beautiful natural harbourside spots which are great for photography. Highly recommended for a break from city life.

Hawkesbury Visitor Centre tel: (02) 4588–5899
Ku-ring-gai Chase National Park tel: (02) 9457–9853
Royal National Park tel: (02) 9542–0666
Sydney Harbour National Park tel: (02) 9585–6444

13

HIGH COUNTRY

Namadgi • Kosciuszko •

Yarrangobilly

*A*ustralia *is not renowned for its mountains, but its highest peak lies within the Kosciuszko National Park. This 'high' country, the largest national park in New South Wales, also contains the Yarrangobilly Caves and thermal pool as well as a number of ski-fields and resorts. Next door, lying in the south-west corner of the Australian Capital Territory (ACT), is Namadgi National Park. Some of the highlights within these wilderness areas are bushwalking, cross-country skiing, whitewater rafting and horseback safaris. Both the Namadgi and Kosciuszko national parks have camping areas.*

Travel Tips

There is a major airport at Canberra and a regional one at Cooma. Road access to Namadgi National Park from Canberra is via the Boboyan Road, which is unsealed along parts of its route. To get to Kosciuszko from Canberra you can take the Monaro and Snowy Mountain highways or the Kosciuszko Road from Cooma. Visitor centres in Canberra, Cooma and Jindabyne can supply all the maps you will need. Permits, available at the entrance, are required to enter Kosciuszko. Winter driving can be hazardous even without snow, as ice can build up on the roads' surface so tyre chains are required by law to be carried in all vehicles. Alpine roads can be closed during inclement weather, so check beforehand. The region is at times extremely cold, even in summer, so always take warm clothing. Organised tours can be arranged from Canberra, Cooma and Jindabyne.

ABOVE *In winter Perisher Valley is covered in snow, enticing skiers. The resort town of Perisher is open throughout the year to cater for other sporting activities, including trekking to the top of nearby Mount Kosciuszko, the continent's highest point.*

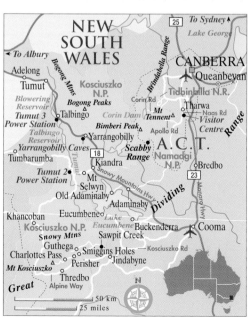

NAMADGI NATIONAL PARK

Namadgi National Park comprises almost half the area of the ACT, the home of the national capital. There are dozens of marked trails and walks, from jaunts of a few kilometres to longer multi-day trips. Information is available at the park's visitor centre, located about 2km south from Tharwa on the Naas Road. Beware of regular snowfalls in the Brindabella Range in winter, which make some of the roads impassable.

Namadgi acts as a natural stepping stone between the formal parks of Canberra and the rugged wilderness of Kosciuszko's high country. The park's dry lowland forests make way for the wet gum forests on the slopes of the Brindabella Range, followed by the snow gums and alpine flower meadows at the top. Rare sphagnum peat swamps are also found scattered along the range. Commonly seen wildlife includes grey kangaroos and wombats.

Annual feasts

Before European expansion into the region, Aboriginal groups used to visit the rocky sites in Namadgi and Kosciuszko during summer months to feed on bogong moths. Bogongs migrate to the mountains in their millions during this time to hibernate. The Aborigines used to extract by hand the masses of fat-laden moths that clogged the cracks in the boulders, and roasted them in hot ash for an easy and delicious high-protein meal. Normally living in groups of a dozen or so, the Aborigines would gather in camps of hundreds when they exploited this rich food source.

Mountain and forest walks

Mount Tennent is a prominent peak of almost 1400m at the northern edge of the park, immediately adjacent to the visitor centre. A summit walk starts 3km along the Apollo Road from its junction with the Naas Road, about 8km south of the visitor centre. A fire trail climbs the peak and makes an invigorating five-hour-return trek. The views across to Canberra and over the Brindabella Range are breathtaking.

A second popular walk leads to Booroomba Rocks and starts a further 5km up the Apollo Road at the end of a 3-km, unsealed, dry-weather-only track. The track head has a

ABOVE *Booroomba Rocks in Namadgi provide a wonderful vantage point from which to survey the surrounding wilderness.*

delightful, isolated small picnic area set amongst tall gums. The walking track climbs less than 2km through imposing forests and huge granite boulders to a rock platform perched above a 120-m cliff. Booroomba Rocks is a great lookout point and a popular local climbing and abseiling location.

The third recommended walk is the Yerrabi track which, although only 4km return, reaches a very high vantage point. It crosses a more alpine landscape and starts at the marked car park about 19km south of the Orroral Road turn-off on the Boboyan Road, heading towards the ACT–New South Wales border. An open alpine swamp marks the trail's beginning before the track slowly climbs to the Boboyan Trig. The top of the peak is open and rocky and a great spot for solitary contemplation or a picnic as the views, stretching across most of the park and particularly into the Bimberi Wilderness, evoke a powerful sense of isolation and mystery. This large wilderness area is formed from parts of the Kosciuszko and Namadgi national parks and the Bimberi and Scabby Range nature reserves. The area within these parks and reserves is given special status by park rangers and is subject to particularly sensitive eco-management.

Camping

Two basic camp grounds with toilets and fireplaces are located in the park. One is on the Orroral Road, about 16km south of the visitor centre. The other at Mount Clear is adjacent to the Boboyan Road and is only 5km north of the ACT–New South Wales border.

How to get there

An organised bus tour can be arranged from Canberra but the main parts of Namadgi National Park can easily be reached by car along the sealed Naas and Boboyan roads through Tharwa. The less developed northern parts of the park can be reached by the Cotter or the unsealed Brindabella roads.

ABOVE *A boardwalk to the summit of Mount Kosciuszko helps to protect the fragile alpine meadows in the park.*

If travelling through the region from north to south by car, it is recommended to head west from central Canberra along the Cotter Road, turn into Tidbinbilla Road and then south to Tharwa and the Namadgi National Park visitor centre. Camp overnight at either of the camp sites and try a number of the walks. The next day head south on the Boboyan Road to Adaminaby, then either keep heading south into the Kosciuszko region and onto Victoria or swing north through the Yarrangobilly areas of Kosciuszko and circle back to the ACT via the Tumut and Brindabella roads.

Namadgi National Park tel: (02) 6237–5222

KOSCIUSZKO NATIONAL PARK

Kosciuszko National Park contains the continent's largest alpine area but its highest peak, Mount Kosciuszko, is only 2228m high. It comes as a disappointment to many that Kosciuszko doesn't stand out as a grand, isolated peak like the famous summits of other continents, and that it is in fact only one of a number of peaks that dot this high country plateau.

The lack of dramatic high peaks dates back to a time when the area was a vast, flat, uplifted plain of mainly granite rock with a few isolated peaks. Over the aeons, the land's shapes became weathered and rounded, but remained largely unchanged. Weak glacial activity in the past 2 million years created interesting features such as cirque lakes, moraines and polished rock pavements (Lake Albina and Lake Cootapatmba were created by this sort of glacial activity), while rivers forged their way through the plateau's western edge, creating the ravines that divide the peaks.

Alpine walks

Kosciuszko has hundreds of great walks. Comprehensive lists and brochures with up-to-date information are available at each of the park's five visitor centres. A word of warning: Kosciuszko is a true alpine area and freezing weather, accompanied by snow, can strike at any time of the year. On all walks, especially those on the high plateau, and even in summer, precautions should be taken in case of sudden weather changes.

CORROBOREE FROG

Buried beneath the winter snows in the alps of southern Australia lives the tiny, extraordinarily coloured corroboree frog (*Pseudophryne corroboree*). The most easily recognised of all Australia's frogs, it grows no bigger than a matchbox. The corroboree's upper body is yellow with black lines from nose to tail. The head, legs and toes are also beautifully patterned with the same detailed lines. Underneath is a marbled pattern of black, white and yellow.

Corroboree frogs occur in the high country generally above 1000m. They are most common around Mount Kosciuszko, Australia's highest point, although small isolated populations are scattered throughout the mountains.

Unlike most Australian animals this tiny frog hibernates. Hibernation is a rare behaviour for any Australian animal and is only recorded for a handful of species. Before winter the corroboree frog burrows deep into the soil or vegetation, where temperatures always remain a few degrees above freezing. At the end of winter, female corroboree frogs travel to the edge of sphagnum bogs where they prepare a moist burrow beside a pond or creek. From January to March they lay up to 30 large eggs onto the floor of the burrow. Although not in water, the eggs do not dry out and the baby tadpoles develop inside them, eventually reaching an advanced stage before rain stimulates them to hatch. Water then floods the burrows and allows the tadpoles to swim into the pond or creek, where the normal process of developing from tadpole into frog takes place.

Corroboree frogs cannot hop or jump as their legs are tiny; forward movement is a curious clumsy crawl or walk. To overcome obstacles the corroboree frog elevates its body and moves along on the tips of its toes.

LEFT *The entrance to Kosciuszko National Park is marked by the Thredbo River.*

BELOW LEFT *The walks to the lookouts at Mount Kosciuszko are well signposted.*

Glacial lakes

Another excellent walk includes one or more of the five glacial lakes. A short hike of 10km to and from the car park at Charlottes Pass to two of these lakes, the Blue Lake and Headley Tarn, will take about five hours to complete.

Alternatively, all five lakes can be taken in on a longer loop walk that takes in the main dividing range. This route affords spectacular views of Lake Albina with Mount Townsend, the country's second-highest peak, towering behind. Again this walk can be started either from Charlottes Pass or Thredbo.

There is an overlap between the lakes' loop walk and the summit climb, but both are worth the effort. To attempt both the summit and lakes' loop in one day would require top fitness as it is over 20km and you might miss the opportunity to fully appreciate all that the landscape has to offer.

One of the many enjoyable short walks below the treeline is to Rainbow Lake. Access is from a car park near Rainers Gap south of Smiggins Holes on the Kosciuszko Road. The walk is an easy 3-km-return and the lake is a pleasant place to picnic. The track passes through a mix of open woodland and forest. Open meadows are carpeted with a variety of wildflowers including trigger plants.

Alpine camping

Camping is permitted anywhere in the park except in the resort areas, at Yarrangobilly Caves, in the catchments of the glacial lakes, within sight of roads or close to watercourses. A camping ground with all the facilities is located near the information centre at Sawpit Creek and there are also over 20 basic camping sites, with only pit toilets and fireplaces, located along the main roads within the park.

How to get there

The main road access from Canberra is the Monaro Highway to Cooma and then via Jindabyne or Adaminaby. From the west Tumut and Khancoban are entry points. Recommended back-country access is via the unsealed Boboyan Road through Namadgi to Adaminaby. In summer, the Barry Way is a great alternative route to western Victoria.

Kosciuszko National Park tel: (02) 6450–5600

The 'must do' walk of the high country is the climb to Kosciuszko's summit, which is perhaps also the most rewarding. The summit walk can be completed in a day's outing from either Thredbo or the car park at Charlottes Pass. If you are travelling with two vehicles, the trip can be made more interesting and rewarding by starting at Thredbo and finishing at Charlottes Pass.

From Thredbo the easier option is to take the Crackenback chairlift to the top of the range. To the summit and back is a 12-km walk which will take between four and six hours to complete. The whole of this walk is above the treeline with most of the track on a raised metal boardwalk, except for the last kilometre or so where it is across a flat swampy terrain.

From Charlottes Pass the climb follows the old road. This route is about 16km in length with a steady rise of over 400m.

YARRANGOBILLY

The huge northern section of Kosciuszko National Park is centred on the Yarrangobilly Caves. It is quieter and more relaxed since it is away from the popular resorts around Jindabyne. There are vast areas that can be explored on long hikes or on cross-country skis, depending on the season. The Tumut River and Talbingo and Blowering reservoirs provide great sites for canoeing, sailing and boating. For those in four-wheel-drive vehicles there are many remote tracks to explore, but access to these can depend on the weather and the condition of the tracks, so it's best to check at the ranger stations before you start out. For those in conventional vehicles, there are still plenty of remote and out-of-the-way spots to explore.

Caves of limestone
Yarrangobilly is a limestone region honeycombed with caves of outstanding aesthetic and scientific value. A stockman took shelter during a storm in two caves in 1834 and since then over 200 caves have been separately identified, all rich in a variety of calcite formations. Adjacent to the caves is a spectacular rocky gorge cut deep into the limestone hills. None of the main Yarrangobilly

Caves supports colonies of breeding bats since the temperature inside is far too cold for them to survive.

There are regular tours through three caves while the Glory Cave has a self-guided trail. Numbers on all tours are limited and booking can be made ahead or on site. There are also a number of short walking trails in the area, like Castle Track and Glory Farm Walk, each an hour's duration.

A thermal swimming pool is located near the information centre. The mineral water is fed from deep underground and maintains a constant temperature of 27°C.

Camping
Camping is not allowed, nor is accommodation provided around the caves; it is strictly a day-use area. However, 10km north on the Snowy Mountains Highway there are several delightful basic sites on the banks of the upper Yarrangobilly River. This is a good place to base yourself for a day or two while you explore the region.

ABOVE *The tranquil alpine meadows near Kiandra were once alive with the endeavours of miners working at their gold diggings.*

Historic highland huts

About 100 historic and rustic huts are scattered throughout the high country. They date mainly from the grazing days prior to the declaration of the park in 1944. Cattle were brought up from lowland farms to graze and the huts were built by the stockmen for temporary shelter. Many of the huts are located in some of the most remote and beautiful parts of the high country and are now available to cross-country skiers or bushwalkers for overnight shelter. Maps showing the detailed location of huts are supplied by the park's visitor centres.

Some people would prefer to have all the huts in the national park removed, but others, bearing in mind their historical significance and the safe havens they create in heavy weather, work to preserve the old huts. An association has been formed for the latter purpose. A night or two in a remote hut in winter or summer is a truly rustic experience.

Overland walking trail

In 1824–25, the explorers Hamilton Hume and William Hovell made the first overland crossing from Sydney to a site near present-day Melbourne. An historic walking trail winding through the Yarrangobilly area commemorates this feat. It is well marked and a section of the trail starts at the Blowering camp site near the wall of the reservoir. This section runs south to Buddong Falls picnic site, south of Tumut's power-station. It takes about three days to complete the walk and at various points the trail connects up with public transport.

Skiing and goldmining

Mount Selwyn is the only ski resort in the northern region of Kosciuszko. It is mainly for beginners and offers inexpensive skiing. There is no accommodation. Access for vehicles is from the Snowy Mountains Highway at Kiandra.

Kiandra is a famous historic goldmining area. For a short time in the 1860s the town had a population of 10 000 miners. Today there is nothing left but ruins and a name on the map. A short drive up the Cabramarra Road is Three Mile Dam, a pleasant place to set up camp as there are a number of short interesting walks.

How to get there

The Yarrangobilly area of northern Kosciuszko National Park is most easily accessed via the Snowy Mountains Highway between Tumut and Adaminaby. Alternate access is via Tumbarumba and the Elliott Way to Kiandra in summer (in winter there may be closures due to snow). From Canberra, the Brindabella Road to Tumut is recommended during dry weather.

Kosciuszko National Park (Tumut) tel: (02) 6947–4200

DON'T MISS...

ADVENTURE EXPERIENCES

The high country is a great location for many adventure pursuits. In winter visitors can indulge in the full range of winter sports, including downhill and cross-country skiing, and snowboarding. The main winter resorts are Thredbo, Perisher and Guthega, while Mount Selwyn offers family-orientated facilities. Adventure winter sports such as mountaineering and cross-country ski touring are also on offer. In late winter and spring there are many great locations for whitewater canoeing and rafting. During the summer there are safari horse rides, mountain bike riding and river canoeing. Closer to Sydney visitors can go whitewater rafting on the Shoalhaven River near Nowra.

OTHER INTERESTING AREAS

Tidbinbilla Nature Reserve is a scenic reserve near Canberra, with tame and semi-tame native animals, including emus, grey kangaroos and koalas, making it a great spot for wildlife photography. No camping is allowed.

The **Brindabella Range** near Canberra was the site for three important Apollo space-program land stations in the 1960s and 1970s. One of these, Tidbinbilla Deep Space Communication Centre, remains and is still operated by NASA and has a well-

Toboggans are popular with children on the snow slopes.

appointed facility specialising in space history. Access to the space centre and the reserve is from Tidbinbilla Road west of Canberra.

Paddy Palin (adventure tours), Jindabyne tel: (02) 6456–2922
Cooma Visitor Centre tel: (02) 6450–1742
Tidbinbilla Tracking Station tel: (02) 6201–7800
Tidbinbilla Nature Reserve tel: (02) 6237–5120
Hume and Hovell Walking Track tel: (02) 6921–2503
Shoalhaven Rafting World Experiences tel: 1800 803688

RIVERINA

Cocoparra • Willandra • Lake Mungo

Australia is often described as 'the land of sweeping plains' and this is especially true of the Riverina, a district of vast plains in southwestern New South Wales. Bush camping is allowed in many of the reserves with a few established sites, and there are a number of opportunities for four-wheel-drive exploration as most of the local roads are unsealed. The best times to visit are in autumn and spring when the weather is neither too hot nor too cold.

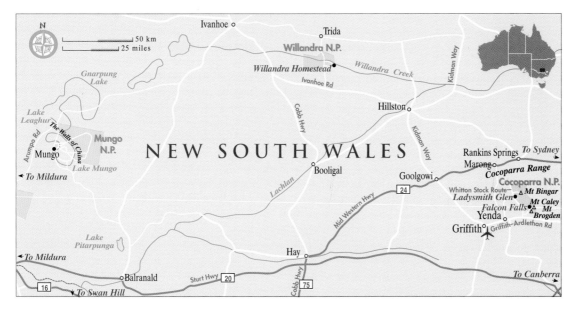

ABOVE *When you are driving through the Riverina region, be aware that flat, dusty plains can become vast bogs after rain.*

OPPOSITE TOP *Cocoparra is a little-visited park with an interesting history.*

OPPOSITE BOTTOM *The emus of Cocoparra are curious, ungainly birds with an appetite for picnic food.*

COCOPARRA NATIONAL PARK

The low-rise Cocoparra Range runs approximately north–south between the Mid Western Highway and Griffith–Ardlethan Road. The range, which is a point of topographic relief in an otherwise flat landscape, is composed of sandstone and conglomerates, and is the eroded remnant of a high range originally formed under the sea approximately 410 million years ago. Rounded and flattened over a period of millions of years, the range is a good example of what geologists call a 'hogshead' – folded sediments that have been eroded into a steep-sided range.

Rugged routes

An historic drive on an original stock route skirts the western edge of the Cocoparra National Park. The unsealed Whitton Stock Route was used to drive stock before the advent of modern truck transport and was also used by the famous Cobb and Co coaches at the end of the last century as part of their route from Melbourne to Queensland. Many of the old cypress mile posts as well as the foundations of several staging stations and hotels can still be seen along the way. Just within the boundary of the Cocoparra National Park, the remnants of a bridge hang over Steamboat Creek.

Cocoparra's peaks

The highest peaks on the Cocoparra Range are mounts Caley, Bingar and Brogden. A lookout road goes to the summit of Mount Bingar with access off the Whitton Stock Route, 18km north of Yenda. From Yenda, a road and short walking track lead to the top of Mount Brogden. Toilets and a picnic area are provided at the track head. The Barry Scenic Drive from Yenda cuts across the southern end of the range providing access close to Mount Caley for those wishing to climb to its summit. Note, though, that there are no marked trails.

A series of about 10 short, westward-flowing streams drain the range after the infrequent rains. The streams have cut attractive gullies into the ancient sandstone creating secluded and shady spots that are ideal for a short walk or picnic. Alongside most of the streams are formal picnic sites which are often accessible from the Whitton Stock Route. The most spectacular deep gully is Ladysmith Glen, which is over 30m deep and cut by Jack's Creek below Mount Bingar. Access to the gorge is off the Whitton Stock Route, 17km north of Yenda.

Scenic valleys

The scenic drive along the Whitton Stock Route also provides access to Pleasant Valley and the picnic area at Spring Hill in the north of the park. Even during dry weather when no water is falling, nearby Falcon Falls is worth the short walk.

Nature and wildlife

Wildlife in the park includes grey kangaroos, echidnas and emus, but feral goats have displaced the euros that once lived in the rocky ranges. The area is a birdwatcher's paradise, with many species of rare inland honeyeaters and other desert nomads recorded, while the rare glossy black cockatoo has also been seen in the park.

Both the white and black cypress pines, two of the continent's few commercially used softwood timber species, grow abundantly. Large specimens of the brightly green-coloured kurrajongs are found dotted across the flats and creek valleys. Many wattle species are common and their yellow flowers make a fine winter and spring display.

Adjoining the park to the north is the Cocoparra Nature Reserve which conserves a similarly sized section of the main range – altogether, over 13 000ha of this thickly wooded range is protected. There are no public facilities within the reserve.

Camping
Bush camping is permitted, however no facilities are provided. Campers should note that no water is available and there is no visitor centre or other facilities. The closest place for supplies is Yenda. Cocoparra is recommended as a stop-over for those travelling from the Sydney and Kosciuszko regions to the parks of New South Wales' west or for those heading north from Victoria. However, for travellers who have the time and a specific interest in wildlife, it is a rich area that merits deeper exploration.

How to get there

Cocoparra is located 25km north-east of Griffith. Turn north off the Griffith–Ardlethan Road at Yenda. Alternatively take the Mid Western Highway from Sydney and turn south at Marong, west of Rankin Springs. Note that after wet weather the roads may be closed, even to four-wheel-drive vehicles.
Griffith National Park and Wildlife Service tel: (02) 6962–7755

GOANNAS

Lizards are very prominent creatures in Australia's wildlife fold. In parts of the inland there can be over 40 species living on 1ha of grassland. Australian lizards fall neatly into five main categories: dragons, geckos, skinks, legless lizards and the giants of the lizard world, the goannas.

Over 20 Australian species of goanna are known on the continent and they occur in all habitats and all parts of the country. Goannas have long, forked tongues that flick in and out of their mouths adding to their image of ferocity.

Gould's goanna is the most widespread, found right across the country except for the forests of the south-east. It has a variable appearance, ranging from pale yellow with dark spots to almost black, and it lives on the ground.

A common large eastern goanna is the lace monitor (pictured). Usually dark blue on its back, it grows to about 2m. Occasionally seen scavenging on the ground, this species lives in tall forest trees. The lace monitor's diet is mainly birds' eggs and their young.

The Mertens water goanna is a small aquatic lizard. Frequently seen along the banks of wetlands and rivers in the tropical north, this brown lizard feeds on fish and frogs.

The largest Australian lizard is the perentie which grows to over 2.5m in length. It is the world's second-largest lizard, outclassed only by the Komodo dragon from Indonesia.

A legendary bush tale claims that a bite from a goanna will never heal – which is not exactly true. Goannas do, however, feed on rotting carrion and bites can become easily infected. The creature's claws, especially those of the tree-dwelling species, are also dangerous weapons. Goannas that hover around picnic spots can be tame, but it is wise to observe and photograph them from a distance.

WILLANDRA NATIONAL PARK

Willandra National Park is for those who like huge open spaces, observing wildlife, indulging in scenic photography, riverside camping, swimming, four-wheel-drive exploring, river canoeing or star gazing. The park was once part of the Big Willandra Station, one of the biggest merino stations in the late 1900s. Today, it is a place in which to absorb the traditions of the past. For such a seldom-visited, remote location, the facilities are surprisingly good.

The weather in the park is usually dry. In summer it is hot and in winter, after very cold and frosty nights, delightfully warm. The skies are generally cloudless and seemingly vast. There is usually water in the creek for swimming and sometimes there is a little water in small pools scattered across the plain. However, when inland thunderstorms deluge the deserts 150km to the west, the Willandra National Park and much of the surrounding region can become a huge lake within days.

Secluded homestead
The historic Willandra Homestead in the most eastern section of the park was, for over a century, a major centre for the wool industry. Its name is embedded in the folklore and songs of the outback and much of the original homestead and station buildings remain. The thatch-roofed ram shed and the shearing complex are all preserved. Here you can absorb the atmosphere of the traditional outback way of life with its constant struggle against the elements.

Winding creek
The Willandra Creek, winding its way from west to east and forming the park's northern border, is the major focus of the park. The whole area lies on the red and grey clays of the vast Lachlan River floodplain. The vegetation is dramatically divided between the tall riverine forests and the semi-arid grass plains.

The creek and the Willandra Billabong are refuges for large numbers of waterbirds. Ducks, herons, ibis and moorhens can all be found feeding and roosting amongst the trees or on the water. Quiet wildlife-watching from a canoe on the billabong can be rewarding.

ABOVE *A number of the outbuildings at Big Willandra's home-stead have been restored for use as accommodation, like this old thatched-roof ram shed.*

Black box gums

The broad creek flats of the park are dominated by the black box tree. This is a type of open-shaped gum tree which can grow to about 20m. The name 'box' was given to the species by early bushmen as it appeared similar to the European box tree. Scattered amongst the black box are the long drooping leaves – reminiscent of the hanging leaves of a willow – of the river cooba, a species of wattle that grows into a small tree. This species is flushed with yellow flowers throughout summer and early autumn.

Black box can form small forests in areas where, scattered across the plains away from the creek lines, depressions fill with water after rain. Each of these little 'islands' of trees has its own flourishing wildlife community which comes to life when the depression fills with water. These areas are good places for wildlife observation, especially if only a small patch of water remains.

Grasslands of wildlife

Away from the creek lines most of the park is flat grassland stretching to the horizon. These plains were once covered in sheep but are now reserved exclusively for native wildlife.

Apart from the larger species, such as red kangaroos and emus, there are also many cryptic and rare species to be found. Due to the impact of sheep the native saltbushes and wallaby grass have largely disappeared and have been replaced by other grasses. Over time it is hoped that the original native grasses and low shrubs will return and the area will become an oasis for nomadic native birds and other wildlife.

Park facilities

Facilities in the area are simple but comfortable. There is a ranger station at the historic homestead and a picnic and basic camping area. Toilets and showers are provided. Overnight cabins are located at a spot between the homestead and Willandra Billabong and many delightful picnic areas are scattered along the Willandra Creek. There are also a number of marked short walking trails and the Merton Motor Trail for a car-based self-guided tour.

How to get there

Willandra National Park is remote and access is only by vehicle or light aircraft. The park is 64km from Hillston, off the Ivanhoe Road on the way to Willandra (main area), or off the road to Trida. Many roads are suitable only for four-wheel-drives. Beware of road closures after rain.
Griffith National Park and Wildlife Service (02) 6962–7755
Cabins (02) 6967–8159

MUNGO NATIONAL PARK

Mungo was declared Australia's first World Heritage site in 1981. Its significance lies in its unrivalled collection of Aboriginal cultural artefacts and its historic landscape. Harsh and unforgiving, Mungo is not a classic national park or reserve – some have observed that its juxtaposition of ancient and modern makes Lake Mungo a schizophrenic place.

Ancient lakes and shifting dunes
About 45 000 years ago, Mungo was an area of huge freshwater lakes. Full of fish, yabbies and tortoises, these 10-m-deep lakes covered an area of 1000km². However, with the changes in climate across the Australian continent, the lakes began to dry out around 25 000 years ago and, over the next 10 000 years, the wind formed huge 30-km-long crescent-shaped sand dunes along the lakes' eastern edges.

These deep dunes buried and preserved all evidence of human activity that had occurred on the lake shore. Modern erosion is now exposing the remains of these ancient camps and has also sculpted a harsh face to the white sand dunes. The craggy west-facing slopes are known as the Walls of China, a reference to the Chinese immigrants who built the shearing shed in 1869. For the best photographic effects, with optimum shading on the dune faces, visit just before midday.

Buried secrets
From anthropological research carried out on the exposed human remains and the charcoal left from fires, it is now known that Aborigines lived at Mungo for at least 40 000 years.

The evidence comes from an invaluable and amazingly complete collection of ancient skeletons. A tall man, known as Mungo III, lived in the lakes area about 35 000 years ago. At his death, parts of his body were painted with ochre and he was buried in a shallow grave. A young woman, known as Mungo One, was cremated about 30 000 years ago. Her bones, among the oldest human remains found in Australia, had been broken into over 150 pieces and then buried in a small grave beside the cooled funeral pyre. As well as being one of the earliest known cremations in the world, the rituals displayed by these people are also the earliest known funeral rites in the world.

Sheap shearing and desert trails
Much more recently, Mungo formed part of the huge Gol Gol sheep station. From the 1860s until it was declared a park in 1979, the barren landscape was scoured by sheep searching for food. Over 50 000 sheep were shorn annually in the Mungo shearing shed, which stands today as an interesting historic reminder of those times.

Conspicuous wildlife includes both red and grey kangaroos and emus. The desert vegetation is now regenerating after the impact of a century of stock grazing on the fragile arid landscape.

A 'must do' while in the Mungo region is the 60-km drive through the park. The drive takes several hours to complete and highlights 14 major sites of natural and cultural significance. Picnic spots are provided at a number of spots along the way.

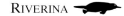

ABOVE *The Mungo Woolshed is an historic reminder of the days when the area was a centre of rural activity.*

OPPOSITE *Mungo National Park is a strange landscape of long eroded sand dunes and ancient lake beds that are slowly revealing the history of the continent's past inhabitants.*

There are three marked walking trails within the park, each one taking in a different natural feature. The Grasslands Nature Trial is 1km long and takes in the area around the camp site. The Foreshore Walk begins near the visitor centre and provides an introduction to the varied landscape. Finally, the Mallee Walk focuses on the multi-stemmed eucalypt that grows in inland areas of the continent. This walk is best done in the early morning when there is a good chance of seeing some of the unique mallee bird species.

Staying the night
Three accommodation options are available in the park. There are two basic camp grounds; one is near the park entrance and the other, Belah Camp – for those who want a true wilderness experience – is at the back of the Walls of China. The old shearer quarters are available for a modest charge to those needing creature comforts, while the motel-style Mungo Lodge is located outside the park.

How to get there

Day tours and car rentals are available. Driving from Mildura, head through Buronga towards Wentworth and then turn off at Arumpo Road and travel 100km north. Via Balranald or Euston, connect north to Pooncarie and Kinchega. It is possible to make a long daytrip to the park from Mildura or Balranald.
Mungo National Park and Wildlife Service tel: (03) 5023–1054

DON'T MISS...

ADVENTURE EXPERIENCES
The Forbes Soaring and Aero Club is located 400km west of Sydney via the Great Western Highway. With the enormous daily hot-air build-up over the central plains, this is one of the greatest gliding spots in the world. Flights of up to nine hours are possible and the distances travelled can exceed 500km. Paired flights can be arranged and photography from the air can be spectacular.

The large Murrumbidgee, Lachlan and Murray rivers, and some of the minor watercourses like Willandra and Merrowie, have long stretches suitable for canoeing enthusiasts. The annual 400-km Murray River Marathon Canoe Race takes place between Yarrawonga and Swan Hill just after Christmas. It is held over five days, covers 80km of paddling each day, and is followed by a New Year's Eve bash. Whether for the serious competitor or just for fun, it's all for the Red Cross – a good cause.

OTHER INTERESTING ACTIVITIES
There are many nature reserves scattered throughout the Riverina which are worth visiting for those with an interest in wildlife. Contact the national park service offices in Griffith and Cobar for more information.

Paddle-steamers offer a pleasant way to explore the Murray.

Swan Hill and other centres along the Murray River promote the interesting river life of the last century, offering part-day or overnight tours on restored paddle-steamers with bushcraft demonstrations.
Forbes Soaring and Aero Club (02) 6852–3845 or (02) 6852–1430
Murray River Marathon (03) 9685–9999
Griffith National Park and Wildlife Service (02) 6962–7755
Cobar National Park and Wildlife Service (02) 6836–2692
Swan Hill Visitor Centre (03) 5032–3033

CAMERON CORNER

Kinchega • Mootwingee • Sturt

Western New South Wales is best experienced by travelling in a four-wheel-drive vehicle, as this is the only way to access many of the region's remote locations. However, the most popular areas are generally accessible in conventional vehicles, although most of the local roads remain unsealed. Don't forget insect repellent or fine insect nets at night as flies in summer and mosquitoes near the rivers can be a problem.

Travel Tips

The main access to western New South Wales is by road, or light aircraft to the regional airport at Broken Hill. Bus tours also set out from Broken Hill but there is no public transport. The main road access is via the sealed Barrier Highway, which links Sydney and Adelaide, and the Silver City Highway, which runs north from Mildura. The Silver City is unsealed past Broken Hill.

Always carry sufficient supplies, including drinking water, and fuel for the car as distances between supply stations can be long. It is also wise to check ahead of arrival in case there are any permits that the parks' authorities require with regards to entry, camping and camp fires.

Words of caution for drivers:
- After heavy rain the clay soils on the Darling River floodplain become a huge bog.
- Take care on the loose road surfaces, especially around corners.
- Sheep and cattle often wander onto the roads.
- Stock grids on the back tracks are often poorly aligned with the surface and substantial washouts around them are frequent.
- Kangaroos and emus are often a hazard.
- Avoid night driving.

ABOVE *On the way to Mootwingee, roads often cross dry creek beds, which can become raging torrents after rain.*

OPPOSITE *Kinchega National Park is a desert oasis of freshwater lakes, abundant wildlife and delightful camp sites amongst tall gum forests.*

KINCHEGA NATIONAL PARK

Kinchega National Park is a place of great contrasts. Set amongst the parched sand dunes are the freshwater Menindee Lakes, an oasis for waterbirds. Dust from the dry saltpans blows across green shady riverbanks along the Darling River, and where 6 million sheep were once shorn, there are now peaceful camp sites.

Kinchega is easy to explore and conventional vehicles can traverse most of the park roads. A ranger station and an information centre are located in the park. The Bend Nature and Historic Drive, a self-guided car trail, is highly recommended. With 16 information points, the trail takes in parts of the Darling riverbanks, the old Kinchega homestead and the four main park habitats – the lakes, the floodplain woodlands, the lunettes (semi-circular shaped dunes), and the red sand dunes – each with its own features of interest. Short marked walking trails are located throughout the park.

Early pioneers

European history in the area goes back to the early explorers Major Thomas Mitchell (1834), Charles Sturt (1844), and Robert Burke and William Wills (1860). However, pastoral grazing put the area on the map in the 1850s and, by 1876, 40 shearers worked in the huge Kinchega shearing shed. The shed with much of its equipment and machinery still stands as an historic reminder of those pioneering days.

Lakes teeming with life

Lake Menindee and Lake Cawndilla are large overflow freshwater lakes filled by the Darling River. The water creates an important inland breeding haven for many species of wildlife, including ducks, swans and pelicans. Ibis, several species of cormorant and herons breed in extensive rookeries along the tree-lined lake shore. Native freshwater fish, including Murray cod and golden and silver perch, are so abundant that they are fished commercially. Boating and recreational fishing are popular activities.

Floodplains of trees

The Darling River, one of inland Australia's most important waterways, is bordered by old river red gums and behind them are the black-soil floodplain woodlands. This area is dominated by black box gums and coolibahs and is the nesting habitat for many birds, including corellas, cockatiels, finches and blue bonnets. A quiet night-time stroll with a strong torch may even reveal a possum or two, or other nocturnal wildlife. Wildlife watching and bushwalking in this region are also great in the early morning as both visitors and wildlife escape the heat of the day.

Curved dunes

The lunettes are linked closely to the main lakes where wind- and wave-blown sand has built up high dunes on the eastern shores. Bluebush and other desert shrubs grow on these dunes and have stabilised them for thousands of years. Apart from the fossil evidence found here of Aboriginal settlement from 26 000 years ago, the remains of the charcoal from their cooking fires have revealed the bones of a variety of giant marsupials, including extinct giant kangaroos and wombats. Fossils of modern Australian mammals have also been located, among them the Tasmanian tiger, numbats and several species of hare wallaby, a type of small kangaroo. None of these species now lives in the Kinchega region.

Seas of sand

The red desert sand dunes, the last main habitat of Kinchega, cover most of the park area and are dominated by bluebush, wattles and the belah, a beautiful desert she-oak. After rain, these dunes become a sea of red, yellow and white wildflowers. Notable species include billy buttons, poached egg daisies, Sturts desert pea and the Darling pea. Conspicuous sand-dune wildlife includes kangaroos, emu and sand goannas.

Staying the night

Over 30 delightful camp sites are located in idyllic settings amongst the river red gums along the banks of the Darling. Other camping spots are by the sandy shore of Lake Cawndilla. In the winter months, and outside the busy school holiday periods, these are ideal places to set up base camp for a few days.

Supplies are readily available from the historic Menindee village adjacent to the park. The shearer quarters can also be booked for any large group accommodation and there is also motel and hotel accommodation (try the historic Menindee Hotel) at the park's front gates.

How to get there

Road access is via the 110-km sealed Menindee Road from Broken Hill. An alternative route in dry weather is via Pooncarie on an unsealed road. From Ivanhoe or Wilcannia access is difficult as the tracks are poor and unsealed. Most of the park's roads are suitable for conventional vehicles but a number of roads are suitable only for four-wheel-drive.
Kinchega National Park tel: (08) 8091–4214

MOOTWINGEE NATIONAL PARK

Mootwingee is really two protected areas in one – a national park and an historic site. The historic site was originally proclaimed in 1967 to protect areas of value as well as significant Aboriginal sites, but is now surrounded by the much larger national park. Access to particularly sensitive areas is strictly controlled, but visitors can book a special tour. These tours do not run every day, so you'll need to ring ahead to confirm.

Mootwingee is a great expanse of rich-brown rocky sandstone hills breaking away into narrow gorges filled with waterholes. The streams are lined with river red gums tortured by the limitations of the harsh landscape. Struggling to get a hold on the broken rocky ledges, twisted trees, such as mulga and cypress pines, dot the plateau. Euros hide amongst the rocky ledges during the day, emus wander across the grassy flats and wedge-tailed eagles soar high over the ranges. Many other birds are common including corellas, ringnecks and budgerigars. Goannas and various colourful dragon lizards can be seen, especially when disturbed by a passing vehicle.

RIVER RED GUM

Gum trees and wattles cover most of the Australian continent, dominating virtually every landscape with the exception of small areas of rainforest, treeless desert and mangrove swamp. Although regarded as typically Australian, wattles are found in many parts of the world and only about half of the known species are native to this continent.

Gum trees on the other hand are mostly Australian. Of the 600 or so species, only two (both found in Timor) are not native to the country. The tall river red gum is probably the best known and the most widely distributed.

Throughout inland Australia river red gums are most likely to be seen growing along watercourses. They line the Murray River and can be seen growing in the gorges at Katatjuta. The famous Aboriginal artist of central Australia, Albert Namatjira, made household images of these gums.

Occasionally the river giants can grow to 45m with a trunk diameter of 4m. Germination of the seed occurs after the ground beneath the adult has been flooded. Flooding does not occur ever year, so the rejuvenation of red gum forests is patchy rather than prolific.

Old river red gums are habitats for a large range of wildlife. The thick, tall foliage provides food and shelter for insects and birds, while deep, cool, dry hollows provide nests and shelter for mammals such as possums, birds such as parrots, and reptiles such as goannas.

Given the majesty of these trees and their location beside rivers and lakes, camp sites are often located near them. Beware, though, the large tree limbs fall frequently and usually without warning. It is wise to position tents and vehicles clear of large overhanging limbs.

ABOVE *Road signs in western New South Wales highlight the incredible distances between towns, warning drivers to be prepared.*

take from 30 minutes to three hours. For the more experienced walker the challenging, three-hour Byngnano Trail is a scenic pleasure, affording great elevated views of the rugged gorges. Mootwingee Gorge has a short and easy walk to its tranquil waterhole which is surrounded by craggy red cliffs. The best time to do most of these walks is early in the morning when the wildlife is on the move and you can avoid the heat of the day which makes walking exhausting.

On the western side of the entry road there is a three-hour walk which takes in the ridges. This walk should be done late in the day as the setting sun casts long shadows across the range.

The Old Coach Road drive has been marked for self-guided touring. This 10-km drive takes in much of the diverse landscape of the park. The route also travels on parts of the old Cobb and Co coach road from Broken Hill to White Cliffs, past many Aboriginal art sites and strangely eroded rocky outcrops which make good places to stop.

An ancient art gallery

Many centuries ago Aborigines were the first to discover the craggy beauty of the Byngnano Ranges and the protection afforded by the shady rock overhangs. The waterholes not only provided them with fresh water but also food in the form of the wildlife attracted to the pools. The ranges are extremely rich with paintings and engravings. The paintings, depicting stencils of human hands and domestic implements, were done in various shades of ochre on the walls of caves and overhangs. Engravings, many illustrating wildlife, such as emus, and animal tracks, were picked out on the broad pavement-like sandstone slabs on the ridge tops. Many different stories are told in the rock art and some images carry deep spiritual significance for the Aboriginal people.

The more recent history of European settlement is evident by the ruins of the old Mootwingee Homestead and the remains of the Rockholes Hotel. The site was also a base camp for the famous but ill-fated trek by the explorers Burke and Wills in 1859–60.

Rugged walks and an old coach route

Many of the park's walks wind through the ranges' gorges and rocky oases. From the Homestead Creek there is a group of walks – exploring regions known as the Rockholes, Homestead Gorge and the Thaakaltjika Mingkana Cave Painting – which

Camping

In addition to its historic and cultural value, the craggy desert beauty and plentiful wildlife make this a special place in which to spend a few days. Note, however, that in busy times the rangers encourage campers to stay for only two nights. The holiday periods during the cooler months of the year should be avoided as the park is popular. The camping ground, which has basic facilities, is located about 6km into the park in Homestead Gorge. Pre-booking a camp site is recommended. Water is available but only in limited supply. There are no stores in the park and visitors need to be entirely self-sufficient, particularly in holiday periods.

How to get there

Mootwingee National Park is readily accessible by road from Broken Hill. First head north on the mainly unsealed Silver City Highway for 55km, and then head east on an unsealed but good road. There are a number of four-wheel-drive access routes via White Cliffs and from Fowlers Gap on the Silver City Highway.

Mootwingee National Park tel: (08) 8088–5933

STURT NATIONAL PARK

The Sturt is New South Wales' third-largest national park with only Kosciuszko and Wollemi being larger. There are numerous opportunities to explore the area by four-wheel-drive since there are over 300km of tracks and roads within the park. The information centre at Tibooburra is a good place to finalise plans for a visit to the region.

In search of inland riches
In 1846 the explorer Charles Sturt established a base camp at Fort Grey while searching for the fabled inland sea, which at that time many believed existed in central Australia. During the winter and spring months he set out on expeditions north, west and east to Lake Blanche, along Coopers Creek and close to the edge of the Simpson Desert. One expedition member, James Poole, died of scurvy and is buried at Mount Poole just south of the park.

After Sturt, the goldminers moved into the region in 1880. They did not stay long and pastoral interests began to develop. In the 1970s conservation interests led to the start of the land purchases which resulted in the declaration of the 3500-km² Sturt National Park.

Diverse landscapes
Sturt National Park can be divided into four landscape types or sections. In the west, close to the South Australian border, the country consists of spinifex-covered red sand dunes typical of the Strzelecki Desert further west. The dunes rise to a height of 15m. In the east of the park, around Mount Wood and scattered in small pockets elsewhere, are the riverine floodplains. This landscape is typical of the Bulloo Overflow country. In between these two are the 'jump-ups' around the Grey Range and the stony treeless gibber plains. A fifth type could also be included – the patch of granite boulder country near the Dead Horse Gully camp site. An easy 2-km loop walk through the Granites starts at the camp site.

Desert wildlife
Large conspicuous wildlife abounds in the Sturt. There are huge populations of emus and red kangaroos. From mid-winter adult male emus are often seen with chicks.

In the rocky outcrops of the jump-ups euros like to hide amongst the overhangs during

ABOVE *The incredibly long dog fence was built to keep dingoes away from the sheep farms and settled districts.*

LEFT *Road warning signs alert drivers to potential danger, particularly when the inland roads narrow to just a car's width.*

the day while the riverine forests are the home of small numbers of grey kangaroos. Goannas are frequently seen on warm days and the strange shingleback lizard is common, as is the bearded dragon.

Lake Pinaroo near Fort Grey is the terminal drainage point for much of the park. It often has water and is an important habitat for many birds. Birds of prey are also abundant including wedge-tailed eagles and the smaller black kites. There is a lot of movement at night by wildlife such as nightjars, owls and kangaroos. Night wildlife-spotting can be interesting but drive slowly.

Keeping the dingoes out
The Sturt is bounded to the east and north by the world's longest fence, erected to prevent dingoes from entering sheep grazing areas to the south. The Dingo Fence runs for over 5700km from South Australia to Queensland. Fifteen boundary riders patrol the 664km of New South Wales' fence.

Four-wheel-driving

Roads suitable for conventional vehicles link all the park sites (except for Olive Downs) with Tibooburra. The road to Olive Downs is accessible by four-wheel-drive only. A new four-wheel-drive track has recently been opened, connecting Olive Downs with Fort Grey and completing the circular route that links most of the features of the park. There are also four-wheel-drive loops linking Tibooburra and Olive Downs, and Tibooburra and Mount Wood. Informative national park self-guided leaflets are available for these roads, but note that all roads are impassable after rain.

Camping

The main camping area is at Dead Horse Gully, 1km north of Tibooburra, the local service town. There are toilets, picnic areas and drinking water at the camp site. Other sites are at Mount Wood 27km east of Tibooburra, at Olive Downs 55km north, and at Fort Grey 105km west. Park staff ask visitors to use these sites rather than bush camp as it is easier to provide prompt attention in emergencies.

ABOVE *The Sturt National Park is a region of beautiful and resilient desert flora, and contains an extensive network of roads suitable for four-wheel-drive trekking.*

How to get there

Access to Sturt National Park is by vehicle or light plane. The eastern edge of the park straddles the unsealed Silver City Highway, which provides the easiest and best scenic route north from Broken Hill. Many roads are only suitable only for four-wheel-drive vehicles. Access to western Queensland and the Strzelecki Track in South Australia is also open to four-wheel-drive vehicles only.
Sturt National Park tel: (08) 8091–3308

DON'T MISS...

ADVENTURE EXPERIENCES

Cameron Corner was named after the man who surveyed the area in 1880. The trek to the junction where three states join is hardly a serious challenge today – there is even a 'corner' store now – but it is still an adventure. A conventional vehicle will get you there, but a four-wheel-drive provides some extra security.

The Murray–Darling is the longest river system in Australia and canoeing its length from Tenterfield in New South Wales to Lake Alexandrina in South Australia would have to be one of the great adventures. However, the Darling River is not on any tourist routes and sometimes it is not possible to canoe along it due to a lack or over-abundance of water. This journey therefore requires careful planning.

OTHER INTERESTING PLACES

Silverton, 25km outside Broken Hill, is an historic ghost town now used as a movie set. Built in 1876, this town once boasted a population of 3000. Most recently it has been the location for the Australian movies *Mad Max II*, *A Town Like Alice*, *Hostage* and *Razorback*.

The boundaries of three states intersect at Cameron Corner.

White Cliffs is, like Coober Pedy in South Australia, a town built underground. Opal mining is the main industry in this hot, out-of-the-way place. Tours of the mines are possible and the solar power station is of international interest.

The area has many well-known outback pubs including Menindee, Milparinka and Tibooburra.
Cameron Corner Store tel: (08) 8091–3872
White Cliffs Visitor Centre tel: (08) 8091–6614
Broken Hill Visitor Centre tel: (08) 8087–6077

NORTHERN RANGES

Warrumbungles • Pilliga •

Mount Kaputar

*T*he northern inland areas of New South Wales are accessed easily from Sydney. The Warrumbungles and, to a lesser extent, Mount Kaputar are very popular, especially in the winter, during the school holidays and on weekends. Both the Warrumbungles and Kaputar have very good facilities and a variety of options for wilderness activities. Either would make a good base for a three- to five-day stopover. If you want to escape from the crowds, the Pilliga is an excellent option. Coonabarabran is the best town for supplies.

ABOVE *A trail to Crater Bluff is one of the many wilderness walks within Warrumbungle National Park. The park also contains remote camp sites for overnight hikers.*

OPPOSITE *The Breadknife at the Warrumbungles is a challenge for adventurous rock climbers and also provides a striking image for photographers to capture.*

Travel Tips

Dubbo and Coonabarabran have regional airports but the best access to all the northern parks is by road. All the access roads are good, the main ones being the sealed Mitchell, Oxley and Newell highways. For a shorter and much more interesting back route from Sydney see the Warrumbungles entry. Conventional vehicles will get to most areas, but there is a four-wheel-drive-only camp ground at the Warrumbungles. Although the Pilliga is usually dry, four-wheel-drive is recommended after wet weather. Roads are fenced and on open farm country kangaroos and emus are less common so night driving is relatively safe. There are no clay soils or floodplains so the unsealed roads are not usually affected badly by rain. As with many national parks there are restrictions on where to camp and light fires. Check with the park authorities. Plants within national parks are protected, so don't be tempted to remove them.

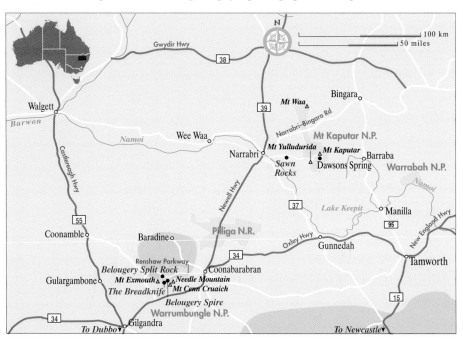

WARRUMBUNGLE NATIONAL PARK

This is one of the most popular inland national parks in New South Wales. Set like a huge forested island in a sea of grassy farmland, its towering stony peaks with their strange names dot the high ridges. Biologically it is where east meets west with an unusual mix of plants and animals living side by side. Bushwalking, camping and rock climbing are the park's most popular pursuits while the varied landscape and wildlife beckons photographers and naturalists. A ranger station and a comprehensive visitor centre are located on the flats near the centre of the park, just off the Renshaw Parkway.

Huge basalt lava flows formed a raised caldera in northern New South Wales about 13 million years ago. Many volcanic vents broke open, creating numerous small lakes, dyke lines, cones and basalt flows. The volcanic activity was neither the result of one big explosion nor caused by a single volcano, but rather continuous activity in a massive area that slowly built up a volcanic pile – a caldera – over 25km wide. This is what is now known as the Warrumbungle Range, and formations such as the 90-m-high Breadknife, Belougery Spire and Needle Mountain are remnants of that volcanic activity which created such striking images.

The disintegration of the volcanic rocks created rich soil which now supports a wide range of plants. Gum tree woodlands cover the lower slopes and valleys of the range. Higher up, heathlands cling to the rocky hillsides and curious grass trees dot the landscape. In winter and spring dozens of wattle species enrich the green and brown bushland with their splashes of golden yellow. In spring, after good rain, the park is a profusion of wildflowers.

Wildlife galore

Five species of kangaroo occur in the park, the most abundant being eastern grey kangaroos, euros and red-necked wallabies. Koalas are common and may be seen in many areas, but especially around the Spirey and West Spirey creek flats. Echidnas are also common.

Of the large numbers of birds present in the park two groups, the parrots and the eagles, stand out. About a third of the continent's parrot species have been recorded here, including the red-winged parrot, blue bonnet and many cockatoos. Peregrine falcons nest on the high rock faces and wedge-tailed eagles soar overhead. Typical inland birds, like the red-capped robin and babblers, are also common.

A choice of walks

Of the many marked trails in the park there are several less than 2km long, around the picnic spots and lookouts in the valley floor. The best of these are Wambelong Nature Track and the Burbie Canyon Walk. Both, however, can be very busy.

The best walks are those that lead to the high points of the park; these vary between 4 and 12km in length. Belougery Slit Rock, about 5km long, is highly recommended as an introductory walk. It starts on the Parkway adjacent to Camp Wambelong. A comprehensive, 15-km day walk leads to the Breadknife from Camp Pincham, returning via Ogma Saddle.

Those wanting to observe the wildlife should take the Mount Exmouth trail that goes via West Spirey Creek, returning via the Boulevarde. This would make a good day walk, so start early. The total distance is about 16km but coming home is downhill.

33

Back-country wilderness walks lasting several days are also possible. It is easy to select a route that can loop back to a vehicle without retracing your steps. As with all the walks, it is essential to carry sufficient water supplies.

Camping

Camping is encouraged in the park and the five main sites – Pincham, Elongery (near the visitor centre), Blackman, Wambelong (for group camping), and the Woolshed – have good facilities. Each camp ground is located on or beside the Parkway. No wood fires are permitted and all campers are advised to have their own cooking facilities. Free electric barbeques are available.

Burbie Camp is only accessible to those with four-wheel-drive vehicles. It is located south of the Parkway near the western park border. Bush camping is allowed in many parts of the park and seven back-country sites are available for walkers.

How to get there

The recommended route from Sydney is via Lithgow, Mudgee, Gulgong, Mendooran and Tooraweenah. From Coonabarabran in the east, it is only 35km to the park boundary on a sealed section of the John Renshaw Parkway. From Gulargambone in the west it is 42km along sealed and unsealed sections of the Parkway. Other minor access routes are via Tooraweenah to Gunneemooroo Camp.

Warrumbungle National Park and Wildlife Service
tel: (02) 6825–4364

THE PILLIGA FORESTS

The Pilliga region is the largest area of inland plain forest on the Australian continent and has been referred to as a 'million wild acres'. Most of the Pilliga landscape is either undulating or flat. A large part of the forest grows on the deep sandy soil, which drains well and makes vehicle travel easy, even after rain. Occasionally, on the lesser-used tracks, creek crossings may become a little boggy in wet weather.

Most of the Pilliga is in public ownership and is accessible to visitors. About a quarter of the forests are in the 75 000-ha Pilliga Nature Reserve with the balance managed by the State Forestry Commission who actively encourage recreation use. For administrative purposes there are over 30 separately named forestry areas: Denobollie, Wittenbra and Jacks Creek State Forest to name only a few. From a recreational point of view, however, the Pilliga is one large 400 000-ha forest with 2700km of public roads and tracks to explore and half a dozen established picnic areas and camp sites.

Swamp oak

The word *pilliga* is the Aboriginal name for the area. The local Kamilaroi people lived along the Namoi River and referred to the nearby forested country by this name, which means 'swamp oak'. Today it also refers to a township on the northern side of the forest.

The most prominent tree of the region, and the one of most interest to the foresters, is the white cypress pine. This native tree has a pretty conifer shape when young and its timber is highly sought after for its characteristic durability and resistance to termites. It also regenerates readily.

BUDGERIGARS

It comes as a pleasant surprise to see thousands of wild, free-flying budgerigars when the common perception of this bird is that they are usually caged. Around the world, budgerigars are the most popular parrot in captivity. They are also the most widely known Australian bird. Budgerigars can be encountered anywhere in inland Australia.

The best location for observing flocks of these nervous desert nomads is at a waterhole at dusk. If local conditions have been dry and there are few water sources, your chances of seeing a variety of interesting wildlife, including colourful parrots, increase markedly. Wheeling flocks of synchronised fast-flying budgerigars over a waterhole during sunset is one of Australia's most breathtaking and unforgettable sights.

Seeds of low-growing plants form the main diet of wild budgerigars. They breed whenever the desert rains bring on flushes of new growth and pairs may have several broods if food remains abundant. It is normal for budgerigars to breed in large colonies and hundreds of birds often nest together in one small area. Nests are a simple scrape on the floor of a gum tree hollow and the average clutch is five eggs. Chicks are reared in the nest for between four and five weeks, however young budgerigars become independent of their parents within days of taking their first flight.

Wild budgerigars are always green. Under artificial breeding conditions, they are seen today in dozens of different colours, from yellow to blue. However, all wild birds have finely marked black zebra lines across the back, a yellow face and a general green appearance. Males can be distinguished from the females by the slightly darker blue band on the top of the bill.

ABOVE *Johns Crossing is a quiet waterhole within the extensive native pine and ironbark forests of Pilliga. Noisy flocks of parrots, including budgerigars, come to drink here in the evenings.*

Other common tree species are ironbarks and red gums. Watch out for the koalas and red-necked wallabies which reside in the forests of the region.

Driving trails

One of the easiest ways to see the Pilliga is to follow one of the marked driving trails. The longest drive is a circle linking Coonabarabran and Narrabri via the Newell Highway and the Pilliga Forest Way. This is probably the most comprehensive way to explore the area. It can take as little as two and a half hours but can also be enjoyed at a more leisurely pace if time allows. If only passing through the area, part of this trail could be taken from Coonabarabran to Narrabri, or vice versa, avoiding the Newell Highway on this leg.

Camping

Unlike most state forests, camping is permitted at any of the prepared picnic areas. In addition, there is a basic camping ground at Salt Caves, an area which takes its name from the wind-blown sand caves. Other features of the forest include lookouts at Pantons and Baileys, and water depressions which attract a variety of wildlife at Gilgai Flora Reserve.

Warrabah National Park

The Warrabah is a little-known riverside park located away from most of the tourist routes. It is well worth a visit for those wishing to enjoy a more remote experience and is a good half-way stopping point between the Warrumbungles region and the rainforest country around Dorrigo. The park is a great area for rock climbing, canoeing, liloing, swimming and bushwalking with most of its activities being based around the Namoi River. This boulder-strewn river cuts a winding course deep down into the surrounding granite-base hills, creating 15km of swimming holes and waterfalls. The river is a grade three canoeing river and should not be tackled by the inexperienced. One set of falls lies about 6km upstream from Thunderbolts Hole.

The vegetation is fairly uniform with dry gum forest, cypress pines and she-oaks. Most of the mammals are nocturnal but there is a good range of birds to be seen. Reptiles, including skinks and dragon lizards, are common along the river during the warmth of the day. Watch out for the red-bellied black snakes as their bite is fatal.

Bush camping

Camping facilities are simple and bush camping is permitted. There is only one access point to the camping area near the park entrance at Thunderbolts Hole. Bush tracks lead to the swimming spots at Willow Hole, Billys Hole and Gum Hole. There is no ranger station, information centre or source of supplies. For a stay of any period of time, you'll need to bring everything with you.

How to get there

Access to Pilliga is reached from a number of roads north and south of Baradine or from the Newell Highway between Coonabarabran and Narrabri. The Warrabah National Park lies 35km north of Manilla via Tamworth, or from Coonabarabran via the Oxley Highway, turning north 30km east of Gunnedah.

Baradine State Forest tel: (02) 6843–1607
Armidale National Park and Wildlife Service
tel: (02) 6773–7211

MOUNT KAPUTAR NATIONAL PARK

Most of the rugged Mount Kaputar National Park is wilderness with over 80 per cent of its rough mountain tops and gullies having been formally zoned as park wilderness areas. There are dozens of great day and part-day walks starting from and around Dawsons Spring. Experienced walkers can spend many days exploring its remote corners.

To the top

A must for the first-time visitor is the Mount Kaputar Summit Walk. This gentle walk takes about an hour and starts on the Nature Trail. The view from here is expansive, across the park and over to the New England Tableland and the Warrumbungle Range. The Kaputar Plateau Circuit, which takes in Rangers and Lairds lookouts and travels through euro and rock wallaby habitat, is more challenging. Its 6km of energetic walking should take about five hours.

Crater walks

Away from Dawsons Spring and Bark Hut there are numerous shorter and longer walks. Many of these, including the Yulludunida walk, Waa Gorge and Sawn Rocks, can be treated as daytrips from Dawsons Spring. Yulludunida Crater, a strenuous four-hour walk, is perhaps the most rewarding of all and, if time is taken to explore the crater, it can easily lead to a full day's excursion. Access is from Dawsons Spring Road about 14km down from the main information centre. The snow gums of other high-country areas are replaced here by cypress pines and grass trees. Brush turkeys are frequently seen lurking in the undergrowth. The final climb to the crater peak is a taxing 100-m scramble up a rocky gully.

Basalt organ pipes

Sawn Rocks is considered to be one of Australia's best examples of 'organ piping' or basalt columnar jointing. Located on the Narrabri–Bingarra Road near a small picnic ground 32km from Narrabri, a visit to Sawn Rocks is a great midday activity. Not only is the walk short and shaded but the cliff face is seen at its best just after noon. A short stroll up

ABOVE *The dramatic Sawn Rocks at the foothills of the Nandewar Range are pillars of solidified lava that resemble organ pipes.*

the shady creek under the rusty figs brings you to the precisely sculpted 40-m-high rock face. These great pillars of solidified lava are coloured with varying degrees of intensity depending on the time of exposure to the elements. Each five-sided pillar of basalt has neatly broken off at a different length to create an impressive natural rock sculpture.

Vast floral variety

From the flat surrounding plains to the 1510-m peak at Mount Kaputar, this is a national park with great contrasts in vegetation. Figs and lilly pilly trees are common and, extra-ordinarily, here and there in tiny moist pockets are patches of dry rainforest. Higher up the slopes, drier gum woodlands dominate and native cypress pines cling to the shallow soil. Higher still, short heathlands cover the rocky outcrops. Where the soil is deep enough, snow gums make delightful alpine forests. At these altitudes on poorer soils and more exposed sites, heath and stunted woodland occur. On the wetter east-facing slopes patches of wet gum forests are dominated by various species of messmates and mountain gums.

A diverse wildlife habitat

Wildlife in the park is diverse due to the wide range of habitats. Four marsupials are common – the larger eastern grey kangaroo, the euro, and the smaller swamp and red-necked wallabies. The tall gum forest is home to three species of nocturnal glider and two species of possum.

Camping

Camping is permitted at three sites and facilities are extensive. There are toilets, hot showers, laundries, free electric barbeques, water tanks and fireplaces at Upper Bullawa Creek, Bark Hut and Dawsons Spring. Dry wood is in short supply so it must be brought in with campers. The main information centre is at Dawsons Spring. There are also two furnished cabins which require prior booking. For those seeking a remote wilderness experience, bush camping is permitted away from formed roads and picnic areas. Note that conditions can often be cold and misty. Heavy frosts are to be expected and there are occasional snow falls above 1200m.

How to get there

Access by car is 50km east of Narrabri, which is 570km north-west of Sydney. The best areas are at and on the way to Dawsons Spring and Upper Bullawa Creek. The Narrabri–Bingarra Road also crosses the park and access to the Mount Waa section of the park is off this road.

Narrabri National Park and Wildlife Service
tel: (02) 6792–4724

Don't Miss...

Adventure Experiences

The Warrumbungles are considered to have some of the best long, rock-climbing routes in Australia. The main routes are on Belougery Spire, Crater Bluff, Bluff Mountain and Tonduron. As well as the technically difficult climbs there are many easy day climbs that can be done on your own or as part of a group. Local clubs and a number of groups from Sydney and interstate head to this area on climbing expeditions.

Whitewater rafting and canoeing on the Gwydir River, downstream from Copeton Dam near Inverell, through granite gorges and in glorious hot weather is rated as some of Australia's wildest. Multi-day trips are available.

Other Interesting Places

Siding Springs Observatory is one of the most important observatories in the Southern Hemisphere because of the clear inland skies and its mountain-top location. The largest instrument is a huge 3.9-m Anglo–Australian telescope. Located west of Coonabarabran, just outside the park, the observatory has a public information centre.

Macquarie Marshes is one of the most significant swampland locations in the state. Historically, regular flooding from the

Whitewater rafting is available on the Gwydir River.

Macquarie River would fill the marshes and trigger the breeding of thousands of waterbirds. Deliberate flooding is now planned through the releasing of water from Burrendong Dam. Access is difficult since it is mainly surrounded by private land. There are views from Coolabah to Coonamble Road about 40km west of Quambone. Open days are sometimes arranged.

Coonabarabran National Park and Wildlife Service (rock climbing at Macquarie Marshes) tel: (02) 6842–1311
Siding Springs tel: (02) 6842–6211
Rafting World Expeditions tel: 1800 803688

RAINFOREST RANGES

Dorrigo • Washpool •

Border Ranges

*R*ainforest was once prolific along the coastal plain, but over the centuries many of these areas were felled to make way for farmland. Fierce conservation battles have ensured that the remaining forests will not be lost for future generations as they have been declared national parks. However, the parks comprise only a fraction of the northern ranges' wild country. Watch out for the road signs pointing to the state forests. Camping is permitted in many of these and local state forest maps are available from local rangers.

Travel Tips

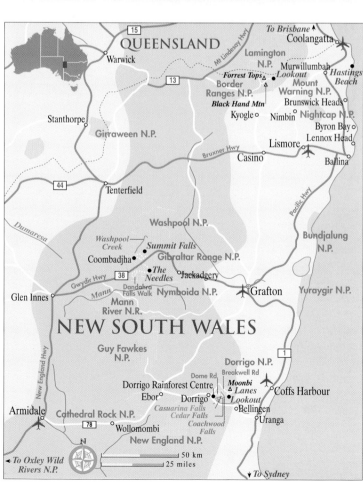

The main airport to the region is at Coolangatta with regional ones at Coffs Harbour, Armidale, Grafton and Lismore. Rental cars are available at these centres but it is perhaps best to hire a vehicle at Sydney or Brisbane and travel between the areas. If you want to hire a four-wheel-drive vehicle, book ahead as they are popular. By car, take the opportunity to experience the wilderness and avoid the main roads. Both the inland New England Highway and the busy, coastal Pacific Highway run north–south, but use them only for long-haul travel. A number of east–west-running roads link the coast and the tablelands and allow you to experience more of the countryside. Buses also travel regularly to the region, and there are a number of daytrips from the bigger coastal centres. Trains also travel between the larger cities.

ABOVE *The short but memorable Wonga Walk, which heads out from the visitor centre at Dorrigo National Park, passes the Crystal Shower Falls and then meanders through the rainforest.*

OPPOSITE *The lookout at the end of the purpose-built Skywalk at Dorrigo National Park offers fabulous views over the rainforested region without causing damage to the precious and extremely delicate ecosystem.*

DORRIGO

The Dorrigo region consists of a number of wilderness areas, including the Oxley Wild Rivers, Cathedral Rock, New England and Dorrigo national parks.

The World Heritage-listed Dorrigo National Park now protects what was once the great Dorrigo Scrub. The first tiny reserves were declared in 1902, one of the earliest rainforest areas to be protected in the country. The deep basalt cap of the plateau is covered in rich volcanic soil and the landscape has been dissected by mountain streams creating deep gullies and waterfalls off the escarpment.

Luxuriant plant life

The plateau is covered mostly in subtropical rainforest with a rich assemblage of plants, including strangler figs and booyongs. Red cedar and giant stinging trees grow with a luxuriant undergrowth of ferns and orchids. Warm and cool temperate rainforest with coachwoods and Antarctic beech is found in patches of poorer soils and in the higher altitudes. Dry rainforest also occurs in pockets as well as a rich mix of wet gum forests dominated by blackbutts and Sydney blue gums.

Dorrigo boasts one of the most impressive rainforest information centres in the country. In addition to a range of facilities, there is a rainforest lookout known as Skywalk, which allows close inspection of the rainforest canopy.

A wildlife Eden

The huge variety of vegetation supports an equally diverse birdlife, including some rare rainforest species. Marbled frogmouths, paradise riflebirds and rufous scrub-birds are found here, as are the more common green catbirds and satin bowerbirds. However, the avian highlight is the mound-building brush turkey, which stalks around the rainforest openings.

Most of the region's resident mammals are nocturnal. but in the early morning or late afternoon red-necked pademelons are seen quite frequently in open areas.

Rainforest walks

The park has delightful marked trails, including the 6-km Wonga Walk, which starts at the Glade Picnic Area and takes in the dramatic subtropical rainforest habitats and Hardwood Lookout, affording views across to the coast. For those wishing to really experience Dorrigo, however, head to the Never Never Picnic Area located to the west of the Glade on the Dome Road. Several longer walks set out from here and explore the warm temperate rainforest. Of these the best are the Rosewood Creek Track including Cedar Falls side-track, a 6.5-km circuit.

Lanes Lookout camp

No overnight camping is allowed in the popular areas of Dorrigo but a bush camp site is available on the Wild Cattle Creek near Lanes Lookout, 10km east of Dorrigo. Take the Prakes Road from Dorrigo, then the Breakwell (Slingsby) Road which enters the park on the Killungoondie Plain. The camp is about two hours' walk along Slingsby Trail.

New England: a rugged escarpment

There is only one entry point to New England National Park, off the Armidale–Ebor Road 14km west of Ebor. The landscape is varied but the feature that draws most visitors is the cool temperate rainforest near the escarpment rim. Only the central and high areas are easily accessed, with most of the rugged country falling away to the east. The central area has a number of good marked walks but the rest of the park is for wilderness exploration only. There is a good range of accommodation from basic camp sites – like the Styx River Rest Area 3km outside the park and the Thungutti Camping Area just inside the park – to cabins at Banksia Point, where booking ahead is essential.

Cathedral Rock's granite towers

Cathedral Rock National Park, 15km from Ebor Falls and 50km from Dorrigo, is rarely visited. Its dominant features are huge granite outcrops and gum forests. There is a variety of long walks and two good bush camp sites, one at Barokee Rest Area in the centre of the park and the other at Native Dog Creek Rest Area on the Guyra–Ebor Road.

Oxley Wild Rivers

Home to deep gorges, swimming holes and rivers ideal for canoeing, Oxley Wild Rivers National Park is located east of Armidale and south of Wollomombi. This park comprises a number of separate regions with different access routes. At Wollomombi there is a gorge containing one of the continent's highest waterfalls with a good swimming hole at the bottom. Also try Georges Creek on the Wollomombi–Kempsey Road. Bush camping is permitted in most sections of the park.

How to get there

The main road access to the Dorrigo wilderness area is off the Armidale–Urunga Road, which starts south of Coffs Harbour, and runs through the towns of Wollomombi, Ebor and Dorrigo.

Dorrigo Rainforest Centre tel: (02) 6657-2309
Armidale National Park and Wildlife Service (Oxley Wild Rivers) tel: (02) 6773-7211

WASHPOOL

This wilderness area includes the Washpool, Gibraltar Range and Nymboida national parks, which are all connected. Conservation battles in the late 1970s focused on the Washpool region and resulted in compromises that allowed for some forestry activities to continue, but also protected many large areas with new national parks being formed and rainforest sections being added to existing parks.

Protected forests

The Washpool National Park was one of the new parks, with the pristine rainforest of the Washpool and Coombadjha valleys north of the Gwydir Highway being included in 1983. The open woodland and heath of the Gibraltar Range National Park, sitting on the range astride and south of the Gwydir Highway, were set aside in 1967. These two parks share a long border and both have World Heritage status.

Rainforest walking trails

The Washpool Walk in the Washpool National Park is one of the best marked rainforest trails in the state. Starting at the Coombadjha Rest Area the walk winds its way through 10km of many types of warm temperate rainforest. The track passes Summit Falls and then goes through

---

REGENT BOWERBIRD

The Regent Bowerbird is one of Australia's most striking birds. Males are dramatically adorned in black and gold, and the bill and eyes are also golden. The bird's colours are particularly dazzling against the verdant dark forest in which it lives. As with all species of bowerbird, the female is sombrely attired; her mottled green and brown plumage is suited to the camouflaged role she performs at the nest.

Like all bowerbirds, the male regent builds a stick bower to entice potential mates. Consistent with the theory that the duller species build showier bowers, this handsome bird builds a simple one. The main arena consists of two walls of short sticks standing upright and forming a central avenue. This avenue may be decorated with a selection of leaves, snail shells or fruit. The male paints the walls of the bower with chewed fruits applied with moistened saliva. All this is apparently very impressive to the females.

Once a potential mate approaches the bower for a closer look, the male begins a bounding dance, churring and squeaking and flashing his brilliant golden plumage. If the female is impressed

by this performance, mating may take place either in the bower or on a simpler display ground nearby. The female then has the task of nest building, incubating the eggs and rearing the young on her own.

Regent Bowerbirds are usually elusive and will remain hidden in dense tangled vegetation. They are found in subtropical rainforest along the coast from Mackay in Queensland to Sydney. In winter, mixed groups of males, females and youngsters may venture away from the thickest parts of the forest, sometimes making cautious appearances in more open country. The normal food of this bowerbird is fruit which it collects in the upper branches of the forest.

ABOVE *Coombadjha Creek at Washpool National Park can be reached via a short walk through rainforest from any of the camp sites in the park's south.*

a rainforest gully that is home to some huge red cedars. One of the trees has a circumference of over 7m. Washpool also contains the world's largest undisturbed coachwood forest.

Wilderness challenge
For independent trackers, a 30-km trek from Coombadjha to the Baryulgil entrance of the park via the Washpool Creek is a real wilderness challenge. Depending on the route chosen, this trek can include old forestry trails or can cross the Willowie Scrub rainforest wilderness. The walk is highly recommended and being drenched by waterfalls and rain is invigorating. There are also wild rocky streams suitable for swimming. Before setting out, though, check with the park staff or at least register your proposed route at the ranger station.

Gibraltar walks
The many excellent tracks in the Gibraltar National Park include the walk to the 240-m Dandahra Falls, a 5-km-return

hike that takes in the granite tors known as the Needles and the Barra Nula Cascades. The granite faces and tors present a challenge to rock climbers.

Nymboida's wild rivers
Nymboida National Park adjoins the southern border of the Gibraltar Range National Park and contains the confluence of the Mann and Nymboida rivers. Bush camping along the sandy river flats or exploring the area by whitewater raft or canoe are the main attractions of this region.

On the edge of the main range just east of Glen Innes is a peaceful small reserve on the upper reaches of the Mann River. The Mann River Nature Reserve's mountainous terrain is covered in wet gum forests and there is a good selection of rock holes for swimming. Steep mountain walks of up to 7km are marked and lead to the reserve's high points. Watch out for six species of kangaroo, including rock wallabies.

Camping
There are several picnic areas and a basic camp site along the Coombadjha Road, south of the Washpool National Park. An isolated basic camp site and picnic area exists at the northern lowland end, just inside the Baryulgil entrance.

The Gibraltar Range National Park's visitor centre is located at the main entrance road to the Dandahra Falls. Good facilities including cold showers are available at the Mulligans Hut camping area.

In the Nymboida National Park facilities are few but there is a delightful riverside camp ground at Ramomie in the state forest south of Jackadgery. Simple camping and picnic facilities are also provided along the river's edge in the Mann River Nature Reserve.

How to get there

From Grafton the Washpool region is 80–100km (or 60–80km from Glen Innes), along the Gwydir Highway. There is also an unsealed road from Baryulgil via Coaldale.

Access to the rugged rainforests of the Washpool and Gibraltar Range national parks is along the Coombadjha Road, north off the highway beside the Hakea Picnic Ground, which is 6km to the east of the visitor centre. Some of the lower sections of this road are steep and slippery so take extra care while driving to avoid accidents.

The Gibraltar Range National Park is 69km from Glen Innes on the Gwydir Highway.

Road access to Nymboida is from the Gwydir Highway via Cooraldooral, the Fire Trail in the west or the Jackadgery Road to New Zealand Falls in the east.

The Mann River Nature Reserve is 35km east of Glen Innes, also off Gwydir Highway.
Glen Innes National Park and Wildlife Service
tel: (02) 6732–1177

ABOVE *The walk to the summit of Mount Warning reveals a delightful kaleidoscope of rainforest trees, wildlife and views.*

BORDER RANGES

This region, along with the Washpool area further south, was the focus of some of Australia's most bitter and physical wilderness conservation battles. Intense media and political conflict in the 1970s culminated in the 1979 clashes in the forests of Terania Creek, now part of Nightcap National Park, between supporters of forest logging and conservationists. As a direct consequence, many of the rainforest areas of northern New South Wales were placed under the care of national parks and reserves. Protesters Falls beside Terania Creek commemorate this period. The Border Ranges, Mount Warning and Nightcap national parks were all inscribed as Rainforest Reserves and placed on the World Heritage list in 1986.

Circles of fire
The Nightcap, Tweed and McPherson ranges, part of the New South Wales–Queensland border, form a huge circle of rugged rainforest-clad mountains which surround the remnants of a 23 million-year-old shield volcano. The craggy peak of Mount Warning, named by Captain Cook, was the central magma chamber from where eruptions spread for over 40km. Remnants of the volcano's eastern edges now form reefs in the ocean off Hastings Beach, and Mount Warning is, today, the largest shield volcano in the southern hemisphere.

The shade of the rainforest
Nightcap National Park is an area of rich subtropical rainforest, and trees such as red cedar, yellow carabeen and strangler figs shade the forest floor. On the higher and drier ridges are huge brush box trees, some over 1500 years old. The box trees were the main target of the loggers in the past. Picnic areas are located at the top of Mount Nardi at the end of Newtons Drive from Nimbin. From here there are a number of walks along the top of the range. A loop walk of about 5km is possible from the Mount Nardi car park to Mount Matheson and back via Pholis Gap. The most accessible area of rainforest is at the Terania Creek picnic area, and a 1-km walk leads to Protesters Falls.

The spectacular scenery and rainforest of the Border Ranges is a haven for wildlife watchers, naturalists and bushwalkers. Connecting with the Lamington National Park in Queensland, it forms a vast 70-km region of mountain rainforest. The best landscape views are available along the Tweed Ranges Scenic Drive. Dotted along the drive are picnic areas with toilets and numerous rainforest walks. A day spent exploring the drive and its trails is definitely time well spent.

The central section of the park along Lions Road offers little opportunity to explore on foot but there is, however, good scenery from the road. It is also a more scenic route into Queensland than what the coastal road offers. West of Lions Road, access to the park is limited with no facilities. All exploration is on foot in difficult and unmarked terrain.

Wildlife of the rainforest

Over 170 species of bird, including many rare ones, such as the sooty owl and Albert lyrebird, and some more widespread rainforest species such as bowerbirds and fruit-pigeons have been recorded in the park. Platypus inhabit the creeks and many different possums and gliders may be spotted at night with the aid of a strong light. Over 40 species of frog, mainly nocturnal, also live in the park.

Mount Warning

The climb to the summit of Mount Warning is worth the challenge. For those of moderate fitness the 9-km-return walk will take about six hours. There are many stops along the way and chances to observe sting trees, figs, palms and flame trees. Observant and quiet walkers may see brush turkeys or logrunners.

The short Lyrebird Walk gives access to a palm forest on a raised walkway. It is best to start either walk early so as to increase the chances of seeing the more timid wildlife that hides during the day.

Camping

There are two basic camping areas in the Border Ranges National Park, at Forest Tops and Sheep Station Creek, and both are on the Tweed Range Scenic Drive. Either would make a good base to explore the region. Camping for one night is allowed near the Terania Creek picnic area in Nightcap National Park. No camping is allowed in Mount Warning National Park but there is a private camping ground with good facilities at the park's entrance.

How to get there

Mount Warning National Park is 12km west of Murwillumbah on the Pacific Highway. To reach Nightcap National Park, head north from Terania Creek or Nimbin. The eastern sections of the Border Ranges National Park are accessed via the Tweed Range Scenic Drive from Kyogle north of Casino on the Bruxner Highway.

Alstonville National Park and Wildlife Service
tel: (02) 6628–1177

DON'T MISS...

ADVENTURE EXPERIENCES

The Nymboida River is one of the country's top whitewater rafting and canoeing regions and in terms of rafting is a great area for beginners through to the more advanced. Multi-day trips are for experienced rafters wanting a wilderness experience. Rapids in the Nymboida Gorge include 'The Mushroom', 'Devils Cauldron' and 'Off the Wall'.

Whitewater canoeing can be undertaken on the Mann River. The best time is in winter and spring, subject to water levels. There is a choice of companies operating in the area.

Caldera Rim Walk is a world-class wilderness walk along the top of the rainforest ridge dividing New South Wales and Queensland. There are several possible start and finish points and the longest walk extends over four days. A recommended starting point is at the Booyong Walk in Border Ranges National Park, finishing in Lamington National Park in Queensland. This is only a one-way trail so you will need to make arrangements for the return journey.

OTHER INTERESTING AREAS

There are many coastal national parks with great beaches and good camping facilities. Try **Bundjalung National Park** with camping access from Iluka, **Yuraygir National Park** with camping access south of Yamba, and **Hat Head National Park** with camping access south of South West Rocks. Detailed maps or directions are available from National Parks and Wildlife Services offices. Avoid school holiday periods.

Whitewater rafting on the Nymboida River provides numerous challenges.

Grafton Visitor Centre (Washpool tours) tel: (02) 6642–4677
Coffs Harbour Visitor Centre (whitewater rafting)
tel: (02) 6652–1522
State Forestry Kempsey tel: (02) 6562-1341
Grafton National Park and Wildlife Service (coastal parks)
tel: (02) 6642–0613
Port Macquarie National Park and Wildlife Service
tel: (02) 6583–5518

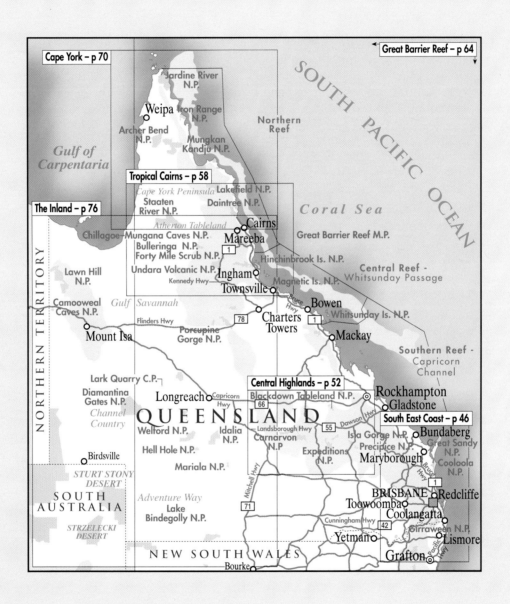

Cape York – p 70

Great Barrier Reef – p 64

Jardine River
N.P.

Weipa

Iron Range
N.P.

Archer Bend
N.P.

Mungkan
Kandju N.P.

Northern
Reef

*Gulf of
Carpentaria*

Tropical Cairns – p 58

Cape York Peninsula   Lakefield N.P.

The Inland – p 76

Staaten
River N.P.

Daintree N.P.

Coral Sea

Atherton Tableland   Cairns

Chillagoe–Mungana Caves N.P.   Mareeba

Great Barrier Reef M.P.

Bulleringa N.P.
Forty Mile Scrub N.P.

Hinchinbrook Is. N.P.

Central Reef -
Whitsunday Passage

Undara Volcanic N.P.

Kennedy Hwy   Ingham

Magnetic Is. N.P.

Lawn Hill
N.P.

Townsville

Camooweal
Caves N.P.

Gulf Savannah

Bowen

Bruce Hwy

Whitsunday Is. N.P.

Flinders Hwy

Charters
Towers

Mount Isa

Porcupine
Gorge N.P.

Mackay

Southern Reef -
Capricorn
Channel

Lark Quarry C.P.

Central Highlands – p 52

Diamantina
Gates N.P.

Longreach

Capricorn
Hwy

Blackdown Tableland N.P.

Rockhampton

Gladstone

*Channel
Country*

QUEENSLAND

Dawson Hwy

South East Coast – p 46

Welford N.P.

Idalia
N.P.

Landsborough Hwy

Carnarvon
N.P.

Isla Gorge N.P.

Bundaberg

Hell Hole N.P.

Expeditions
N.P.

Precipice N.P.

Great Sandy
N.P.

Mariala N.P.

Maryborough

Cooloola
N.P.

Birdsville

Mitchell Hwy

Bruce Hwy

*STURT STONY
DESERT*

BRISBANE

Redcliffe

SOUTH
AUSTRALIA

Adventure Way

Lake
Bindegolly N.P.

Toowoomba

Coolangatta

*STRZELECKI
DESERT*

Cunningham Hwy

Girraween N.P.

Yetman

Lismore

Pacific Hwy

NEW SOUTH WALES

Grafton

Bourke

NORTHERN TERRITORY

QUEENSLAND

SOUTH-EAST COAST

Girraween • Cooloola • Fraser Island

Queensland's south-east region is richly blessed with an equable climate, vast sandy beaches and inviting waters. The summer months can be humid, however, and the nights frosty, especially when camping inland from the coast. Outdoor activities in summer can also leave you vulnerable to sunburn so take extra precautions. Slap on the sunscreen, wear suitable clothing, always wear a hat and avoid the midday sun.

Travel Tips

Brisbane is the closest major centre for domestic and international flights, rental cars (including four-wheel-drives), bus and safari tours, and trains. Brisbane is also a good place to obtain up-to-date information and maps from the National Parks' visitor centres or the Water Resources and Forestry Service.

From Brisbane, the main sealed highway to Fraser Island is the Bruce, which heads north along the coast. The Cunningham heads west, connecting with the New England Highway, the Warrego heads north-west to the central highland region and the Pacific heads south along the coast to Sydney.

Bear in mind that salt water can cause damage to vehicles so if you are tempted to do a beach drive think about hiring a vehicle instead of using your own. There are many car hire firms in Brisbane, Noosa Heads and Hervey Bay and four-wheel-drives can be hired for a day or longer.

GIRRAWEEN NATIONAL PARK

The Girraween National Park lies inland from the bustling coast, and with its interesting mix of wildlife, classic granite stone arrangements and mountain camping, it is a great place for bushwalkers. This is not normally an overcrowded park, so a bush camp site is nearly always available.

Girraween abuts the border of New South Wales and the adjacent Bald Rock National Park. Other major wilderness parks south of Toowoomba include Sundown, Main Range and Mount Mistake. All have good bush camping facilities and are not as busy as the coastal parks. Sundown is particularly wild and remote, an ideal winter refuge away from the more popular places.

Girraween's majestic landscape is dominated by an extraordinary array of amazingly arranged granite tors and boulder fields. The rocky peaks including Mount Norman, the highest, are all the result of great lava intrusions dating back to over 225 million years ago.

Girraween is an Aboriginal word meaning 'many flowers'. Late winter and spring flowers form a strong contrast to the rounded and sombre grey landscape. Granite rocks do not produce rich soils, however, and the park's vegetation consists principally of wattle and pea heathlands with scattered pockets of gum and native pine forests. In places, where the granite boulders impeded water flow, swampy conditions have developed. Most of the taller gums grow in the steeper valleys where the soil extends deeper.

Wildlife, heard but unseen

At dusk or in the early morning, wildlife watchers will be rewarded with grey kangaroos, red-necked wallabies and swamp wallabies in the grassy clearings, especially around the camp sites. A number of possum species are present in the park but are unlikely to be seen unless nocturnal spotlight rambles are undertaken. Brush-tailed possums often visit the camp grounds in the evenings. Wombats are frequently heard at night and rarer marsupials, such as quolls, have been observed, while owls and frogmouths are also heard and sometimes seen on spotlight trips. Many common birds, including parrots and wrens, may be seen, but the park's avian highlights are the rare turquoise parrot and exquisite diamond firetail.

Shorter walks

On cool summer mornings or during the mild winters, forest walks are a sheer delight. For the less ambitious the Granite Arch Walk from the camp ground takes less than half an hour. Alternatively, there is the Dr Roberts Waterhole Walk, featuring the ground orchids of the woodlands. This walk starts near the northern exit of the park.

Climbing the rock formation known as the Pyramids is a strenuous trek of about two hours return. Several combinations of longer walks including climbing Castle Rock, the Sphinx and Turtle Rock are worth the challenge. The climb to the summit of Mount Norman is the most energetic marked walk but the views are breathtaking. This hike starts at the information centre and takes about six hours.

Walking treks

Girraween provides an ideal opportunity to enjoy several days of delightful wilderness walking in all but the hottest months of the year. It is a relatively quiet area that allows a level of solitude and reflection that is less likely on the coast. The other nearby inland parks in New South Wales and Queensland provide similar walking opportunities. One- or two-day wilderness walks can conveniently link both the Girraween and Bald Rock national parks.

BELOW *Mount Norman is dotted with giant granite boulders, and the climb to the summit and back is a full day's walk.*

An exposed slab of grey

Bald Rock is a huge granite slab 750m long, 500m wide and rising 200m above the surrounding landscape. The slab is one of the largest exposed granite domes in the world. Swimming holes are located in Bald Rock Creek and at the Junction, and during popular times of the year park rangers run nature walks. Whilst days in winter are balmy, nights can be very cold.

There are two delightful bush camp sites in the park with excellent facilities including hot showers. Information can be obtained at the ranger centre at Bald Rock Creek. The established camp sites are rotated to allow regeneration of each area in turn.

How to get there

Girraween is located 260km south-west of Brisbane on the Highway. The sealed Pyramids Road leaves the New England Highway 26km south of Stanthorpe. There is also an unsealed road from Eukey.

Access to Bald Rock is from the Mount Lindesay Highway 33km north of Stanthorpe. Access to the parks south of Toowoomba is from the Stanthorpe–Glenlyon Dam Road.
Girraween National Park tel: (07) 4684–5157
Sundown National Park tel: (02) 6737–5235

COOLOOLA NATIONAL PARK

Cooloola National Park is a complex coastal region with many facets. The 30-km-long beach is backed by 200-m-high coloured sand dunes, towering gum forests and dune lakes. In addition the freshwater Noosa River winds its way through the park and empties into a series of freshwater lakes. This unusual natural diversity creates a range of wildlife observation and recreation activities within a relatively small area.

Four-wheel-driving

Beach driving is allowed within the park, but only in four-wheel-drive vehicles. Access to the main beach, variously known as Ocean, Teewah, Cooloola or Forty Mile beach, is via Rainbow Beach in the north, via the Noosa River Crossing in Tewantin from the south, or, in the centre, via Rainbow Beach Road. Access to the coloured sand dunes along the central and northern beachfront is via the beach, and beach camping is allowed. The wreck of the *Cherry Venture*, just south of Double Island Point, is also accessible via the beach.

HUMPBACK WHALES

One of the great environmental tragedies of the last century was the hunting of whales to near extinction throughout the oceans of the world. Nineteenth-century whalers hunting in Australian waters decimated populations of several whale species. It is a joy that in the final decades of the 20th century whale numbers are recovering to the extent that observation of migrating and breeding whales in Australian waters has become a popular nature activity.

Humpback whales are huge and have a distinctive fin on their back which, together with enormous flippers stretching over 5m across, distinguishes them from other large whales. A large male's total body length may reach 15m. They are known for their confidence around boats and their apparently 'playful' antics – above-water behaviour includes breaching, rolling, tail splashing and somersaulting.

Humpbacks have regular migration routes. Every year they swim from the summer feeding grounds in the Antarctic to the winter breeding grounds in the relatively warmer waters around the eastern and western Australian coasts. Moving at speeds of around 8kph, the young males arrive first, followed by mated pairs and finally the mothers with older calves. The mothers and calves leave the tropical waters at the end of winter after all the other whales have departed.

During the winter, migrating whales can easily be observed off Cape Byron, Korogoro Point at Hat Head National Park and Camden Head at Camden Haven in New South Wales. The best viewing areas in Queensland are around Hervey Bay, Point Lookout on Stradbroke Island and between the Great Barrier Reef and the coast, especially around the Whitsunday Islands.

In Western Australia, humpbacks are most often seen at Ningaloo Reef, off Point Quobba at Shark Bay and around the Dampier archipelago.

ABOVE *Rainbow Beach is world famous for the variety of sand colours in its dunes. Beach driving is permitted along this beautiful stretch of coastline.*

Coastal walks

Coastal wilderness walking is at its best in Cooloola. A well-planned, marked trail runs 46km from Elanda Point, the main centre in the south, to the park edge at Rainbow Beach Road. The trail could be completed in a couple of days but to really appreciate the region allow two nights of camping. The trail crosses many park habitats and can be boggy.

There are six points of vehicle access to the trail allowing for shorter sections to be completed. It is wise to always carry sufficient fresh water despite the abundant supplies as conditions may affect the quality of the water. There is an information centre at Rainbow Beach for maps and advice.

Coloured sand walks

Carlo Sand Blow is a short walk from Rainbow Beach. From the Bymien picnic area are several options for interesting forest walks. Poona Lake is just over 2km from the picnic area and the walks to Freshwater and Rainbow beaches are both around 7km return. The Rainbow Beach Walk follows the old telegraph line, and a longer walk heads south and circumnavigates Freshwater Lake.

Waterway exploring

Walkers and four-wheel-drive explorers will enjoy Cooloola, but quietly gliding down the Noosa River by canoe is a highlight that is unsurpassed. Short evening walks from the camp site by the river is an unforgettable experience.

The activities in the southern section of the park also centre on its waterways. The freshwater upper Noosa River has almost 30km of waterway navigable by small boats, and even more if you are prepared to do a few portages.

Walks from boat landings include the 4-km-return Teewah Walk across the dunes to the main beach. Beginning at a landing on the Noosa River, the Cooloola Sandpatch is a delightful 12-km-return walk through a variety of open forests and dune formations. On Kinaba Island there is an information centre accessible only by walking or by boat. The centre has a mangrove boardwalk.

Womalah State Forest

Enclosed within the park is the Womalah State Forest. It extends south from Rainbow Beach on the eastern side of the Noosa River, almost to the Cooloola Sandpatch, a distance of nearly 20km. There are many rough tracks in the forest and care should be taken traversing the area as a car can easily get bogged in sand.

Staying in the park

The best-equipped camping grounds are behind Rainbow Beach at Freshwater. Other camp sites are located at Poverty Point on the quiet salt waters of Tin Can Inlet and along the main beach south of Little Freshwater Creek.

The Cooloola Wilderness Trail has five camp sites along its length, two of which are inaccessible except via the trail. There is a private camp ground at Elanda Point with further camp sites at Harrys Landing and Fig Tree Point. There are also many bushwalker camp sites and locations for boat camping within the park.

Towns around the park have a full range of accommodation, from the luxury facilities at Noosa Heads to more modest facilities elsewhere.

How to get there

Noosa Heads is around 200km north of Brisbane via the Bruce Highway, turning off at Cooroy, or 30km west of Gympie on the sealed Tin Can Bay Road to Rainbow Beach. The unsealed Cooloola Way south from Rainbow Beach Road goes to the west of the park. Some four-wheel-drive-only tracks include beach access at Freshwater. There are also many bus and safari tours from Brisbane and Maryborough.

Freshwater National Park and Wildlife Service
tel: (07) 3449–7959

ABOVE *A camp site is located at Lake Boomanjin, renowned for its rich colour that has been enhanced by tannins from vegetation.*

LEFT *Near Central Station on Fraser Island are tall eucalypt forests which have flourished despite their sandy floor.*

FRASER ISLAND

Fraser Island should not be missed, both for the beach camping and quiet exploration of the perched lakes. This is a place with a wild untamed feel and a few days roaming its tracks and beaches, either on foot or by four-wheel-drive, will enliven the spirit. The northern half of the island is part of the Great Sandy National Park and the main centre is located at Central Station in the southern section of the island. Information offices are located at Waddy Point and Dundubara.

Fraser Island is the world's largest sand island and is over 120km long with dunes rising over 200m. Because of its remarkable beauty and its intriguing natural history, the whole island was given World Heritage status in Australia's bicentennial year. Forestry operations ceased in 1992 and the whole island is now managed by the National Parks Service.

Given that the island is composed only of sand, it supports an amazing wealth of plants. Huge blackbutt forests, once felled for their timber, grow in protected areas, while rainforest patches, heathlands and mangrove forests skirt the island's southern edge.

Lakes perched on sand

Across the island there are 20 major lakes and a variety of other swampy areas. These lakes are located high on the sand with accumulated leafy deposits on the lake bed providing a seal to stop the fresh water draining away. Half the world's perched lakes reside on Fraser Island. Lake Boomanjin, the world's largest, covers an area of over 200ha and is surrounded by beautiful wide, white sand.

It is fascinating to see small freshwater creeks draining the sandy island; here and there they spill across the coastal beaches and out to sea.

Although shallow, the freshwater lakes are safe for swimming. Eli Creek is popular but swimming at the ocean beach is dangerous and not encouraged by park rangers.

Teeming with wildlife

The abundant wildlife is a feature of the island. Birds of prey are conspicuous, particularly sea eagles and brahminy kites. Over 200 birds have been observed on Fraser Island.

Many species of possum and swamp wallaby hide in the thicker forests. Several species of tortoise live in the freshwater lakes, including some very friendly residents of Bowarrady Lake. As with all wild animals they should not be fed for their own nutritional good.

Fraser Island's dingoes are the purest strain of dingo remaining on the continent, since the mainland canines have interbred with domestic dogs. The dingoes can often be too friendly, and as they are wild animals they should also not be encouraged with food.

Walking the sand
There are dozens of marked walking tracks on the island, ranging in length from 1km to long day walks. One of the most popular is the Circuit Walk from Dilli Village on the ocean beach to Lake Boomanjin, Central Station and back to the beach at Lake Wabby.

Driving the sand
Most visitors explore the island by four-wheel-drive vehicle. There are hundreds of kilometres of sandy tracks and beach driving is allowed. Special techniques are required for driving on this type of terrain and if visitors are renting, either on the island or at Hervey Bay, inexperienced drivers should be given some basic instruction.

Colour-coded, marked four-wheel-drive trails help new venturers find their way. The northern, red-marked circuit starts at Central Station and passes Lake Mackenzie and Lake Wabby. The southern, green-marked circuit visits a number of southern lakes and meets the ocean beach at Dilli Village. Both these circuits cover about 30km.

Two other routes start at Happy Valley. The southern, yellow route is short and visits Lake Garawongera and the ocean beach. The longer northern blue route covers 36km through the Yidney Scrub to Lake Allom and then to the ocean beach. The southern beaches are usually less frequently visited by fishermen and provide the perfect opportunity for quiet reflection.

Staying on the island
There are seven main camping areas on the island and beach camping is allowed. There are also four resort areas with all styles and standards of accommodation.

How to get there

Fraser Island lies 190km north of Brisbane. Transport to the island is either by light plane, vehicle or passenger ferry, or private boat. Ferries operate from the Urangan and River Heads near Hervey Bay to Kingfisher Bay, and Inskip Point to Hook Point.
Central Station National Park and Wildlife Service tel: (07) 4127–9191
Fraser Coast Visitor Centre tel: (07) 4122–3444

DON'T MISS...

ADVENTURE EXPERIENCES
Cooloola National Park is one of the few places in Australia that has an organised canoe camping trail. The park service has produced a canoe trail brochure which identifies 15 camp sites from Boreen Point along the Noosa River to the junction of Teewah Creek. The total distance is 36km one way and several days to a week could be spent exploring the trail. Canoes are available at Elanda Point camping ground and Harrys Landing.

Hang-gliding from the dunes in Cooloola National Park has a strong following and the brisk sea breezes provide the necessary lift for exciting flights across the park.
Elanda National Park and Wildlife Service tel: (07) 5449–7364

OTHER INTERESTING ACTIVITIES
Boat-based whale watching on **Hervey Bay** is one of the highlights of an Australian adventure holiday for many visitors. There are many tour operators and most have full- or part-day trips during the winter months. Some boats have hydrophones (an instrument used to detect sounds underwater) and underwater viewing facilities.

Lake Wabby, Fraser Island, is accessible by four-wheel-drive.

The whole of **Moreton Island** north of Brisbane is a sand island and national park. It has huge sand dunes and is accessible only to four-wheel-drive vehicles. This is a good vantage point for shore-based whale watching.
Moreton National Park tel: (07) 3408–2710
Queensland Travel Centre (whale watching) tel: 13 18 01
State Forests Gympie tel: (07) 5482–2244
Borumba Dam tel: (07) 5484–5106

CENTRAL HIGHLANDS

Carnarvon Gorge • Dawson River Gorges •

Blackdown Tableland

The Central Highlands is a good stopover between the Queensland coast and western New South Wales or the Northern Territory. From Brisbane it can become part of a round trip up the coast to the Whitsundays, then returning inland. As summer can be hot and wet, the best time to visit is from about April until October. During these months the days are balmy and the nights cool, but some nights can be bitterly cold and frost is common. All the well-known areas are busy at this time of year, so booking camp sites before arriving is advisable.

Travel Tips

The major airport is at Brisbane with regional ones at Roma, Gladstone and Longreach. Extended safari tours are available from Brisbane.

Road access is via the sealed Warrego Highway west of Brisbane and north on the Leichhardt or the part-sealed Carnarvon and Fitzroy development roads. Alternative routes are the Bruce Highway from Brisbane to Gladstone and then via the Dawson, or via the Capricorn Highway from Rockhampton or the Gregory from Charters Towers. If you are travelling from New South Wales, take the Mitchell Highway.

Rental cars are available from most centres. Four-wheel-drives are useful, and essential after rain as roads can be impassable for conventional vehicles and even the main roads are subject to flooding. Carry extra supplies in case of delays.

Flies can be a nuisance and animals wander onto the roads at any time, especially at night so avoid driving then.

ABOVE LEFT *Carnarvon Gorge is an oasis in the middle of a dry inland region.*

OPPOSITE *Aboriginal rock art at Carnarvon Gorge is thought to be over 3600 years old. The history of the early inhabitants is unknown.*

QUEENSLAND

To Clermont / Charters Towers
To Longreach
Jericho
Gregory Hwy
66
Capricorn Hwy
Emerald
Rockhampton
1
Peregrine Lookout
Blackwater
Dingo
Duaringa
66
Charlevue Lookout
Fairbairn Dam
Stony Creek Falls
Officers Pocket
Mimosa Creek
Rainbow Falls
Springsure
Blackdown Tableland N.P.
To Gladstone
17
Mantuan Downs
Nogoa
55
Fitzroy Dev Rd
Great Dividing Range
Ka Ka Mundi Section
Rolleston
Dawson Hwy
Moura
Burnett Hwy
To Brisbane
Salvator Rosa Section
Carnarvon N.P.
Bauhinia Downs
Mt Moffat Section
Carnarvon Gorge Section
Lake Nuga Nuga
Theodore
Tambo
Warrego
Carnarvon Gorge
Visitor Centre
Oasis Tourist Lodge
Expeditions N.P.
Isla Gorge N.P.
Landsborough Hwy
Robinson Gorge
Cattle Dip
Precipice N.P.
Augathella
71
Taroom
Dawson
Injune
N
100 km
50 miles
Charleville
To Cunnamulla
Carnarvon Dev Rd
To Roma

CARNARVON GORGE

This national park covers an area of inland Australia that is not to be missed. At least three days should be allocated to fully appreciate the region, even for those with only a little time to spare. The landscape at Carnarvon is dominated by a sandstone plateau that is dissected by a number of streams and rivers. In various parts of the park the sandstone has weathered into a great diversity of landforms. The Carnarvon region also has a myriad wild animals and is well-known for its possums, lizards and birds; platypus can also be seen.

When the explorer Sir Thomas Mitchell stumbled upon the gorges of this region in 1846, he described them in literary superlatives: 'Some resembled gothic cathedrals in ruins, others forts… It was a discovery worthy of the toils of pilgrimage. These beautiful recesses of unpeopled earth could no longer remain unknown.' His reflections on the geological features of the region remain unquestioned but his assessment of its lack of inhabitants was inaccurate. The evidence of Aboriginal occupation of the gorges in the form of grand rock-art sites is a significant feature of Carnarvon Gorge National Park.

Main gorge: walk of treasures

Carnarvon's main gorge is a 30-km serpentine-shaped oasis of cool forests, running water and spectacular scenery. To visit all the outstanding features a 10-km, full day's excursion from the visitor centre is required, and it is one of the most rewarding day walks on the continent. On the way to the jewel in the gorge's crown at Cathedral Cave there are Aboriginal paintings, stencils and engravings. Big Bend is just beyond the end of the main gorge walk and from here the more adventurous can explore the upper reaches of the gorge and enjoy the commanding views from Battleship Spur. For those with the energy, the Moss Garden, Amphitheatre, Hell Hole Gorge and Wards Canyon are all captivating side trips off the main gorge walk.

Mount Moffat

The Mount Moffat section is located 160km northwest of Injune. The gorge is a narrow slit gouged into the soft white sandstones and the towering cliffs shade the floor of the valley, enabling a rich ancient rainforest to persist in the cool recesses. This is one of the most popular regions of the park but a four-wheel-drive is needed to reach many of the places of interest.

Wilderness treks

The Ka Ka Mundi section is bounded by 30km of sandstone escarpments and its high peaks form part of the Great Dividing Range. This remote area of the park is only recommended for visitors with four-wheel-drives. The region has no marked walking tracks so the wilderness walks along the high sandstone ridges, especially to Mount Ka Ka Mundi, are through very remote country.

Salvator Rosa

In the Salvator Rosa section to the west, the soft sandstone forms a rounded landscape with luxuriant springs which seep water onto the dry plains, forming swamps and peatbogs. This area so impressed the explorer Sir Thomas Mitchell that he named it after the famous 17th-century Spanish artist.

Accommodation and facilities

At Carnarvon Gorge, the main centre for all sections of the park, there is a visitor centre, toilets, showers and car-based camping facilities. Access is easy for conventional vehicles. A comfortable range of accommodation, which can be used as a base, is available at the entrance, and back-country camping is an option at either Big Bend or in one of the other park sections. Oasis Lodge provides cabin

accommodation just outside the park, 3km from the visitor centre. There are four basic bush camp sites at Dargonelly Rock Hole, West Branch, Mount Moffat and Kenniff Lookout. There are also camp sites at Nogoa River and Louisa Creek and both of these can be reached in conventional vehicles.

At Ka Ka Mundi there are, unfortunately, no formal facilities but pleasant car-based bush camping is possible under the forest gums at Bunbuncundoo Springs. This is 36km south of Yandaburra Homestead, which is located 130km west of Springsure.

How to get there

Carnarvon Gorge National Park lies between Roma and Springsure, 106km south of Rolleston of which only the first 20km is sealed road. Mount Moffat is reached via Injune. Access to Salvator Rosa and Ka Ka Mundi is via Springsure and Tambo, almost 200km from Tambo via Mantuan Downs. Most of the access to and within the park is reserved for four-wheel-drive vehicle as the unsealed roads are subject to flooding.

Carnarvon Gorge tel: (07) 4984–4505
Salvator Rosa tel: (07) 4984–1716
Ka Ka Mundi tel: (07) 4984–1716
Mount Moffat tel: (07) 4626–3581
Oasis Lodge tel: (07) 4988–4503

DAWSON RIVER GORGES

Sandstone escarpments and gorges rise up from the flat brigalow plains in a broad band of country stretching over 400km from Jericho, west of Emerald on the Capricorn Highway, south to Taroom on the Leichhardt Highway. The biggest area of this range country is found in the west, and comprises various sections of the Carnarvon Gorge National Park. The Dawson and its tributaries also cut through this sandstone block in many places.

A cluster of remote and beautiful gorges makes up the Isla Gorge and Expedition national parks, providing protection and access to this little-known sandstone region. These rugged gorge-filled parks are a delight for those who appreciate remote wilderness walking in areas with little evidence of human activity.

Robinson Gorge

Expedition National Park (previously known as the Lonesome and Robinson Gorge national parks) is the largest park in this sandstone region. Its dramatic feature is Robinson Gorge, 12km long and 100m deep. This is real wilderness walking country and high sandstone cliffs overlook the Dawson River and Arcadia Valley. In the deepest valleys pockets of rainforest plants, including cabbage tree palms, take refuge. Most of the plateau is covered in a variety of open gum forests. The park is also

EASTERN BROWN SNAKE

The Australian continent is known for its poisonous snakes and yet most visitors to the bush rarely see them. The nine potentially most lethal snakes in the world are found only in Australia. The most lethal snake is the inconspicuous and little-known fierce snake of the remote deserts of eastern central Australia. Bites inflicted by this snake are almost unknown.

The second-most lethal snake in the world is the common eastern brown snake. They occur, not surprisingly, in the eastern half of the continent and are found in dry country where they feed on mice and small birds. Frequently occurring around human dwellings, this species is active during the day. Growing to over 2m in length and with a slender streamlined shape, its colour is variable – adults are normally a uniform brown or black. This is an egg-laying species and the normal clutch numbers between 10 and 30 eggs. Eastern brown snakes move very quickly and, if cornered, are ferocious and can inflict multiple bites. Unusual for Australian snakes, this species rears up to strike and often bites adult humans above the knee. Fortunately, it is very wary and will move away from human activity if at all possible. Nevertheless this species is, after the tiger snake, responsible for most of the serious snake bites in the country.

Since a series of scientific breakthroughs in the 1970s, the human survival rate following dangerous snake bites has increased remarkably. With the advent of species-specific antivenom, plus efficient tests to identify the species of snake from its venom, as well as new first aid techniques, the chances of a bite causing death are now greatly reduced. Recommended first aid for a snake bite is to immobilise the bitten limb, apply heavy-pressure bandaging and ensure immediate hospital care.

a haven for many interesting mammals; the whiptail wallaby is regularly seen in open forests, and in the rocky gorges the brushed-tail wallaby reaches its northern limit of distribution. The aggressive, little northern quoll is an elusive resident.

Exploring the gorge

The main gorge can be explored on foot and liloing on the deep clear pools is popular. One favoured walk is to the waterhole known as the Cattle Dip, which gets its name from the sheer vertical cliff walls surrounding the 300-m-long pool. Access to this swimming spot is from the Starkvale Junction car park. Another point of foot access to the gorge is the Get Down, which is reached via a 2-km walk from the Starkvale camp site. Above the gorge there are marked walking tracks, however there are no marked routes within the gorge. A trek through this region offers sculpted rock formations and Aboriginal art sites within some of the caves, but any exploration of this area should be attempted only by experienced and well-equipped walkers.

Isla: twisting gorges

The Isla Gorge National Park boasts scenic views over deeply dissected sandstone ravines and is a good wayside picnic and recovery stop. The area is a maze of intertwined outcrops and strangely carved rock formations. Much of the park is open gum forest with remnants of brigalow shrublands. There is also a rich showing of wildflowers in spring. Unusual features are the patches of dry rainforest with bottletrees in the northern region around Flagstaff Hill. It is also an area particularly rich in birdlife. Here one can examine the remnants of a stone road believed to be part of an 1860s coach route.

ABOVE *Weathered sandstone cliffs, deep wet gullies, bush camping sites, and walking trails are the attractions of Robinson Gorge.*

Into the gorge depths

There is a lookout with splendid views close to the highway at Isla. For really adventurous bush-walkers, this park is a paradise. The descent into Isla Gorge is difficult but rewarding, revealing a huge range of stone arches, rock overhangs and complex gorges and amphitheatres. David Gordons Spring is a lush oasis tucked away in the depths of this gorge.

Remote riverside magic

Precipice National Park is a little-publicised, remote park located 50km north-east of Taroom and south of Isla Gorge. The gorge's prominent landscape feature is a huge, 10-km frontage to the Dawson River. Access to the frontage is difficult, but the effort is worthwhile. The Taroom park service office has the most up-to-date information.

Camping

All three parks are most suitable for the well-equipped and experienced walker. Picnic areas and basic camp sites are provided at Oil Bore and Starkvale in Expedition National Park. This park has been expanded several times in recent years and new facilities are currently being developed. Isla has a basic camping site and picnic area near the lookout.

How to get there

Expedition has vehicle access from Moura. Travel either 89km west of Taroom on the Leichhardt Highway or 70km south of Bauhinia Downs on the Dawson Highway. Access to Isla is adjacent to the Leichhardt Highway, 35km south of Theodore. Four-wheel-drive access is available at the northern end of Isla, adjacent to Flagstaff Hill. Precipice lies north-east of Taroom.

Taroom National Park and Wildlife Service
tel: (07) 4627–3358

BLACKDOWN TABLELAND NATIONAL PARK

The undulating Blackdown Tableland is a northern outlier of the huge sandstone plateau. It is also a junction for the three main upland areas – the Expedition, Shotover and Dawson ranges. The Blackdown Tableland National Park and adjacent state forest are located on an 800-m-high plateau surrounded by precipitous cliffs. The long spectacular cliff lines form the core of the park and range in height from 60 to over 300m. This plateau has many varied wilderness bushwalking opportunities. Park trails access many of the more dramatic lookouts but some tracks are suitable only for four-wheel-drive vehicles.

For those travelling through central Queensland this is a good stopover between the Carnarvon Gorge and the coast at Rockhampton. It is especially recommended as an off-the-beaten-track type of place to visit.

Pockets of wildlife

In spring, the best time to visit, waterfalls are a feature of the park. The falls drop into moist gullies, containing pockets of palms, tree ferns and lilly pillies. Most of the tableland's heaths and dry gum forests are in flower in spring and blooms of the rare local callistemons and wattles may be observed. The tableland is habitat for few large animals but boasts a great diversity of birds. The heathlands provide refuge for species of honeyeaters and the cliffs make great nesting sites for many birds of prey, including peregrine falcons.

Trails with inspiring vistas

There are over 20km of marked trails in the park. From the camp ground at Mimosa Creek there are two short walks. The 2-km-long Mimosa Culture Track investigates the art shelters and food plants of the Gungaloo Aboriginal people, who once lived on the plateau. This track also explores the history of European settlement and utilisation of the area.

A slightly longer walk to Officers Pocket leads to the head of the Mimosa Gorge. From here, there are distant views from the cliff tops across to Mimosa Creek and the Dawson Range.

Two short walks leave the main park road near the entrance. The Peregrine Lookout and Sunset Lookout tracks lead to spectacular viewing points on the northern rim of the plateau. There is another short walk to Mimosa Gorge 5km south of the camping area. This walk leads to Rainbow Falls, with a steep flight of stairs taking visitors to the bottom of the waterfall.

A branch track above the falls leads to a series of pools known as the Rock Holes. A 10-km-return walk to Stoney Creek Falls provides an inspiring view of the narrow gorge country on the northern rim of the park. Access to this trail is from the unsealed Park Loop Track.

ABOVE *For those that venture beyond the main tourist routes and visit Charlevue Gorge at Blackdown, the rewards are breathtaking views.*

Adventure walks

The adventurous can undertake longer overnight walks in the less developed, southern regions of the park. Care should be taken when attempting to find routes that descend from the escarpment. Some routes are well known and local advice is highly recommended.

Park Loop Track

The Park Loop Track begins and ends at a point 4km north and south of Mimosa Camp, off the main park road. This 18-km-long vehicle track is, in part, for four-wheel-drives only and leads to the northernmost point on the plateau rim, Charlevue Lookout. There are many awe-inspiring cliffs situated around the plateau and lots of options for exploratory abseiling. However, it is not a good area for rock climbing due to the crumbly nature of the sandstone.

Tall gum forests

Adjacent to the Blackdown Tableland National Park is a large area of state forest stretching south and east of the park. It is dominated by tall gum forests with small permanent streams.

The Fitzroy Development Road, south of the Capricorn Highway and 7km west of Duaringa, cuts through this area. Other access points are located both in the south and north of the national park.

Camping

The main camping ground at Mimosa Creek has basic amenities and a ranger station. Several picnic areas, toilets and car-based camp sites are provided. There are no stores in the park and the nearest supplies can be obtained in Dingo. Bush camping is usually permitted in the state forest, however there are no facilities.

How to get there

From Rockhampton, head west for 144km, or travel 106km east of Emerald on the sealed Capricorn Highway. The main access from the highway is 11km west of Dingo. The park is 20km south of the highway on an unsealed road and the camp ground is another 20km further on.

Blackdown Tableland National Park tel: (07) 4986–1964

DON'T MISS...

ADVENTURE EXPERIENCES

Wilderness walking in the Carnarvon Gorge is the pick of this region's adventure activities. Three- to five-day trips with a variety of itineraries are possible. The biggest difficulty is in arranging one-way trips with convenient pick-up arrangements. This is best done with two vehicles.

Detailed contour maps of the park are available from the National Parks and Wildlife Service.

Carnarvon Gorge tel: (07) 4984–4505

OTHER INTERESTING AREAS

Outside the major parks are several pleasant riverside camp sites with facilities including showers on the Dawson River downstream of **Theodore** and south of **Moura**. These areas are suitable for canoes. Contact the Taroom Council.

There are many other interesting areas for bush camping in national parks and in state forests on the coast and on the tablelands. For details contact the local National Parks and Wildlife Service and Forestry offices.

The tiny **Gemini Mountains** (previously Peak Range) **National Park**, located between Clermont and Dysart north of Emerald, has caves and volcanic plugs and is visible from the Peak Downs Highway. The Gemini Mountains (Pollux and Castor) rise abruptly from the wooded grasslands. Sturdy footwear is required to climb the summits. Bush camping is possible but it is recommended that you carry your own water

Bushwalking is popular at Blackdown Tableland National Park.

supplies. This area, despite its small size, has very strong scenic appeal and an interesting geological history. Bush camping is permitted away from roads and car parks.

Taroom Council tel: (07) 4627–3211
Rockhampton National Park and Wildlife Service
tel: (07) 4927–6511
Rockhampton Forestry tel: (07) 4931–9700
Gemini National Park tel: (07) 4982–4555
World Wide Maps Brisbane tel: (07) 3221–4330

TROPICAL CAIRNS

Daintree • Undara • Chillagoe Caves

*C*airns is an excellent base for a wide range of *wilderness* activities with new challenges always on offer. In this region, two seasons prevail: the 'Wet', beginning in November and lasting until April, and the 'Dry' for the rest of the year. During the summer months it can be difficult to move about due to flooding and boggy roads, but this is also when the wildlife is at its most active, waterfalls are gushing and the landscape comes to life. Tropical cyclones can occur during this time, but the full effects are less pronounced on the tablelands.

Travel Tips

Cairns has both an international and domestic airport with daily flights to all the Australian capital cities. There are also interstate coach and train services to Cairns from Brisbane. The country's widest range of safari and special interest tours head out from here, including treks to Cape York Peninsula. Rental cars, including four-wheel-drive vehicles, are readily available in Cairns.

The Bruce Highway along the coastline is the major north–south road. The Kennedy Highway heads inland through Atherton, and major road links to the Northern Territory head out from Townsville.

Insects can be a big problem when camping, particularly mosquitoes and sand-flies. Carry repellents, keep your skin covered and have sealed sleeping arrangements if possible.

ABOVE RIGHT *The coast road to Cooktown through the Cape Tribulation region is suitable only for four-wheel-drive vehicles.*

OPPOSITE *Mossman Gorge in the Daintree National Park became World Heritage-listed because of its incredible rainforest habitat.*

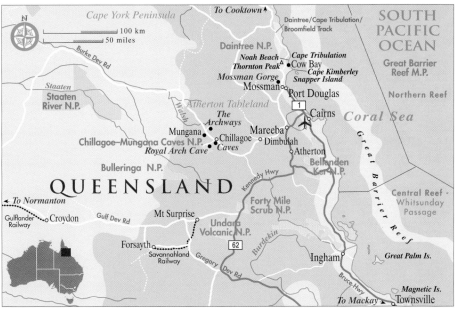

DAINTREE NATIONAL PARK

The Daintree region is the ultimate tropical paradise, combining reef and forest. Unfortunately it is very popular, so it is wise to try to have your own transport and get away from the masses a little if you can. The area is a joy at any time of the year, but best in winter.

The world-famous Daintree National Park protects some of the continent's most valuable World Heritage forests. When it was declared, the park's natural regions met all four of the World Heritage criteria: evidence of major stages in the earth's evolutionary history, diverse animal and plant life, habitat for threatened species and spectacular scenery.

Rare rainforest
Most of the Mossman section of the park is a wilderness of upland tropical rainforest. Waterfalls cascade into fast-flowing streams which feed the Mossman and Daintree rivers. The landscape in this remote region is rain-drenched and precipitous, making access very difficult. The high cloud-shrouded mountains are refuges for tree frogs, tree kangaroos and possums. Tropical birds such as bowerbirds, figbirds and fig-parrots fill the forest canopy with colour and sound, adding to the attractions.

Mossman Gorge
One section of the park, located just west of the town of Mossman, has been developed to provide a taste of the whole region. Watching for platypus or freshwater turtles in the Mossman River provides a welcome excuse for a quiet picnic. A 400-m walk leads to a suspension bridge which hangs over Rexs Creek. From here, there is access to a 3-km walk through the rainforest and along the edges of the stream in the lower section of the gorge.

Cape Tribulation
The most accessible region of the Daintree is the Cape Tribulation National Park. On this stretch of coast two great World Heritage regions come together: the rainforest of the Queensland's Wet Tropics and the magnificent coral wonderland of the sprawling Great Barrier Reef.

Palms, treeferns, orchids, climbers and hundreds of other plants grow in luxuriant profusion. From the mangroves on the edge of the reef to the 1400-m mountain-top heathlands and forests of Mount Thornton, the Daintree National Park is a botanical paradise.

The wildlife is equally rich and diverse. Although rarely seen, the Bennett's tree kangaroo is a unique local resident. Road signs warn of the very real danger of car accidents with the cassowary, a fascinating large flightless bird. Cassowaries can be dangerous when nesting and have been known to land a fatal kick. Saltwater crocodiles live in the rivers and are extremely dangerous. Not all the wildlife, however, is potentially life-threatening and reptiles, birds and mammals abound.

Beach walking
Beach walking is not to be missed and is possible at low tide at Cow Bay, Noah Beach, Emmagen Beach and between Myall and the Cape. A good four-hour-return walk runs along the shore from Emmagen Beach to Myall Beach. It is best to start on the outgoing tide. At Oliver Creek, a 1-km-long boardwalk explores the rainforest and mangroves, while at Cape Tribulation a short boardwalk culminates in a viewing platform on the headland. From here, there are idyllic vistas over the coast and ocean. Some picnic areas are situated nearby.

Four-wheel-driving
If travelling by four-wheel-drive, take the Daintree–Cape Tribulation–Bloomfield track along the coast to Cooktown. Side roads head east to Cape Kimberley and Cow Bay. The northern section of the track, from Cape Tribulation to the Bloomfield River, has very steep gradients while the river crossing is safe only at low tide. Wildlife is abundant and roads are narrow, so drive carefully.

Accommodation and facilities

No car-based camping is allowed at Daintree National Park, however keen and well-prepared bushwalkers can hike into the park and camp in the bush. A range of accommodation is available in Mossman.

At Cape Tribulation there is a park's service camp site at Noah Beach and private camping grounds at Myall Beach and Cape Tribulation. If you have a boat, try camping on the southern side of Snapper Island near Cape Kimberley.

How to get there

There are a number of bus tours from Cairns. By road, the main centre of the Daintree is at Mossman Gorge, 80km north of Cairns and 5km west of Mossman, with easy road access. Cape Tribulation is 104km from Cairns along the Cook Road, then across the Daintree River by barge, which operates seven days a week from 06:00 to midnight.

Mossman Gorge National Park and Wildlife Service
tel: (07) 4098–2188

FLYING FOX

In tropical and eastern Australia it is common to observe vast flocks of flying foxes, also known as fruit bats, flitting across the sky at dusk in search of food. Thousands of these noisy wheeling bats head towards soft fruit and blossom trees and can travel up to 50km from their roost to suitable spots. Many species of rainforest trees, such as figs, depend on the bats to spread their seed pods around.

Flying foxes are herbivorous. With their dog-like snouts, large eyes and simple little ears they are quite unlike the insect-eating bats which use echolocation to find their prey. The wings of flying foxes have fingers at the 'elbows' which enable the animals to clamber about in the tree-tops.

The daytime roost of flying foxes can be very conspicuous – to your eyes, nose and ears – as they gather together in groups sometimes numbering over 10 000 individuals. Flying foxes hang upside-down by their legs during daylight hours in the upper branches of preferred roosting trees. They may set up a roost for a short period or establish themselves in a good spot for many years. The choice of a day roost is not always appreciated by people since the bats can do great damage to the trees and anything below. For example, flying fox day roosts located in the Sydney Botanic Gardens are causing considerable damage to historic trees. The smell of a flying fox camp is also strong and distinctive.

In Australia, eight different species of flying fox are known. Roosts in northern Queensland are found on mangrove islands or other sites safe from predators, and can contain three different species of flying fox camped together.

UNDARA VOLCANIC NATIONAL PARK

Undara Volcanic National Park protects an extraordinary 190 000-year-old volcanic landscape. The main crater is surrounded by a lava field of over 1000km². The usually dry landscape is pockmarked with cinder cones and small depressions caused by the collapse of underground lava tubes. Basalt spreads from the crater occur in patterns similar to those found on the surface of the moon. Undara's curiosities are unique in Australia and rare in the world. Particular highlights are the wildlife and geological features.

The area's volcanic activity centres on the Undara Crater, the 20-m-high rim being the highest point in the district and having an impressive depression almost 50m deep and over 300m across. The rim is still well-formed and the crater shows evidence that it was at one time a lake. The volcanic eruptions left behind lava tubes (Undara is believed to be the longest system in the world), caves, craters and long ridges, now a feature of the park.

Lava tubes

Lava tubes are the remnants of underground lava streams. At Undara, they indicate how the lava flows moved north and west from the crater for over 160km. During volcanic activity, the outer layers of these lava flows cooled and hardened while the inner lava remained hot, continuing to flow. When this inner lava eventually drained away, it left behind the long, horizontal, cylindrical caves – or tubes – of basalt. At Undara some of these tubes are 20m wide and over 10m high.

The caves have rare volcanic features, including laval stalactites, stalagmites, high lava marks, drip lines and ropey lava. The Australian continent's longest-known and best example of a lava tube, the Bayliss, runs underground for 1.5km. The roof has collapsed in several places, creating cool deep craters that have become a refuge for rainforest vegetation in an otherwise harsh dry landscape.

Unexplained phenomenon

Another feature of the park is The Wall, a strange and unexplained formation which extends out from the end of one of the underground lava systems. It is thought that this structure may be the result of an undrained lava tube. This fascinating feature is visible on the surface and extends for many kilometres.

LEFT *The Undara tubes were created by lava which drained away leaving cavernous structures.*

BELOW LEFT *Undara Lava Lodge provides bush tucker for its guests.*

Forty Mile Scrub: a botanic rarity

On the road from Cairns a stopover at the Forty Mile Scrub is highly recommended. This pocket of vine thicket has miraculously survived thousands of years of isolation from other rainforests on the dry range top and the clearing of land for agriculture. The semi-evergreen botanical oddity provides strong evidence of the biological links between Australia, South America, and Antarctica that began to be severed as Gondwana slowly fragmented approximately 300 million years ago.

The park's rich basalt soils support and protect both the rare vine thicket and open gum and native pine woodlands. In the evening black-striped wallabies and red-legged pademelons, which normally seek security in the thickets, venture out onto the open grassy woodland glades. Undara Volcanic National Park is a great location for early morning or dusk wildlife observation.

Accommodation and facilities

The Undara Volcanic National Park has no developed facilities but Undara Lava Lodge, a low-profile resort, is located nearby. There is also accommodation adjacent to the park, ranging from basic camping to lodges in recycled old railway carriages.

Camping is permitted at Forty Mile Scrub.

Flora and fauna

Generally, the region is not noted for its botanical diversity. The surrounding plains are covered in a uniform open-woodland gum forest. The dark green vine scrub is restricted to the collapsed underground laval depressions. Wallabies feed in the grassy glades and a number of species of bat inhabit the caves. The area has a wide range of birdwatching opportunities with large numbers of waterbirds inhabiting the Hundred Mile Swamp.

The park's most interesting bushwalking is around the lava formations. The rest of the region consists of open gum forest with few landscape highlights. Organised four-wheel-drive vehicle and coach tours visit the sensitive cave areas and the Tallaroo Mineral Hot Springs. Night-time spotlight tours reveal glimpses of otherwise rarely seen nocturnal wildlife such as possums and rare bats.

How to get there

A four-hour, 280-km drive along the sealed Kennedy Highway from Cairns will take you to Undara. This road is suitable for conventional vehicles. There are many coach and safari tours available from Cairns. Undara Lava Lodge has a private airstrip and scheduled light aircraft services fly in from Cairns.

Forty Mile Scrub National Park is on Kennedy Highway, 240km south-west of Cairns en route to Undara. Access is from the car parks along the edges of the highway which cuts through two separate sections of vine thicket.

Yarramulla National Park and Wildlife Service
tel: (07) 4097–1485
Undara Lodge tel: (07) 4097–1411

CHILLAGOE–MUNGANA CAVES NATIONAL PARK

At Chillagoe, massive limestone bluffs tower above the surrounding country forming rocky islands covered in rainforest. Underneath the bluffs is another equally rare and beautiful landscape, Chillagoe's limestone caves. These are protected as a national park, which is divided into nine sections. The largest area is at Royal Arch Cave, which is also the main public cave system.

Chillagoe provides easy access to the country's vast and remote northern tropical wilderness. From here, adventurous four-wheel-drive explorers set off to the lower regions of Cape York Peninsula and the Gulf of Carpentaria.

The high limestone bluffs support unusual vegetation. The rocky peaks protect the area from bushfires and so rainforest plants are able to survive. However, with the desiccating dry seasons and the porosity of the limestone, the only rainforest plants that do survive are deciduous. These strange leafless figs, coral trees, kurrajongs and strychnine bushes cluster on the hilltops, while bloodwood and ironwood forests dominate the rolling countryside in between.

Shy wildlife

Although mammals are not easy to observe, rock wallabies are occasionally seen. Other more common wallabies and euros feed amongst the boulders and in the park glades. The time to catch these nervous marsupials is at dusk or during the early morning before too many other people are about.

Birds are more conspicuous and include the noisy and attractive blue-faced honeyeaters and flocking apostlebirds. Flying foxes are attracted to fig trees when they are in fruit.

Life in the caves

Some of the wildlife of the region is concentrated around or restricted to the caves. Three species of bat nest in the caves and other species use them for roosting. Pythons are attracted to the colonies and are major predators. The rare white-rumped swiftlet nests in the caves during the Wet. This unusual cave-dweller shares with bats the ability to echo-locate in the dark. Chillagoe Caves is one of only five known nesting places for this bird in Australia.

Cave tours

Self-guided and guided tours allow you to explore the equable, cool underground caves. Hand-held lamps are the main source of light, adding to the sense of discovery and isolation. The major cave tour is through Royal Arch Cave and is an easy stroll through 13 chambers. Other guided tours include the electrically-lit excursions through the Donna and Trezkinn caves. Open daylight caves offering self-guided

ABOVE *The Archways Cave, one of the limestone caves at the Chillagoe–Mungana National Park, covers 1ha in area.*

walks are the Archways and Pompeii caves. A torch for each member of the party is very useful on these short walks. The entrances to the Donna, Pompeii, Bauhinia and Trezkinn caves are adjacent to the town of Chillagoe. North of Mungana, 15km west of Chillagoe, is the access to the Archways. Booking for the cave tours and camping can be done at the park office based in the town.

Aboriginal art tracks
Between the Royal Arch and Donna cave entrances, there is a short walking track. This stroll passes a strange balancing rock formation. Along the entry road to this section, just north of Mungana, are Aboriginal painting sites. Located just off the road, they are clearly sign-posted.

Nearby wilderness parks
Staaten River National Park is a huge monsoon open-grassland park located on the floodplain of the Staaten River, in the central region of southern Cape York Peninsula. Features of the park include huge termite mounds, gallery rainforest and tropical wildlife.

Bulleringa National Park is a remote wilderness park located 100km southwest of Chillagoe but access is difficult.

Accommodation and facilities
In the Royal Arch section of the park, about 3km south of Chillagoe, is a small basic camp ground. There are no facilities elsewhere in the Chillagoe Caves area, but a variety of accommodation is available in Chillagoe itself. Drinking water is scarce within the park.

The Staaten River and Bulleringa national parks offer no facilities and access is very difficult. Permission by private property owners is required in advance to use four-wheel-drives in the dry season. Access by any vehicle in the Wet is impossible.

How to get there

Chillagoe–Mungana Caves National Park is three hours or 210km by road from Cairns via Mareebah and Dimbulah. The road is mainly sealed and is suitable for conventional vehicles. Safari tours and air charters are available from Cairns. Road conditions should be checked in the wet season.

Lying west of Chillagoe, both Staaten River and Bulleringa are remote and access is extremely difficult. A four-wheel-drive vehicle is definitely required.

Chillagoe–Mungana Caves National Park and Wildlife Service tel: (07) 4094–7163

DON'T MISS...

ADVENTURE EXPERIENCES
Whitewater rafting and inflatable whitewater kayaking on one of several rivers near Cairns is one of Australia's most recommended adventure experiences. A range of tours is available including overnight and helicopter drop-offs. There are several major tour operators, so compare packages and prices. Inflatable whitewater kayaking is more independent and better suited to experienced rafters.

Early morning hot-air ballooning over the coastal plain is available but is dependent on the weather.
Queensland Travel Centre tel: 13 18 01
Cairns Travel Centre tel: (07) 4052–6211

Tjapukai performers enact Dreaming stories.

OTHER INTERESTING AREAS
The Tjapukai Aboriginal Dance Theatre and Cultural Centre is a major Aboriginal initiative based at the beginning of the new Skyrail to the Atherton Tableland. It should not be missed for its environmental and cultural insights.

Bellenden Ker National Park is a haven of waterfalls and luxuriant rainforests. From the Henrietta camping ground there is the Tchupala self-guided rainforest trail. The Upper Johnston River is a major white-water rafting and canoeing location; access is via the Johnston Highway.

Danbulla State Forest surrounds the Tinaroo Dam east of Atherton. The focus is on water-based recreation, including sailing and canoeing, and five established camp sites exist.

The overland train called **the Gulflander** runs a weekly return trip between Normanton and Croydon, while the newly re-established **Savannahlander** runs a twice-weekly return trip between Mount Surprise and Forsayth.

Beach and forest horseriding is offered by several operators in **Port Douglas** and it is a great way to explore the area.

Palmerston National Park and Wildlife Service tel: (07) 4064–5115
Danbulla State Forest tel: (07) 4091–1844
Cairns Travel Centre tel: (07) 4052–6211

GREAT BARRIER REEF

Capricorn Channel • Whitsunday Passage • Northern Reef

*T*he Great Barrier Reef is a huge marine wilderness which was World Heritage-listed in 1981. It has been divided into three zones – southern, central and northern – by the Great Barrier Reef Marine Park Authority, and is actually a series of over 2100 individual reefs stretching for more than 2000km from Papua New Guinea down the Queensland coastline to Lady Elliot Island. In addition, the marine park comprises over 500 continental islands – these were once part of the mainland but became separated from it as sea levels rose. The best time to visit is from April to October, as during the summer the waters are home to marine stingers, cyclones are more common and the weather is hot, humid and wet.

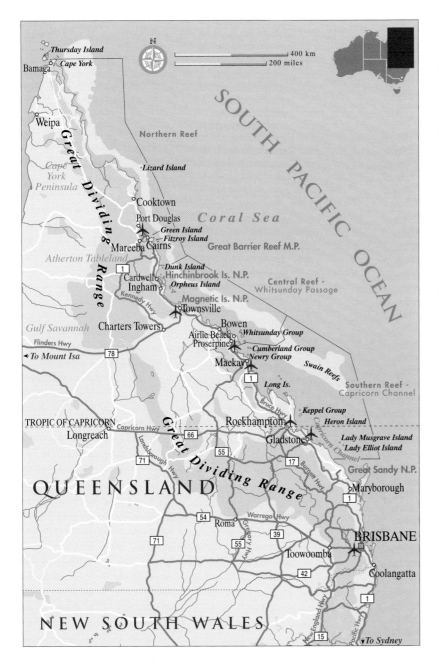

ABOVE *The Great Barrier Reef stretches for over 2000km and is considered to be one of the great natural wonders of the world.*

OPPOSITE *Visitors can snorkel in the turquoise waters off Gladstone near Lady Musgrave Island.*

Travel Tips

There are major international and domestic airports at Brisbane and Cairns. Gladstone, Rockhampton, Mackay, Proserpine and Townsville have regional airports and, besides Cairns, serve as the main access centres to the reef. Over a dozen islands also have small airfields. There is a large choice of car rental companies and tour operators, and a wide range of accommodation is on offer in the larger towns. Rail and coach services run frequently from Brisbane to Cairns with stops along the way.

Other centres for the Great Barrier Reef include Airlie Beach, Cardwell, Port Douglas and Cooktown. The least busy regions are north of Port Douglas, but there are fewer or no facilities. Avoid the cheapest fares for daytrips as it is better to ensure the quality of guides and equipment, and limited numbers in the party.

CAPRICORN CHANNEL

The southern section of the Great Barrier Reef covers the area south of Mackay. The reef lies about 260km off the mainland so daytrips to the outer reef section from the coast can be difficult because of the long distances involved. A viable transport option is the high-speed catamaran, which takes only two hours to reach the outer reef. Closer to the mainland is Lady Musgrave Island which allows visitors to enjoy the reef from the lagoon's floating platform and underwater observatory.

Between the reef and the mainland lie a number of islands that have been categorised into groups. The Capricorn–Bunker Group is about 150km off Gladstone and comprises the islands of Heron, Lady Musgrave, Hoskyn, Fairfax, One Tree, Erskine, Wreck and Wilson. This group also includes the Wistari, Sykes and Irving reefs. The 11 islands that make up the Keppel Group – including Great Keppel, North Keppel, Humpy, Miall, Middle and Conical islands – lie just off Rockhampton.

Resort islands

Many of the islands at the southern end of the reef display the features that led to the Great Barrier Reef's World Heritage listing (the first such listing in Australia). Three islands in the south have resorts: Great Keppel, Lady Elliot and Heron. The latter two are tiny, delightful, vegetated coral cays, where the focus is on presenting the reef to visitors. Half of Heron Island is also a national park with a marine research station and visitor centre. Lady Elliot Island is the only coral cay along the Queensland coast to have an airstrip.

Great Keppel is a continental island located 150km from the edge of the reef. Like the other islands that are part of the Keppel Group, Great Keppel has unspoilt bushland, fringing reefs and a number of white sandy beaches.

Coral cays

Coral cays are formed by the accumulation, over time, of sand and debris. Over many hundreds of years sand is washed atop the formed cay and seeds, either washed in or dropped by passing birds, take root within the precarious environment. Four small remote coral cays – Lady Musgrave, Masthead, North West and Tryon – now support nesting seabirds such as noddies, tropicbirds and shearwaters, as well as turtles in summer. The average distance of these islands from the mainland is 60km and popular activities on these havens, apart from nature observation, include diving and snorkelling.

Mainland turtle nesting

Queensland's most significant mainland turtle rookery is located at Mon Repos, just 15km north of Gladstone. While turtles breed on many of the reef's islands, at Mon Repos large numbers of ocean turtles come to shore between November and January to lay eggs in the sand dunes. Three species of turtle nest here: loggerheads, greens and flatbacks, and the beach is the largest loggerhead rookery in the South Pacific. From January to March the hatchlings emerge and can be observed from around eight in the evening to midnight. Outside these breeding and hatching months, Mon Repos is a quiet reserve. To get a good viewing spot avoid weekends or arrive late to miss the crowds. The beach is almost 2km long, so comfortable walking shoes, a warm waterproof coat and a torch are useful. A visitor centre is located in the park.

Island accommodation

Great Keppel offers a comprehensive holiday resort. Accommodation options include motels, cabins or camp grounds. Camping is also permitted on the other four

continental islands of the Keppel Group. Book well in advance to reserve sites and ensure you are self-sufficient, especially with drinking water. Lady Elliot has cabin or camping facilities, and Heron Island offers both motel and cabin options. A number of the islands in both the Capricorn–Bunker and Keppel groups are national parks, so bush camping is allowed with prior permission.

How to get there

All the Keppel Group islands are accessed by boat from Rosslyn Bay. Heron Island runs both helicopter and boat services from Gladstone. Lady Elliot Island can also be reached from Gladstone by boat or plane as it has an airstrip. Lady Musgrave, Masthead, North West and Tryon can be reached by air, by private charter or scheduled boat, or from Heron Island where a transfer service link is available.

Gladstone National Park and Wildlife Service
tel: (07) 4972–6055
Gladstone Visitor Centre tel: (07) 4972–9922
Rockhampton Visitor Centre
tel: (07) 4927–2055

BUTTERFLYFISH

Butterflyfish form a large group of brilliantly colourful reef fish which occur throughout the tropical oceans of the world. Typically they have a rather compressed, distinctively plate-shaped body and often have bold striped or spotted markings. The striking patterns are principally yellow, black, orange and white. Frequently there is a large spot or a prominent black stripe through the eye. The markings sometimes change with age and some species have juvenile and adult forms. Australian tropical waters are home to at least 50 species of butterflyfish, which live on every part of the Great Barrier Reef. While most are shallow-water residents, some prefer to live in the deeper drop-offs down to about 30m. They are the most commonly seen fish, and many species can be identified during a snorkel, dive or trip in a glass-bottomed boat.

Many butterflyfish eat small invertebrates including marine worms, molluscs and coral. They have tiny bristle-like teeth and with their small mouth and, in some species, pointed snout, delicately browse on coral polyps. Other species snatch tiny floating organisms from the rich tropical waters. Each species of butterflyfish has its own particular lifestyle. Some are highly territorial and others drift by seemingly disconnected to any particular piece of reef. Others are highly sociable while some live solitary lives.

When alarmed, butterflyfish often take refuge in the coral. At night many species sleep wedged into coral crevices but during the day divers may be able to approach them quite closely. In some popular dive locations butterflyfish have become used to human activity and are consequently quite unafraid.

WHITSUNDAY PASSAGE

The central section of the Great Barrier Reef broadly covers all the reefs and islands between Mackay and Townsville and the outer reefs of Swain and Hardy. It also includes the Whitsunday Passage – the tropical waterway between the mainland and the islands of the Whitsunday Group, synonymous with island-getaway resorts. The Whitsunday Group includes Magnetic, Brampton, Lindeman, Hamilton, Long, South Molle, Daydream, Hook, and Hayman. These are all continental islands and offer resort facilities with a range of accommodation options.

Whitsunday Islands
The region is relatively close to the reef and most of the resorts offer a variety of tours. A number of the islands are either partly or fully national parks and bushwalking tracks have been developed with many leading to the more secluded sandy beaches, pockets of rainforest or forested hill slopes of the larger islands. The wildlife includes rock wallabies, and sea eagles and ospreys which make their nests in trees growing in steep and inaccessible sites.

The ideal way to explore the islands is to camp, and then sail and swim in the lagoons and over the reefs. The islands with the best reefs for snorkelling are Hook, Border and North Molle.

Visits to the reef
A number of tour companies offer daytrips to the inner reef for swimming, snorkelling, diving, and glass-bottomed boat rides. Floating pontoons and semi-submersible boats are permanently moored on the main reef. By far the most popular way to explore the main-land islands and inner reef is by yacht and the Whitsundays is the hub of charter boats on the reef. You can either sail yourself or hire a skippered yacht.

Northern magnet
North from the Whitsundays, located off the coast of Townsville, is Magnetic Island, where visitors can enjoy a wide variety of wilderness activities. Two-thirds of the island comprises a national park and 25km of tracks have been

created. Koalas are common and swimming and bushwalking are popular. The island, including fortifications built during wartime, can also be explored on hired bicycles. A regular ferry service travels to and from Townsville daily.

A marine wonderland

Townsville is home to the Great Barrier Reef Wonderland. This major centre contains a reef aquarium, an environmental centre, an Omnimax theatre, a tropical museum and the offices of the Great Barrier Reef Marine Park Authority. The largest living reef aquarium in the centre has 100 varieties of coral and over 200 species of fish on display. The entertaining exhibits are well presented and a visit is highly recommended.

Wilderness islands

For those looking for an experience more in touch with nature, there are several islands on which bush camping is possible. The islands that make up the Newry Group – Rabbit, Newry, Outer Newry, Acacia, Mausoleum, and Rocky – just off the coast 50km north-west of Mackay, are home to rainforest and are surrounded by marine wonders. Access to the group is by private boat.

Four hilly islands in the Cumberland Group – Carlisle, Goldsmith, Cockermouth and Scawfell – also have camp sites, rainforest pockets, volcanic remnants, beaches and fringing reefs. Access is via the resort at Brampton Island or by private boat. Daytrips are allowed to the Percy Isles offshore from Mackay, however camping is not permitted.

BELOW *A village of tents on Magnetic Island provides comfortable accommodation for backpackers.*

Dryander National Park is located on the mainland coast north of Airlie Beach, and includes 11 small inshore islands such as Gloucester and Saddleback and the Armit Group. Wilderness camping is permitted at a number of island sites and on the mainland at areas accessible from the sea.

Island camping

Within the Whitsunday Islands there are over 20 different places to bush camp. These include Hook, North Molle, Whitsunday, Henning, Border, Haslewood, Shaw, Thomas, and Repulse islands. Commercial boat operators provide transfers for campers. Several easily accessible camping sites are located at Whitehaven Beach on Whitsunday Island and at Cockatoo Beach on North Molle Island. Although there is no national park on Magnetic Island, private camp sites are available.

Information on all the island camp sites and permits are available at the Whitsunday Information Centre located between Airlie Beach and Shute Harbour. Boat transfer tickets must be obtained prior to the issuing of permits. Campers using sites on islands must be well equipped and self-sufficient. Gas stoves for cooking and plenty of drinking water are essential.

How to get there

Mainland access points to the islands are from Mackay, Proserpine, Airlie Beach, Shute Harbour or Townsville. There is also a domestic airport at Hamilton Island.
Mackay National Park and Wildlife Service
tel: (07) 4951–8788
Whitsunday Visitor Centre tel: (07) 4945–3711

The Northern Reef section embraces the reef and islands north of Townsville. It is a huge area with seven main resort islands and many wilderness islands. This region provides easy access to the Great Barrier Reef's kaleidoscope of sea life. There are over 400 species of coral, 1500 species of fish, 400 species of mollusc, 500 species of seaweed and 200 species of birds within this marine wonderland.

Access to the large areas of the reef north of Lizard Island is possible only on a multi-day cruise. This region is the epitome of marine wilderness because of its inaccessibility.

An abundance of choices
For those based on the mainland, there is a huge range of daytrips departing from a number of centres between Townsville and Port Douglas. Many different tour organisations offer trips which include snorkelling, diving, reef walks, and cruises in semi-submersible craft.

The greatest difficulty faced by most visitors is selecting from the range of activities, modes of transport and the island or group of islands or reefs on offer. When making a choice, bear in mind that for some outer reef locations a good portion of the day may be spent travelling. Remember, though, that the further out the destination, the less likelihood there will be of crowds. The ideal reef experience usually involves a number of different activities spread out over several days.

Islands of the north
Popular locations in the northern section of the reef include the Low Isle, Green, Fitzroy, Arlington, and Pearl Farm islands, and the Agincourt and Moore reefs. At some locations floating pontoons moored on impressive pieces of reef allow for closer inspection of the marine life.

North of Townsville are four resort islands: Bedarra, Dunk, Hinchinbrook, and Lizard. These are all continental islands and national parks. Two other islands with resorts are Orpheus and Fitzroy, also continental islands.

Tiny Green Island, located just offshore from Cairns, is a coral cay, national park and a popular resort. Within this group fortunate visitors can experience some of the most exclusive spots on the reef.

Hinchinbrook National Park
A number of islands are national parks and Hinchinbrook, the largest, is one of them. More than 10km wide and 35km long, it rises steeply to its highest point of over 1100m at Mount Bowen. There are many wilderness walks including a four- to five-day trek along the Thorsborne trail on the eastern coast. Walkers can enjoy a swim at many secluded beaches. Among the island's wildlife is the estuarine crocodile, a resident of the mangrove forests. Access to the island is by private boat, charter boat or water taxi from Cardwell or Dungeness.

ABOVE LEFT *The coral cays of the Great Barrier Reef are in a constant state of change. Some of the older cays have vegetation growing on them.*

ABOVE RIGHT *The boardwalk on Hinchinbrook Island, the world's largest island national park, provides easy access to the mangroves and rainforests.*

Orpheus: tiny paradise

Orpheus Island is only 14km² and contains a small, exclusive resort. As well as snorkelling on the fringing reef, this heavily forested island provides many opportunities for wild country bushwalks. Access to the island is by charter boat from Dungeness, or by helicopter or seaplane from Townsville. This island is not served by scheduled daytrips.

Island camping

Wilderness bush camping is permitted on a number of northern islands close to Townsville and Cairns. Hinchinbrook permits campers along the wilderness walks and an established camp site is located at Macushla near Cape Richards and Scraggy Point. Orpheus also has a range of delightful camp sites at Yanks Jetty, South Beach and Little Pioneer Bay.

Goold Island near Cardwell has a camping and day picnic area near the beach on its western shore. The many sheltered beaches, fringing reefs suitable for snorkelling and thick forests make this island a popular destination.

Dunk Island, north of Cardwell, is renowned for its beaches fringed with rainforest. A camp ground located near the jetty is a good base from which to explore the 10km of rainforest walking tracks. The easiest access is by water taxi from Mission Beach.

Two small camp grounds are to be found on the Frankland Islands which can be reached via Russell Island, located between Innisfail and Cairns. Fitzroy Island, close to Green Island and Cairns, offers a council-operated camp ground and the island is the site of wonderful bush rainforest walks and a large fringing reef for snorkellers.

How to get there

To get to the islands of the Northern Reef you can only travel by plane or boat. Flights and cruises depart from Cardwell, Mission Beach, Cairns, Port Douglas, Cooktown, and Thursday Island.

Innisfail National Park and Wildlife Service tel: (07) 4061–4291
Cairns National Park and Wildlife Service tel: (07) 4052–3096
Cairns Travel Centre tel: (07) 4052–6211
Port Douglas Visitor Centre tel: (07) 4099–4588

DON'T MISS...

ADVENTURE EXPERIENCES

Options for exploring the Great Barrier Reef include:

- boat or yacht charters – sail yourself around the Whitsunday Islands or hire one with a skipper on board
- sea kayak safaris
- dive safaris
- reef and Cape York cruises
- a combination of sailing and diving with a group on a classic schooner

The ultimate wilderness experience is to camp on an island or stay on a boat for many days and immerse yourself in the reef atmosphere. Alternatively, accommodation can be booked on an island or coral cay with daily sorties out to the reef.

Speciality activities include:
- helicopter flights over the reef
- seaplane flights and reef exploring at the Whitsundays

Most organised reef trips from the main centres and resorts offer one or more of the following activities: diving, snorkelling, and viewing the reef from a semi-submersible or glass-bottomed boat. Most resorts and coastal centres offer parasailing, windsurfing, sailing and canoeing.

Glass-bottomed boats make frequent trips to Green Island.

Queensland Travel Centre tel: 13 18 01
Australian Bareboat Charters tel: (07) 4946–9381
Peregrine Tours tel: (03) 9663–8611
Prodive Whitsunday tel: 1800 075120
Captain Cook Cruises (*Reef Endeavour* – large boat eg. 168-person, luxury) tel: 1800 221080; (*Kangaroo Explorer* – small boat, 25m) tel: 1800 079141
Whitsunday Adventure Sailing (Coral Trekker – speciality boats eg. racing yacht) tel: 1800 075042
Sail Away tel: (07) 4099–5599
Prodive Cairns tel: (07) 4031–5255
Helireef at Whitsundays tel: (07) 4946–9102
Helijet tel: (07) 4946–8249

CAPE YORK

Lakefield • Iron Range • Jardine River

From Cairns to the tip of Cape York Peninsula, a trek of over 1000km, is the most famous four-wheel-drive adventure in Australia. While the Peninsula Development Road links Cairns with Weipa, parts of the road and the tracks that head off into the region are so rugged that it is only possible to travel along them in four-wheel-drives. This is real wilderness territory with very few people living actually on the peninsula.

Travel Tips

Cairns has an international and domestic airport with regular flights to regional airports at Cooktown, Lockhart River and Bamaga. Ferry services link Bamaga to Thursday Island and a barge service links Cairns to the cape ports. Safari tours also head off from Cairns.

Monsoon rains drench Cape York in the summer months, making conditions hot and wet and many roads impassable. Travelling to Coen is possible in conventional vehicles between May and November. Any travel north of Coen is suitable for four-wheel-drives only, and even then only between June and December. River crossings can be dangerous so the depth of the water at entry and exit points should always be checked.

This is certainly not a trip for the inexperienced. The distances between communities are vast, so preparations need to be extremely thorough as supplies cannot be guaranteed along the way.

Saltwater crocodiles inhabit freshwater streams, rivers and ocean beaches. As a result, you should take care not to swim, prepare food or camp within 50m of deep water. Sandflies, mosquitoes and bush flies can give unpleasant bites so protective clothing, insect repellent sprays and sealed sleeping arrangements are highly recommended.

ABOVE RIGHT *At Frangipani Beach, Cape York, the mangroves retain a fragile hold on the shore.*

OPPOSITE *Lakefield National Park is a wetland paradise with a profusion of waterbirds and reptiles.*

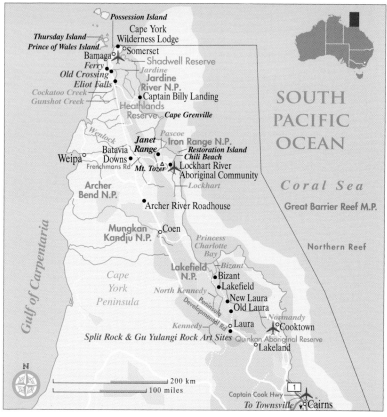

LAKEFIELD

Lakefield is Queensland's second-largest national park after the Simpson Desert. Its open spaces, wide variety of unusual tropical landscapes and wildlife make this a popular winter destination. The park is the most accessible reserve on Cape York, located 146km north-west of Cooktown, and is large enough to provide many wilderness experiences.

Rivers are an essential habitat of Lakefield and the main drainage systems are the North Kennedy and Normanby rivers. In the dry season most of the inland streams stop running but during the Wet the rivers burst their banks and parts of the park become huge bodies of open water.

Mangrove forests and mudflats skirt the ocean beaches facing onto Princess Charlotte Bay. Extensive grasslands, woodlands and open forest sweep back from the rivers which are often edged with gallery rainforests. Much of the park is subject to regular fires and mosaic burning is used to maintain habitat diversity. Occasionally in the early dry season, sections of the park are closed to public access in order for controlled fires to be lit.

Crocodile habitat

The most conspicuous wildlife in the park are the waterbirds, eagles and flying foxes, best observed in the early morning and late afternoon. Wildlife viewing from a boat is also recommended, but caution should be taken in small canoes. Although the many rivers are ideal for canoeing, the park services advise against it because of the danger of crocodiles.

Lakefield is one of only six major saltwater crocodile habitats in Queensland. Hunting during the first half of this century drastically reduced the population but as they are now fully protected, saltwater crocodile numbers are slowly rebuilding. Freshwater crocodiles also live in the park.

One of the most popular activities in the park is fishing. Lakefield is one of the few Queensland national parks to allow this activity. The prized fish at Lakefield is barramundi.

Pioneer spirit

There is an historic homestead near the park entrance that has been restored and dates from the end of the last century. The Old Laura Homestead (1874) stands as a testament to the tough spirit of the first Europeans who moved to the inhospitable region to graze cattle.

Bush facilities

Ranger bases are located in the original cattle homesteads at New Laura, Lakefield and Bizant. Comprehensive camping facilities are available just outside the park at Kalpowar. In addition, there are dozens of bush camping spots throughout the park located alongside lagoons, waterholes and lakes. A boat ramp is located on the Bizant River. The park's main access road runs the full length of the park from Laura to Saltwater Creek and most of the camp sites are adjacent to the road or on short sidetracks. The tropical heat makes walking difficult, however there are some short marked walks near the main camp sites.

An historic gallery

Just prior to reaching Lakefield, in an area between Laura and Lakeland on the Development Road, is a stretch of Aboriginal land that contains some of the most prized rock-art sites in the country. The Quinkan Aboriginal Reserve lies on both sides of the road and thousands of rock-art sites are documented. Elaborately painted figures and stone peckings cover the cave walls, and shelters contain artefacts and

occupation sites. Archaeological excavations have revealed that the art dates back at least 13 500 years and that the area has been occupied for 35 000 years. These discoveries are of international archaeological significance.

Permission from the Aboriginal community is required to visit most of the sites and a community office is located in Laura. There are two sites which can be visited without permission or guides. The Gu Yulangi and Split Rock Art Site is located about 12km south of Laura. Both these areas feature Quinkans, tall spirit beings with helmet-shaped heads. According to the Aboriginal legends, they are evil spirits who lead the unwary to hidden secret places. The caves also have food and animal illustrations. The walking trail is about 3km in length and climbs up onto the escarpment to the rock formation known as Turtle Rock.

How to get there

Access to Lakefield is by light aircraft or by road between April and November. The drive north from Cairns along the Peninsula Development Road takes about eight hours. In dry weather conventional vehicles can usually reach the ranger station at New Laura. From there a four-wheel-drive is recommended. From Cooktown four-wheel-drives can travel through Battlecamp and Coen via Musgrave and Saltwater Creek.

Lakefield National Park (07) 4060–3271

IRON RANGE NATIONAL PARK

Iron Range National Park is primarily an area of high scientific value due to the peculiarity of its wildlife and its extensive lowland rainforest. In addition, the variety of landscapes, in particular the attractive and accessible coastline, provides a contrast to the rest of Cape York. From Lakefield National Park the road north to Iron Range National Park deteriorates from an adequate unsealed road to no more than a bush track in places. Road travel slows markedly and there are many more river crossings. On the way north excellent camp sites can be found on the banks of the Coen River north of the Coen township.

Tropical wilderness

Twenty kilometres north of Coen and adjacent to the sealed airfield, the Development Road crosses into the Mungkan Kandju (previously Rokeby and Archer River) National Park. This is a huge wilderness park stretching from the McIlwraith Range to the junction of the Coen and Archer rivers. Bush camping is permitted in the park, as is fishing. Extreme care must be taken, though, to avoid saltwater crocodiles. Other than along the Development Road, access to this park is only by four-wheel-drive vehicle.

BUFF-BREASTED PARADISE KINGFISHER

Every summer, from Cairns northwards, the lowland rainforests of Queensland ring with the calls of the buff-breasted paradise kingfishers. These spectacular birds migrate south to Cape York every year from central New Guinea. In November the males are resplendent in their fresh and gaudy breeding plumage. Their red legs and oversized bill form a sharp contrast to their azure blue crown and wings, and their orange breast merges with an orange collar under a black eye band. The black-and-white colouring of the male's back runs down to an extraordinarily long white tail – over half the body length is taken up by its tail. The females are similarly brilliantly coloured but their tail is slightly more modest.

These kingfishers establish their breeding territories in November just before the onset of the wet season. A termite mound on the floor of the forest is selected as a nest site and both birds share the job of burrowing a tunnel 15cm into the mound. At the end of the tunnel a large nest chamber is hollowed out. No nest lining is used and the three or four white eggs are laid on the chamber floor. The chicks hatch around Christmas and spend about four weeks in the nest being fed a mixture of insects, small lizards and frogs. The rain-drenched forest is full of suitable prey at this time of year. The adult birds catch the food in typical king-fisher style, waiting on an exposed tree branch watching for movement on the ground below, then dropping to the forest floor to grab the unsuspecting prey.

By March, with nesting finished, the adults migrate north. The young remain for another month or so and then, unaccompanied by their parents, find their way to the wintering grounds in the highlands of New Guinea.

ABOVE *Iron Range National Park is one of the continent's best-known and most popular wildernesses for viewing tropical birds.*

The Mungkan Kandju ranger station is located 70km down a park track which leads from the Coen airfield. The Development Road continues north and crosses the Archer River. This river is a good place along which to camp and the Archer River Roadhouse is well stocked and equipped. From here it is only 20km to where the road to Iron Range heads east from the Development Road. On the slow winding road into Iron Range there are good camping spots at a number of river crossings, including Wenlock and Pascoe.

A diversity of plants

The park contains Australia's largest remaining area of lowland rainforest. Unusual plant species are found in profusion amongst the semi-deciduous vines and palms. The western parts of the park have more typically Australian landscapes with gum forests and heathlands.

On the Janet and Tozer ranges strange pitcher plants and sundews can be found. Mangroves cling to the shoreline along the Pascoe River interspersed with mangrove palms. The alluvial flats also support paperbark forests and other coastal vegetation communities.

A rare array of wildlife

Animals which are otherwise found only in New Guinea find a home in this pocket of Australian lowland forest. Birds such as eclectus parrots, red-bellied pittas and palm cockatoos, and mammals like the grey cuscus are found no further south on Australian soil. Other interesting wildlife includes cassowaries, rare bowerbirds and green pythons. This area is a mecca for birdwatchers.

Human occupation

Traditional occupation of the Iron Range area by the Kuuku Ya'u Aboriginal people occurred up until the 1920s. Their descendants have now settled at Lockhart River. European history of the area started with the ill-fated 1848 Kennedy expedition, the aim of which was to explore Cape York. Of the eight men left at the staging post at the mouth of the Pascoe River, only two survived starvation and illness.

In the 1930s, pearling and goldmining flourished briefly, and a jetty was constructed in 1938. World War II brought thousands of US troops to Iron Range. The region became an important staging area and many wartime facilities were built. Relics of the war days, such as fuel drums, gun emplacements and pieces of bitumen road, can still be found along the coast.

Park facilities

Park service camp sites are located at Chili Beach, Gordon Creek and East Claudie River. Chili Beach is a delightful wide sandy beach with freshwater streams spilling across the shoreline in places. Restoration Island, less than 1km offshore, is part of the park and also has lovely beaches. A national park service ranger is based at King Park Homestead just north of the Lockhart River airfield. Exploration within the park is only recommended in four-wheel-drive vehicles or on foot.

No supplies are available in the park so visitors must be completely self-sufficient. Some supplies are available during limited trading hours at the nearby Aboriginal community store at Lockhart River.

Except for the entry to Iron Range, permits are required to cross any Aboriginal land to the west and south of the park. Heading north to the Cape from Iron Range, the shortest route is via the Frenchmans Road to Batavia Downs.

How to get there

Access to the region is by light aircraft or by road from April to November. Road access is by four-wheel-drive vehicle only via the Peninsula Development Road and the Archer River Road, 130km north from Archer River Roadhouse (about four hours drive). An alternative route is via the Frenchmans Road from the Development Road at Batavia Downs.

Iron Range National Park tel: (07) 4060–7170

JARDINE RIVER NATIONAL PARK

The Jardine River is Queenland's largest perennial stream. More water pours out to sea from this short river than from any other in the state. The Jardine River National Park and two adjoining reserves, Shadwell and Heathlands, form a huge wilderness area on the eastern tip of the Cape. In addition, the coastal waters are reserved as part of the Great Barrier Reef Marine Park. A landscape of broad plateaux with low cliff lines and shallow marshy depressions covers much of the park.

Overland communications
North from the Cape York Peninsula Development Road the route to Australia's most northerly point follows the original Queensland Overland Telegraph Line. This line forms the western boundary of the Jardine River National Park. It was built in 1885 to carry morse messages from Bamaga to Brisbane and was used extensively during World War II. The last official morse message was transmitted in 1964. Up until 1987 the line was used for phone services but was then dismantled with the advent of microwave links. The route of the line is bypassed by the track in some places to make the trip to Bamaga easier, but it does give an insight into the hardships endured by the line's engineers.

A wet desert
Plant communities that are typical of the region include tall rainforest growing on broad sandstone ridges, open forest, heath and shrubland. Vine forests dominate the headwaters of the Jardine River. Stands of native pines form part of the rainforest canopy.

Much of the park comprises swampy ground, and sundews, pitcher-plants and orchids are common. The ground is so difficult to cross that the first European explorers described the area as a 'Wet Desert'. The coast is characterised by lines of white sand dunes backed with lakes and freshwater lagoons.

A link with New Guinea
Some of the continent's most unusual wildlife, including rare kingfishers, frogs and reptiles, are protected within the wilderness parks of the Jardine River. Strong biological connections exist with the wildlife of New Guinea and many birds migrate between the two countries. Birdwatching is one of the most rewarding activities in the park.

ABOVE *The Jardine River National Park contains a remote, wild river known for its beauty and challenging waterflows.*

Park facilities

Access to the park is limited to the roads on the western boundary, those around the ranger station at Heathlands and the two roads that provide access to the coast. Camping is allowed on the banks of the Jardine River and at a delightful spot at Eliot Falls just within the park. A third camp site is located on the coast at Captain Billy Landing in the Heathlands Reserve. Just outside the western edge of the park are camp sites at the Gunshot, Cockatoo and Sailor creeks. Picnic facilities are located at Fruit Bat Falls. The nearest supplies are available at Bamaga, near the tip of the Peninsula, or Archer River Roadhouse.

To the tip of Cape York

The Old Telegraph Line bypass track sweeps to the east of the Jardine River National Park's tip. This bypass route then crosses the Jardine River where there is a vehicle ferry. An Aboriginal reserve access permit can be obtained for this last leg to the tip of Australia. The bypass then rejoins the old telegraph route at the old Jardine River crossing where riverside camp sites are available.

There is a choice of accommodation on the Cape. Camping and resort accommodation is available at Pajinka Lodge, and there are camp grounds at Seisia, Punsand Bay and Somerset.

Bamaga is around two hours' drive from the ferry crossing on the Jardine River. From Bamaga to the Cape it is another 33-km journey north via Lockerbie and then to Pajinka. From the camp ground car park, a short walk through the trees takes you to the beach and along to the headland. Cape York is marked by a small rock cairn.

Possessing a continent

Just around the tip of the Cape is a small island, named Possession Island by Captain James Cook. It was here in 1770 that he claimed the east coast of Australia on behalf of the King of England. The island is now a national park and a plaque marks the spot were Cook performed his simple ceremony. It is only a short crossing from Punsand Bay, and boat landings can be made on beaches on the eastern side.

How to get there

Access to Jardine River is by light aircraft or by road (April to November). Road access is by four-wheel-drive vehicle only, via the Peninsula Development Road and the Overland Telegraph Line Road. The park headquarters are 160km north of the Peninsula Road turn-off. Other access roads include Usher Point in the north of the park.
Jardine River National Park tel: (07) 4060–3241

DON'T MISS...

ADVENTURE EXPERIENCES

Canoeing the Jardine River is a challenge partly because of the remote location, partly because of the power of the river, and partly because of the presence of saltwater crocodiles. There are occasional tour parties but you will probably need to arrange a special group and local guide.

Wilderness walks on Cape York require pre-planning and experience. You need to be well equipped and, as no tours are offered, private parties would need to be arranged. Two excellent locations are the CREB track above the Daintree region in the south and the walks in Iron Range National Park. Local guides are available.

For those with time to spare and the urge to try something different, trips on the mail and service planes or commercial boats that service the Cape York and Gulf Country towns can sometimes be arranged. You will need a flexible touring schedule and be prepared to travel light. Try the Cape York Air Services for seats on a mail run or contact the travel centre, airport or port.
Cairns Travel Centre tel: (07) 4052–6211
Cape York Air Services tel: (07) 4035–9624
Treize Bush Guide Service tel: (07) 4052–1552

The Old Telegraph Route provides a rough crossing over the Jardine River.

OTHER INTERESTING AREAS

Dorunda Station near Normanton is a working Gulf Country cattle station with lodge accommodation and plenty of station activities, horse riding, four-wheel-drive exploring, fishing and boating. You can fly in or drive to Normanton.

Try your hand at panning for gold on what was Australia's richest alluvial field, **Palmer Goldfields**, south-west of Lakeland. There is a camping area within Palmer Goldfield Reserve.
Cairns Travel Centre tel: (07) 4052–6211
Dorunda Lodge tel: (07) 4745–3477

THE INLAND

Porcupine Gorge • Lawn Hill • Adventure Way

*S*cattered *throughout the inland of Queensland are numerous remote and sometimes little-developed national parks. These are well worth the extra effort required to explore them as they offer particularly good outback wilderness experiences. It is a region where new parks are regularly being opened for the adventurous, so it is a good idea to enquire ahead of time with national park authorities about any new areas to explore.*

Travel Tips

The inland is subject to wet season rains and high humidity from December to April. The best time to visit is during the winter months from April to October when the days are balmy and nights cool. If you are camping be prepared for frosts during winter. During the school holidays well-known parks can be very popular so it is generally best to book camp sites in advance.

There are regional airports at Mount Isa, Longreach and Cunnamulla with smaller airfields for light aircraft at the larger towns throughout the vast inland area. Tours can be arranged from Mount Isa, Cairns, Townsville, and Brisbane.

The inland is served by many highways and development roads. A conventional vehicle may get you to the larger towns, but if you go off the main roads you will need a four-wheel-drive. South of Mount Isa, unpredictable summer rains can cause widespread flooding. Access becomes unreliable and rivers like the Diamantina, Cooper or Warrego can become virtual inland seas, interrupting road travel for days or weeks.

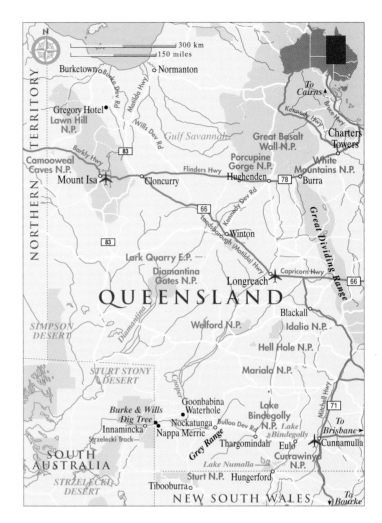

OPPOSITE LEFT *Heavy rains cause flooded roads and washouts, so check water depths before driving through.*

OPPOSITE RIGHT *Porcupine Gorge sweeps through the rugged landscape of the interior, creating extensive vistas.*

BELOW *Long-distance trucks thunder along outback roads, so it is wise to give way as they may not see you.*

PORCUPINE GORGE

Basalt formations feature in a number of remote wilderness parks in Queensland's northern inland. North of the Flinders Highway between Charters Towers and Hughenden is the basalt-capped Porcupine Gorge. Another is the distinctive Great Basalt Wall, while further west the Flinders Highway cuts through the southern tip of the rugged White Mountains National Park. South-west of Winton is the arid and semi-arid Diamantina Gates National Park through which the usually dry Diamantina River flows after prolonged periods of rain.

Lava flows
Located west of Townsville, the Great Basalt Wall National Park is a difficult place to reach, but its landscape discloses secrets of the continent's past. This is an interesting if strenuous landscape to explore. It is the site of the last major volcanic activity in northern Australia and comprises part of an enormous 100-km lava flow. The geological evidence of recent lava flows can be seen in the chocolate-coloured basalt rock formations and the surface volcanic activity. Pockets of dry rainforest are found also amongst the deeper valleys, and the area has a variety of interesting wildlife.

This remote park is ideal for fit bushwalkers. No marked trails exist, so walkers need to be well equipped and experienced. The large basalt masses in the park may affect compass readings so extra care is required in finding your way around remote areas.

Adventurous wilderness walks
The sandstone bluffs and gorges of White Mountains National Park are primarily suitable only for the adventurous wilderness walker. This new park is still mostly undeveloped with no camping facilities. However, some exploration of the Burra Range is possible from the highway. Access to the park is via Burra, about 110km east of Hughenden.

A cool haven
North of Hughenden, and further west in an increasingly dry landscape, Porcupine Gorge National Park features a deep cool gorge with its flowing river, towering cliffs and layers of exposed coloured sandstones – in striking contrast to the dry woodlands of the surrounding landscape.

Young basalt rocks once covered the surface, concealing the sandstone layers which date back millions of years. A river then cut through the basalt creating Porcupine Gorge, and exposing the ancient 500 million-year-old rocks on the valley floor. The park also has delightful swimming spots and in dry weather these provide important refuges for many birds and larger mammals.

Prehistoric footprints
Lark Quarry, located 110km south-west of Winton on the Jundah Road, is a small park with an amazing prehistoric site. Around 100 million years ago a dinosaur stampede occurred when a large carnivorous prehistoric creature attacked a group of smaller dinosaurs. Evidence of the melee is beautifully displayed by footprints preserved in stone. About 250 individual dinosaurs of three species were involved and over 1000 footprints are enshrined. This is definitely worth a stop on the way south to the Diamantina.

Channel deserts
Situated on the usually dry banks of the Diamantina River, this park of the same name preserves a vast region of braided, dry rivers, typical of the Channel country desert ecosystems. The main feature of the park is the narrow gorge between the Hamilton and Goyder ranges. In times of inland floods, this

narrow gap constricts river flow, causing raging torrents and more flooding. During wet periods south of the park, flood-waters spread out across the plains on the way to Lake Eyre.

Camping

At Great Basalt Wall National Park a bush camp site is provided at Red Falls on Lolworth Creek near the entrance to the park. There are few facilities and the falls may dry up at certain times of the year. Camping facilities are provided at Pyramid Lookout in Porcupine Gorge National Park. At Diamantina Gates National Park, the best camping area in dry weather is along the river at Hunter Gorge Waterhole. Visitors should ensure that they are entirely self-sufficient.

How to get there

Porcupine Gorge is located 40km north of Hughenden on an unsealed road. The park becomes inaccessible to conventional vehicles after rain. Access to Great Basalt Wall is by four-wheel-drive vehicle only, and even then extreme care is needed, particularly after rain. The Great Basalt Wall can be reached on a variety of unsealed four-wheel-drive access roads. The best access at present is west from the town of Dalrymple, 39km north of Charters Towers. Diamantina Gates National Park is 300km south-west of Winton via the Lark Quarry and Cork.

Charters Towers tel: (07) 4721–2399
Hughenden tel: (07) 4741–1113
Diamantina National Park tel: (07) 4657–3024

LAWN HILL GORGE NATIONAL PARK

Situated in the vast black soil plains of the Gulf Country, the Lawn Hill Gorge National Park is an unexpected, luxuriant tropical oasis. Fed by springs in the limestone hills on the Northern Territory border, the gorge contains deep waterholes year-round. The Riversleigh sections of the park are World Heritage-listed because of their internationally important mammal fossils. Aboriginal paintings also occur throughout the park and the permanent water attracts an abundance of wildlife. To the south is the Camooweal Caves National Park, where caves have been carved underground by the wet season rains.

Oases in the stony plains

Lawn Hill National Park's dry flat plateau contrasts markedly with the pools of deep water edged by rich vegetation. Bushwalking is possible and there are over 20km of trails. However, most visitors prefer to explore by canoe, lilo or inflatable boat. Fan palms are conspicuous botanical oddities growing abundantly within the moist gorges at Lawn Hill. These dark green tropical plants are seemingly incongruous next to the hummock grasses and low shrubs of the stony plains which surround the watercourses.

Attracted to the water and the waterside trees are mammals such as wallabies and possums. Fish are an important element of the aquatic

RED KANGAROO

The largest living marsupial, the red kangaroo, is very much a symbol of the Australian continent and, along with the emu, appears on the national coat of arms. It is also the symbol of Australia's national airline, Qantas, in the form of a flying kangaroo. Large red kangaroos have a body and tail length of 2.5m and may weigh up to 85kg. This species prefers to dwell in the dry inland deserts and arid woodlands. Males are usually red and the smaller females, sometimes known as 'blue fliers', are blue-grey in colour.

Red kangaroos have an extraordinary capacity to breed in large numbers after the rare desert rains. In good seasons, breeding females may have a young at foot, another in the pouch and a third in a suspended state in the reproductive tract. In extended dry conditions, the red kangaroo's reproductive cycle becomes inactive and no attempt is made to breed.

Sometimes red kangaroos drink at stock watering points, although they are capable of surviving without surface water, gathering their nutritional needs from grasses and small herbs.

Most of their feeding is done in the cool of the night; during the day animals are seen usually resting in the shade. A family group may consist of a dozen kangaroos with one dominant male, while in dry seasons wandering mobs of up to several hundred individuals are not unusual. A few old animals may live beyond 20 years of age but life expectancy is usually much less. Most individuals fail to reach the age of two.

Red kangaroo numbers fluctuate widely because of seasonal conditions, however the species' survival has never been under threat. In fact, red kangaroos are probably more abundant today because of the provision of stock watering points than at any time in the past.

wildlife of the gorges. Common species such as archerfish, salmon catfish and bony bream form a substantial part of the diet of waterbirds such as snakebirds and storks. Several species of turtle are found in the deep pools. These, together with fish, comprise much of the diet of the harmless freshwater crocodiles. The latter can be best observed in the lower gorge.

Aboriginal history

Excavations in the area have revealed a continuous human presence in the region for up to 30 000 years. Huge shell middens, occupation sites, ochre painting sites, stone peckings and grinding stones all provide insights into the culture of the Waanyi people, who occupied the region at the time of first European contact. Important spiritual stories associated with the waterholes form part of their culture. Marked trails and boardwalks provide access to the Wild Dog Dreaming and Rainbow Dreaming art sites. Some of the Aboriginal sites and walking tracks are accessible only by canoe.

Unique fossils at Riversleigh

In the south of the park, the Riversleigh section is world famous for its uniquely rich World Heritage-listed fossil records. Human understanding of the evolution of mammals is being rewritten on the basis of these huge and comprehensive chronicles. Dating back 25 million years, the fossils reveal the existence of egg-laying mammals, marsupials and bats, who were the forerunners of many of Australia's present unique fauna. It will require decades of study before the whole evolutionary picture is fully revealed. Although these sites are widely reported on popular television and in geographic magazines, they are not as yet open to the public and camping facilities are not available.

A percolated land of sunken caves

South of Lawn Hill is the Camooweal Caves National Park. The open woodlands, comprising snappy gums and

ABOVE *Canoeing on Lawn Hill Creek is a rare treat as this is a welcomed oasis in a dry landscape.*

bloodwoods, and the extensive plains of Mitchell grass conceal the dramatic nature of the park's subterranean landforms. Unlike caves elsewhere, these are subject to wet and dry seasons and do not have the features traditionally expected, such as stalactites. The annual wet season deluges that regenerate the grasslands flood Nowranie Creek. Here the water percolates into the ground and erodes the underground layers of dolomite to create the huge cave systems.

In the winter the caves are usually dry and often dusty. There are no guided cave tours and exploration is only for the well-prepared and experienced caver. Access to one of the largest caves is from the base of the sinkhole, 70m deep and a third of a kilometre long, at Great Nowranie Cave.

Camping

There is a well-equipped camp site at the middle gorge of Lawn Hill Creek and camping facilities are also available outside the park at Adels Grove. A ranger station is located near the camp ground at Lawn Hill. In Camooweal Caves National Park there is a good camp site with basic facilities at Nowranie Creek.

How to get there

Road access to Lawn Hill is unpredictable due to seasonal flooding. Summers are hot, wet and unforgiving for the ill prepared, so always carry plenty of water. The park lies 400km north-west of Mount Isa and comprises several sections. Vehicle access is gained from a road to the west of Gregory Hotel. An alternative route for those with four-wheel-drives is to travel 220km west of Mount Isa on the Barkly Highway and then 215km north on the Gregory Downs Camooweal Road. Camooweal Caves is 8km south of Camooweal.

Mt Isa National Park and Wildlife Service
tel: (07) 4743–2055

ADVENTURE WAY

The Adventure Way is 570km of inland roads that connect Innamincka in South Australia to Cunnamulla in Queensland. It travels through some remote arid country in south-western Queensland, twice crossing the usually dry Cooper Creek and the low 'jump-up' hills of the Grey Range.

South-west Queensland has abundant areas of arid wilderness to explore. Two desert national parks, Idalia and Currawinya, are located north and south of this route respectively, and offer further arid-land wilderness exploration. There are many other parks, some with restricted access like the Mariala, Hell Hole Gorge and Welford national parks. It is useful to enquire ahead of time to find out about new developments and seasonal conditions.

Starting at Innamincka in South Australia, the Adventure Way heads east to Nappa Merrie, past Aboriginal art sites and, unceremoniously, across the state border. About 5km short of the junction with the Tibooburra Road, there is a 5-km sidetrack to Cooper Creek. Across the creek at the Bulloo Bulloo crossing and a little downstream is the famous Burke and Wills Dig Tree where the explorers were meant to meet their party who had actually left a few hours before. Camping is permitted between the tree and the crossing.

From grass floodplains to barren desert

Back on the main route, the road crosses Cooper Creek at a narrow section where one of the most remote large bridges of the inland spans the Nappapethera Waterhole. Heading west again the road leads to the Goonbabinda Waterhole on the edge of the Cooper Creek floodplain. Known as the Channel country this region periodically floods producing some of the country's best cattle-fattening grasslands. In dry seasons the Mitchell grass floodplains are reduced to barren desert.

Nockatunga to Cunnamulla

Approaching Nockatunga the road becomes bitumen, providing relief from the corrugations and dust of the unsealed roads. Shady camp sites are located along the Wilson River. Travelling through Thargomindah the next interesting feature is the freshwater lake at Bindegolly. This national park is important for nesting waterbirds. Between Carpet Springs and Eulo are artesian water upwellings, known as mud springs, which provide good observation points for dry country wildlife. Around Eulo there are good camping spots by the waterholes on the Paroo River. The Adventure Way joins the Mitchell Highway at Cunnamulla. This regional town has good facilities and camping areas on the Warrego River.

Currawinya's wetlands and lakes

West of Cunnamulla the lakes and wetlands of Currawinya National Park are a good detour off the Adventure Way. Heading south from the Way at Thargomindah, there are two unsealed roads, both of which lead to Hungerford. However, it is the northern road that cuts through Currawinya park. An unsealed road north from the park to Caiwarro rejoins the Way at Eulo. Although interesting, taking this route adds at least 100km to the journey.

Lake Numalla is a large freshwater lake in Currawinya, frequently filled by overflows from the Paroo River. Access to this lake and the salt lakes in the park is via four-wheel-drive tracks. Non-powered boating is permitted on the lakes, a major breeding location and refuge for waterbirds. Freckled ducks, avocets and rails are only some of the more unusual birds that visitors to the area are likely to encounter. The park's headquarters are located at the old Currawinya Homestead. Camping facilities are provided at Ten Mile Bore and at a number of sites along the Paroo River near the Old Caiwarro Homestead.

Swinging north

The Adventure Way connects with routes to Tibooburra at Nappa Merrie and Nockatunga. From Nappa Merrie it is now possible to also head north on a new route that connects Melbourne to Darwin. The towns and places connected by the new road are Tibooburra, Nappa Merrie, Arrabury, Boulia and Mount Isa. The road is unsealed but is gradually being developed as an all-weather route.

Idalia: shrubland and sandstone gorges

About 400km north of the Adventure Way, Idalia National Park is a wilderness of mulga shrublands and steep escarpments. The park is conveniently located on the route from Carnarvon to Birdsville and on back roads heading south from Longreach. It is about 100km from Blackall, with only one entrance south of Benlidi. Access is restricted to four-wheel-drive vehicles. Bush camp sites are provided and there are several marked walks exploring the sandstone gorges.

How to get there

To get to and to start at Innamincka, head along the Strzelecki Track. Alternatively, take the Mitchell Highway to Cunnamulla and join up with the Adventure Way at this point. The roads are mainly sealed, but if you plan any side trips they are on unsealed surfaces, so a four-wheel-drive vehicle is highly recommended.
Innamincka Store tel: (08) 8667–5990
Longreach National Park and Wildlife Service tel: (07) 4658–1761
Currawinya National Park tel: (07) 4655–4001

ABOVE *The service station at Innamincka provides a wide range of supplies and is a good source of local knowledge about the surrounding terrain.*

OPPOSITE *The road sign on the Strzelecki Track highlights the need for self-sufficiency while travelling through the outback.*

Don't Miss...

Adventure Experiences
Camooweal Caves offer some of the best adventure caving in the outback. For advice on arranging a tour, contact the National Parks service.

Queensland's outback has its own unique style of professional guide service. Known as Savannah Guides, individuals in different parts of the outback are available to provide specialist services. For details on all options including gold-panning, cave tours and Aboriginal art tours, contact the Gulf Savannah Tourism Organisation on the number below.
Mt Isa National Park and Wildlife Service tel: (07) 4743–2055
Gulf Savannah Visitor Organisation tel: (07) 4051–4658

Other Interesting Areas
There are many opal fields in western Queensland. **Longreach** is one centre where you can arrange to go opal

A statue of a pioneer stands outside the Stockman's Hall of Fame in Longreach.

fossicking. Mine tours can be arranged and the deserted town of Opalton explored.

Ironhurst Station cattle property lies 32km north of Georgetown. Here you can join in with the operation of a working cattle station, go birdwatching or try some gold-panning. The comfortable homestead caters for families or small groups only.

The Stockman's Hall of Fame, located in Longreach, is a modern tribute to the early pioneers. The large air-conditioned centre presents an authentic account of life in the inland as well as the opportunity to ride in an authentic Cobb and Co coach which has been restored.

Stockman's Hall of Fame tel: (07) 4658–2495
Cobb and Co tel: (07) 4658–1694
Longreach Visitor Information tel: (07) 4658–3555
Miners Den (Cairns) tel: (07) 4051–4413
Ironhurst Station tel: (07) 4062–1124

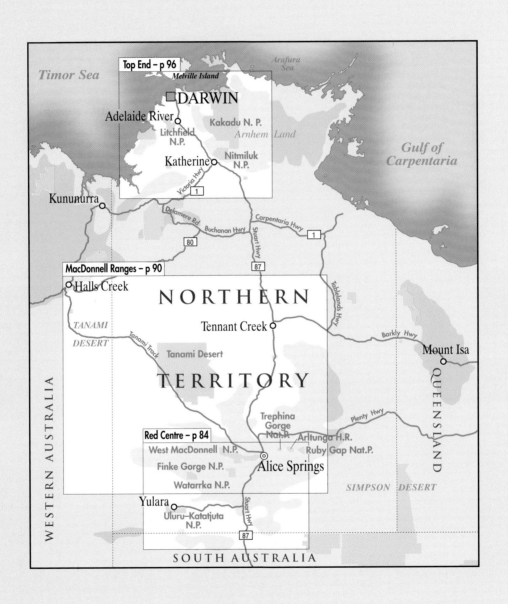

Timor Sea

Arafura Sea

Top End – p 96

Melville Island

☐DARWIN

Adelaide River ○

Kakadu N. P.

Arnhem Land

Litchfield N.P.

Gulf of Carpentaria

Nitmiluk N.P.

Katherine ○

Kununurra ○

Victoria Hwy

Delamere Rd

Buchanan Hwy

Carpentaria Hwy

Stuart Hwy

1

80

1

87

MacDonnell Ranges – p 90

○ Halls Creek

NORTHERN

TANAMI

DESERT

Tanami Track

Tennant Creek ○

Tablelands Hwy

Barkly Hwy

Mount Isa ○

Tanami Desert

QUEENSLAND

TERRITORY

WESTERN AUSTRALIA

Trephina Gorge Nat.P.

Plenty Hwy

Red Centre – p 84

Arltunga H.R.

West MacDonnell N.P.

Ruby Gap Nat.P.

Finke Gorge N.P.

◎ Alice Springs

Watarrka N.P.

SIMPSON DESERT

Yulara ○

Stuart Hwy

Uluru–Katatjuta N.P.

87

SOUTH AUSTRALIA

NORTHERN TERRITORY

RED CENTRE

Uluru–Katatjuta • Watarrka • Finke

*I*n many people's minds, the Red Centre epitomises Australia. Uluru is one of the world's great geological formations and has strong spiritual significance for its traditional Aboriginal residents. Its presence also makes an impact on visitors to the region. Nearby Watarrka National Park and Finke Gorge display too the wonderful formations that distinguish the outback.

All the land around Uluru and to the west of Watarrka is under the custodianship of the local Aborigines and is not accessible to the public unless permission is granted.

Travel Tips

The best time to visit is from April to October, when days are balmy and nights cool. If you plan to camp, be prepared for frosts in winter. In summer the days are hot to very hot, averaging about 37°C. Winds and dust storms can also be unpleasant and flies are a problem. During the winter well-known areas can be busy. Always carry water, even if going on a short walk.

Scheduled flights and coach services leave Alice Springs for Yulara and Watarrka daily. At Yulara rental cars including four-wheel-drives are available. The sealed Lasseter and Stuart highways connect Yulara with the 'Alice' and Adelaide, and the Gunbarrel Highway connects to Perth. The Northern Territory has no set speed limits. At any time, especially at night, stock or wildlife can wander onto the road. If you have problems with your car, do not leave your vehicle.

PREVIOUS PAGE   *The red dunes of the Northern Territory are unlike any wilderness area in the world.*

ABOVE RIGHT   *The steep walls of Kings Canyon at Watarrka create a striking contrast to the surrounding flat desert landscape.*

OPPOSITE   *The vast red monolith known as Uluru rises majestically from a sea of sand.*

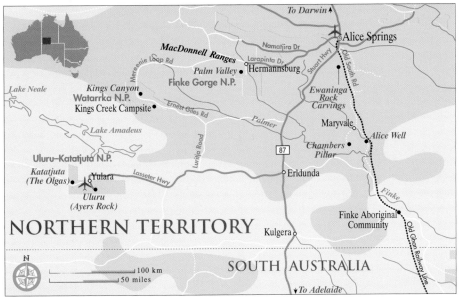

ULURU–KATATJUTA NATIONAL PARK

Uluru is the Aboriginal, and now official, name of the huge monolith that looms out of the central Australian desert. Originally named Ayers Rock by the first white explorers in 1873, it is a single stone mass rising 340m into an almost perpetually blue and cloudless sky. Around its base Uluru measures almost 10km. Geologists have found that this monolith is the exposed tip of a buried slab of rock that may be as much as 5km in depth.

The ethereal quality of Uluru is supported by its apparent changes of colour during the course of the day. The natural sandstone colour is grey, but over the years the rock has turned a deep red because of the blasting it receives from the red desert sands. As the sun appears each morning the first rays are reflected off the surface and the vast expanse of rock sometimes develops an intense pink glow. With the day's progression, Uluru passes through various shades until sunset when the last rays of the day bathe the rock in bright crimson. The intensity of the colour changes during the day depends on atmospheric conditions, the temperature of the air layers, and the amount and location of any cloud cover.

Climbing the Rock

A popular and well-promoted activity at Uluru is the climb to the summit. This has, amongst some visitors, attained the level of a pilgrimage. However, the climb is highly disapproved of by the traditional Aboriginal custodians. They have strong spiritual beliefs tied to Uluru, including the notion that no one other than certain initiated men should ever see the summit. Apart from respecting their wishes, it is wise to bear in mind that the climb to the top is beyond the reasonable physical fitness of many visitors, and accidents – occasionally fatalities – do occur.

The base of Uluru is circled by a walking track which affords a wonderful opportunity to explore the rock's many caves and gorges. After rain, waterfalls crash down the sides of the monolith, filling deep pools at the base. In shaded locations such as at Mutitjulu, the water is believed to be permanent. Wildlife including euros, parrots, goannas and frogs abounds.

Katatjuta: many heads

Uluru lends its name to the Uluru–Katatjuta National Park, which includes the other extraordinary Red Centre geological formation, Katatjuta. An Aboriginal word meaning 'many heads', it is a collection of about 36 domes located nearly 50km from Yulara. The explorer Ernest Giles was the first European to observe this 'wonderful and grotesque formation' and he named the highest peak Olga after the Queen of Spain. Mount Olga is 1069m above sea level but rises only 546m above the surrounding desert. Like the first white explorers, many modern visitors find Katatjuta a more intriguing landscape than the singularly dramatic Uluru.

Dawn walking

One of Australia's greatest bush experiences is the 6-km Valley of the Winds walk at Katatjuta. The road to the car park on the western side of the domes is clearly marked. Due to the oppressive heat in the gorges during the day this walk should be undertaken only in the early morning. The Valley of the Winds is a magical place to be at sunrise for a truly remote desert wilderness experience. Allow about one hour for the drive from Yulara and half an hour to get to the top of the pass for a spectacular view of the sunrise. The whole circuit takes about three hours to complete.

Olga Gorge: red chasm

The Olga Gorge is a powerful attraction of Katatjuta. A short walk from the car park will take you into the massive ochre-red chasm. It is a dramatic landscape and the towering cliffs are emphasised by the narrowness of the gorge. The area is hot during the middle of the day and popular with visitors an hour or two before sunset. As a consequence, the recommended time to visit the Olga Gorge is after sunrise in the cool of the morning.

How to get there

There is an airport at Yulara. If flying, a recommended way to travel is to break the trip at Alice Springs and catch a one-way coach, tour or rental car to Yulara to appreciate the countryside – one day is all that is needed but organised safaris can take two or three days. You can then reconnect with the flight at Yulara. If driving to or from Alice Springs, you should try to link Uluru–Katatjuta and Watarrka national parks to make a round trip from the Stuart Highway.

Uluru–Katatjuta National Park tel: (08) 8956–2299

WATARRKA NATIONAL PARK

Watarrka National Park is a geological and biological wonder in the desert. Kings Canyon, the main attraction of the park, is a chasm cut deeply into the 440 million-year-old sandstone of the George Gill Range. The name of the park, Watarrka, comes from the Aboriginal name for the locally common umbrella wattle tree.

It is only a short drive to Watarrka's main feature, Kings Canyon. In the open country ghost gums dominate on either side of the highway that sweeps into the park. The root grubs and seeds of this bush were used traditionally by Aborigines as a source of food. There are also dozens of species of water-dependent plants that are protected by the canyon walls from the full harshness of the surrounding desert. These plants are tenacious survivors from a much wetter prehistoric aeon.

Walking Kings Canyon

From the car park, beside the scattered pools of Kings Creek, are two walking trails into the canyon. In general it is wise to start these walks in the cool of the early morning and to finish before the full heat of the day. In summer it would be foolhardy to do otherwise. Carrying water with you on treks is essential.

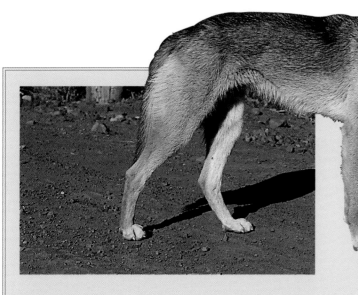

DINGO

One conspicuous member of Central Australia's wildlife is the dingo. A relatively recent arrival on this continent, it is a close but distinct relative of the domestic dog. Around 40 000 years ago the first dingoes arrived in Australia as companions to humans travelling from Asia by boat. They quickly spread and now occur in all parts of the country and in all habitats from desert to the thickest mountain forest.

European occupation after 1788 removed dingoes from the settled regions and, as hybridisation with domestic dogs occurred in many other places, there has been a decline in the dingo population. However, in the central deserts the dingo still holds its own.

Nine out of ten dingoes are a rich yellow-ginger colour. The remainder are various combinations of black, tan, white and brindle. One consistent feature of almost all dingoes is that their feet and the tip of their tail is white.

Like carnivores the world over, semi-tame dingoes are sometimes seen waiting around popular picnic spots for handouts. Although this allows visitors to observe these animals closely, the temptation to provide food to them should be resisted. Wild predators like dingoes can become too tame and become a danger to people and, as a consequence, a danger to themselves.

Wild dingoes are not too particular about what they eat. Mammals such as kangaroos, wombats, rabbits or rats usually make up the main part of their diet. Dingoes also readily take sheep and calves and the country's farmers have gone to great efforts to protect their stock. Sheep country in southern Australia is still separated from the dingoes of the central desert by a fence 5614km long. It is the longest fence in the world and stretches from close to Brisbane to west of Adelaide on the Nullarbor Plain.

ABOVE *The walk up the twisting and labyrinthine trail to the top of Kings Canyon is rewarded by a vista over the chasm and beyond.*

The first track is only 2km long, is relatively flat and it takes about two hours to meander along Kings Creek and up the floor of the canyon. There are fine views of the canyon walls and to the head of the gorge. In places the vegetation is surprisingly thick for such arid landscape.

Depending on how long it has been since the last rainfall, many of the pools may be full of water. The main canyon walk is only 6km long but is very steep and labyrinthine in places. Fortunately it is well marked with multilingual interpretive signs and track numbers. Part of the way along the walk is an emergency box so that, if necessary, contact can be made with the park rangers.

A haunting landscape
Another walk winds along Kings Creek for about half a kilometre and then suddenly launches straight up the wall of the canyon. This is a very difficult stretch and should be taken in easy stages. The reward for reaching the top of the rim is a convoluted walk through bizarre weathered mini-canyons. The track then crosses ancient weathered sandstone surfaces, which in some places have water ripple marks in the stone, reminders of the oceans that retreated 360 million years ago. The track breaks out at the edge of the canyon with dramatic views over 100-m cliffs to the valley below. Desert stretches in

all directions as far as the eye can see while, in the distance, the vast saline Lake Amadeus shimmers on the horizon.

As the walk slowly unfolds, strange and ancient macrozamias – plant relics from the age of the dinosaurs – lie scattered about this haunting landscape. Unusual desert-tortured pines appear as though in a Japanese bonsai garden. Lizards dart for cover under huge slabs of finely layered rocks. The scene is desolate and strangely moonlike.

The track then emerges onto a wooden bridge above a rich wet gorge, the so-called Garden of Eden. Here trees, shrubs and ferns cluster in the cool protection of the upper canyon. On the northern side of the bridge, before the stairs climb out of the canyon, a detour can be made off the main track. Following the creek downstream for 1km it eventually emerges at the head of the main canyon. There are a number of spots with spectacular views out across the top of the usually dry waterfall and down the length of the canyon.

Returning to the main track the best views of the gorge, those from the southern rim, are still to come. It is from here that rock wallabies may be visible sheltering amongst the boulders below. From the southern rim the track then meanders down the scarp to the creek and car park below.

Park facilities
The main visitor centre is located near the entrance of the park and is worth a visit to pick up maps of the walking tracks. Accommodation is available in Watarrka National Park.

How to get there

The park has a light-aircraft strip, daily coach services, and four-wheel-drive safari tours. Car rentals are available from Yulara and Alice Springs. The sealed Stuart and Ernst Giles highways and Luritja Road connect with Alice Springs (310km away) and Yulara (290km). The unsealed Mereenie Loop Road to West MacDonnells National Park is recommended for a round trip back to Alice Springs.
Watarrka National Park tel: (08) 8956–7460

ABOVE *The expansive Kallaranga Valley is located at the upper section of the Finke River, south of Hermannsburg.*

LEFT *Chambers Pillar rises like a sentinel out of the desert and was used as a route marker first by the Aboriginal people and later by the early European explorers.*

FINKE

This expedition heads south from Alice Springs, follows the Old Ghan Railway Line to Finke and then returns via Kulgera and the Stuart Highway. It could be completed comfortably in about two or three days. Preparations should include setting out in a recent-model, reliable vehicle and ensuring you are well stocked with water, food, bush camping gear and a full set of emergency equipment, including specialised maps. Details of travel plans should be supplied to the police.

Ewaninga's rock carvings

About 40km south of the Alice is a small reserve, Ewaninga, which protects a collection of Aboriginal rock carvings. Tiny symbols and motifs cover the flat surfaces of the soft sandstone rock. The age of the art is not known, but it may be thousands of years. The original meanings of these carvings, or petroglyphs, has been lost but the local Aborigines have their own sacred and secret interpretations. Photographing the rock carvings is technically difficult, but pictures are improved if they are taken early or late in the day using the highlighting effect of long shadows.

Rail trekking

The route continues south from Ewaninga, following the Old Ghan railway line. This line was built from Adelaide to Oodnadatta in 1891 and was extended to Alice Springs in 1929. The path of the original railway ran across many low-lying areas which used to flood after heavy rains. A train trip that usually took three days could then extend to a month! The new line was opened in 1980 and is on much higher land adjacent to the Stuart Highway.

Chambers Pillar

At Maryvale Homestead the route leaves the Old South Road via a rough four-wheel-drive track across the usually dry Hugh River. This track then leads for 35km to Chambers Pillar, a strange finger of rock that rises over 50m above the surrounding desert. In early European times, this distinctive formation was used as an important landmark for those heading north to Alice Springs. It is also of significance to the Aborigines – traditional people believe that the Pillar is an embodiment of the shamed spirit of an ancestral dreaming gecko. The best photographs of Chambers Pillar are taken around sunrise and sunset. This is a good place to bush camp and basic facilities are provided.

An ancient watercourse

The route then heads back to the Hugh River and south again on the Old South Road. From here follow the Old Railway and the Hugh River which run side by side. At the picturesque Alice Well (a good spot for a break), the Hugh River then weaves away to the west where it soon joins the Finke River. Close to the township of Finke the route crosses this great inland watercourse which has travelled from Finke Gorge in the West MacDonnells.

Over 700km long and draining a huge area of the west Macdonnell Ranges and the James Range, this major river finally spills out to lose itself in the Simpson Desert. The Finke River is probably the world's most ancient watercourse with its bed and course being estimated at around 100 million years old.

Finke, a community town

The township of Finke is a small, thriving community that was first established in 1929 to serve the Adelaide to Alice Springs Railway. Missionaries soon followed, but with the relocation of the railway the workers moved away. The community became an Aboriginal centre and an Aboriginal council now runs the town. Provisions are available and bush camping facilities are provided nearby. Check at the community store during business hours.

Australia's gravitational point

A few kilometres west of Finke a lonely Australian flag marks the spot calculated by computer to be the continent's centre of gravity. The official 'Centre of Australia' is not widely known and has no facilities, just a flag!

From Finke it is only 150km west on a well-formed unsealed road to Kulgera. The return route then heads north on the Stuart Highway for about 280km to Alice Springs. Accommodation is available at Kulgera or Erldunda Roadhouse on the highway.

How to get there

From Alice Springs access to Finke is via the Old South Road. There are several road signs that point the way to Chambers Pillar and Finke. Except for the return journey on the sealed Stuart Highway, the roads in this region are all unsealed but well marked. It is, therefore, only possible to do this trip in a four-wheel-drive vehicle. Car rentals are available in Alice Springs.

As with all outback travel, it is essential to ensure that you are well-stocked with provisions including drinking water, and fuel for your car. Today it is also advisable to travel with a mobile phone.

Finke Community Store tel: (08) 8956–0966

DON'T MISS...

ADVENTURE EXPERIENCES

A variety of excellent cultural and heritage tours guided by Aboriginal people operate at Watarrka and Uluru. Some tours last a few hours while others may be camping expeditions of many days. Depending on the tour, traditional bush foods such as witchetty grubs may be collected and goanna and kangaroo caught and eaten. Traditional dances, or corroborees, are not usually shared with non-Aboriginal people. For the best experience, plan ahead, be flexible and expect anything. To book, contact the local national park offices or visitor information centres who can supply maps.

One of the most spectacular stretches of scenery in the Australian desert is at Watarrka – a helicopter flight over Kings Canyon is a must for those who enjoy the aerial experience.

OTHER INTERESTING AREAS

Henbury Craters are located about 132km south of Alice Springs and 5km off the Ernst Giles Highway. The group of 12 craters is the result of the impact of a meteor that broke into 12 pieces just above the earth's surface about 5000 years ago. The impact has been calculated at 40 000kph. A basic camping area is provided near the craters.

Impact craters from meteorites can be found at Henbury.

Andado Station is for the truly adventurous and four-wheel-drive vehicles are essential. Located on the edge of the Simpson Desert, east of Finke, the station, the third-largest in the Northern Territory, offers simple bush hospitality to visitors. A remote four-wheel-drive track connects with Finke town. Advanced planning is required.

CCNT Alice Springs (Aboriginal tours, helitours, Andado Station) tel: (08) 8951–8211

Alice Springs Visitor Centre tel: (08) 8952–5800

MacDonnell Ranges

East MacDonnells • West MacDonnells •

Tanami Track

*T*he MacDonnell Ranges form a series of truly
spectacular ridges that run east to west across the
central plain, west of Alice Springs. The Tanami Track
is a rugged outback trail that heads north from near
Alice Springs to the Kimberleys in Western Australia.
The best time to visit the area is from about April to
October when the days are balmy and the nights cold.
Summer is hot to very hot, although there are shady
gorges and places to swim throughout the ranges.

Travel Tips

There is a domestic airport at Alice Springs. The
Ghan train travels from Adelaide and carries
passengers and vehicles. Camping safaris and
coach tours for the West and East MacDonnell
Ranges can include Uluru. If taking an organised
tour, shop around for the best deals.

The sealed Stuart is the main highway south
to Adelaide (1543km) and north to Darwin
(1482km). The main roads east and west
to the major sites of interest are sealed.
This region can be covered in conventional vehicles but four-wheel-drives are
recommended and are available for hire
from the larger centres.

The West MacDonnells have a lot to
offer so plan to spend more time there.
Always carry water and protect yourself
from the sun. During the winter months
well-known areas closer to Alice can be
extremely busy.

ABOVE RIGHT *The MacDonnell Ranges are
ancient craggy mountains that snake across
the central deserts and conceal pockets of
luxuriant vegetation and colourful wildlife.*

OPPOSITE *Emily Gap is a welcome swimming
hole in the MacDonnells, east of Alice Springs.*

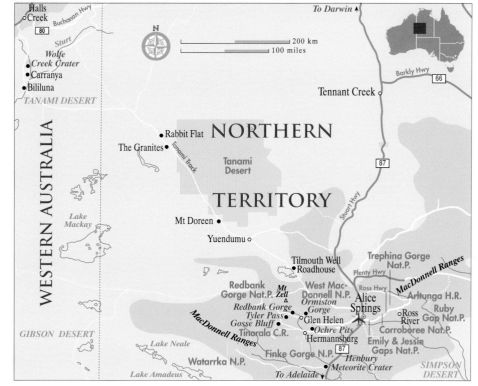

90

THE EAST MACDONNELLS

The East MacDonnells were settled by prospectors in the 18th century and the impact of their diggings on the landscape has left a more noticeable trail than that in the ranges to the west of Alice Springs. But the East MacDonnell Ranges also contain a tapestry of nature parks, reserves protecting sites of Aboriginal importance, areas of mining and exploration history, grand scenery and waterholes which attract wildlife and people alike.

Sacred places
The Emily and Jessie gaps, not far from Alice Springs along the Ross Highway, are scenic red-walled openings in the East MacDonnell Ranges. At Emily Gap there is a small waterhole surrounded by gums, a good spot for a break. The walls of the gorge are painted with Aboriginal art.

With Mount Undoolya on the left, the highway heads further east to Corroboree Rock Reserve, where a large dolomite boulder stands out from the surrounding formations. Aboriginal people kept sacred objects here.

Trephania Gorge: a desert oasis
Trephania Gorge Nature Park is 23km from Corroboree Rock and 85km from Alice Springs on the Ross Highway. The park contains one of the most beautiful gorges east of Alice Springs – tranquil and filled with water, it is truly a desert oasis. The blue skies, sheer red walls and white sands are reflected stunningly in the wide expanse of water, which is a popular swimming hole. There are also many pleasant walks along the river where red gum forest clings to the banks.

Gorge gallery at Ross River
Ross River Homestead is located 9km south off the Ross Highway. The homestead has a range of activities and various styles of accommodation to appeal to most visitors. A four-wheel-drive track that continues south from the homestead winds through an extraordinary, narrow rocky gorge called the N'Dhala. Aboriginal stone engravings decorate the cliff faces of this reserve.

Historic Arltunga
Returning to the Ross Highway, a further 30km east is the Arltunga Historic Reserve, 120km east of Alice Springs. Gold was first discovered in the region in 1887. By the end of the last century about 100 people resided in a bustling small town. The mining operations eventually struggled to survive and the diggings were abandoned during World War I. The site is now a relic of that era and can be fully appreciated during a four-hour car and walking tour of the reserve. For details of the buildings, like the tiny restored police station which closed in 1944, check the visitor centre. Adjacent to the historic reserve there is a commercial visitors' park with supplies and accommodation. There is no camping in the reserve.

Disillusion at Ruby Gorge
For those with four-wheel-drives the 40km of rough tracks to Ruby Gap Nature Park is highly recommended. Information on the Ruby Gorge can be collected from the visitor centre at Arltunga. The deep Glen Annie Gorge is a magnificent chasm cut deep into the ranges. The Hale River, which sometimes rages through this narrow canyon, spills its irregular floods into the sandy country that surrounds the Simpson Desert to the south.

We can only assume that the first European residents of Ruby Gorge in 1878 were less than impressed with their short stay. Over 200 prospectors worked the gorge for a number of weeks before discovering that the rubies they were digging were actually worthless garnets. The name for the gorge stuck but the prospectors moved on, fortunately discovering gold at Arltunga.

Those in four-wheel-drive vehicles can return to Arltunga via the rough 70-km Cattlewater Pass Track, heading north and then turning onto the sealed Plenty Highway and back to Alice Springs. For those in conventional vehicles, the return journey will have to be via the Ross Highway.

Accommodation and facilities
Arltunga has a number of places to stay, either at the homesteads or at camping grounds located along the route. A few days in the region would be well spent. Basic camping and picnic facilities are available at N'Dhala and there are excellent short marked nature walks. Basic camping facilities are also provided in the reserve at Ruby Gap.

How to get there

The main road access to this region is along the Ross Highway, which is sealed to the Emily and Jessie gaps and Trephina Gorge. An unsealed road continues to Ross River Homestead and Arltunga Historic Reserve. Four-wheel-drives are needed to reach Ruby Gap Nature Reserve or to travel north on Cattlewater Pass Track linking to the Plenty Highway.
Trephina Gorge National Park tel: (08) 8956–9765

WEDGED-TAILED EAGLE

The symbol of the Northern Territory Parks and Wildlife Commission, the wedge-tailed eagle is the country's largest bird of prey with a wingspan of up to 3m. In flight, the species is unmistakable due to its sheer size and heavy V-shaped tail. This majestic bird is a close relative of the golden eagles of North America and Europe and can also be found in southern New Guinea.

Wedge-tailed eagles change colour with age – nestlings are white and their first flight feathers are golden brown. The colour then gradually darkens until, at about six years of age, all the plumage is black. Adults live for more than 20 years and form permanent pair bonds. Breeding pairs hold permanent territories.

Using thermal air currents, the eagle soars to great heights above the desert, searching for food over large areas. Prior to European settlement of the continent, it probably fed mainly on various small marsupials such as bandicoots and wallabies. With the decrease in these native animals, eagles now feed mainly on introduced rabbits. Young eagles are frequently seen along the edges of Central Australian highways, feeding on roadside carrion. Groups of young golden-coloured eagles often congregate around the carcasses of dead kangaroos.

Wedge-tailed eagles breed in the winter, ensuring that the main growing time for young birds occurs during the spring when food is most likely to be plentiful. Nests are bulky stick structures, usually located in a fork of the highest available tree. In treeless desert regions, utility poles are often used as tree substitutes. Two eggs are laid in a nest and usually two chicks are hatched. However, it is only in very favourable years, when food is abundant, that both chicks survive. Otherwise it is usual for the older stronger chick to eat its weaker sibling.

THE WEST MACDONNELL NATIONAL PARK

The newest and most spectacular inland Australian national park is the West MacDonnells, officially declared in 1992. The park was created by combining a series of smaller parks with a wide sweep of rugged mountain ranges over 200km long. From the northern fringes of Alice Springs, this magnificent national park includes all the previously well-known sites such as Ellery Creek, Ormiston Gorge and Simpsons Gap. Also included are many new areas such as Mount Zeil, the Northern Territory's highest peak.

Simpsons Gap: biological oasis

The West MacDonnell National Park is a biological oasis in the desert. Of the region's 600 plant species, over 75 have special botanical significance. These include cycads, strange palm-like shrubs left behind from wetter geological ages. The ranges are also a refuge for many species of bird, some very rare. Among the reptile species of this area is the continent's largest lizard, the perentie, which can grow to over 2m.

For many visitors the 'West Macs' are best known as the home of the black-footed rock wallaby. Observing rock wallabies at Simpsons Gap in the cool of the evenings is a Central Australian 'must do'. Although once common and still found in small numbers in remote rocky places, the largest group of these wallabies now resides at Simpsons Gap. Quietly whiling away the heat of the day beneath the boulders, the nimble wallabies emerge from their shelters to graze in the evenings.

Standley Chasm and the Ochre Pits

After Simpsons Gap the next major attraction is to the west at Standley Chasm. Located on the edge of the park, this deep red slash through the ranges is particularly dramatic at midday. Further west is Ellery Bighole, one of the best swimming holes tucked amongst the rocky tors. Close to the main road are the Ochre Pits. Here generations of Aboriginal peoples used ground ochre to make the coloured powder used in their ceremonies. In the past, ochre from these pits was highly valued and traded between communities across Central Australia.

Ormiston and Glen Helen: dramatic ranges

Ormiston Gorge and nearby Glen Helen Lodge are located at the end of the sealed road. Ormiston is high and wide and the nearby pound is bounded by dramatic 200-m-high cliffs. The gorge at Glen Helen has a permanent waterhole in the bed of the usually dry Finke River. Nature walks, lookouts and places for quiet reflection abound in the rocky ranges.

Of the many gorges, the most remote is Redbank. There is enough deep water in the gorge to make liloing down the half-kilometre chasm a sheer delight. Lying, as the gorge does, beyond the end of the sealed road makes it a quiet place in which to experience the surrounding wilderness. Camping nearby gives access to the most remote walks in the park, including the trail to Mount Razorback.

Gosse Bluff: comet crater

A return journey from the western end of the ranges could be via Tylers Pass and the western end of Larapinta Drive. In the south a conservation reserve protects Gosse Bluff, part of a crater formed by the impact of a comet 130 million years ago. Although the access track is only short, it can be impassable to conventional vehicles.

Mission town

Heading back to Alice Springs along Larapinta Drive, travellers will pass through the Aboriginal town of Hermannsburg. Established as a Lutheran mission in 1877, and the birthplace of Aboriginal artist Albert Namatjira, it was returned to Aboriginal control in 1982. Alice Springs is another 132km east of Hermannsburg.

ABOVE LEFT *Cycads are amazing plants that have managed to survive at Simpsons Gap for aeons, despite the harsh environment.*

ABOVE *The dramatic Ormiston Gorge is a highlight of any trip through the West MacDonnell National Park.*

Accommodation and facilities

In the Western MacDonnell Ranges there are basic camping sites at Ellery Bighole, near the Ochre Pits, Ormiston Gorge and Redbank Gorge. Lodge accommodation is available at Glen Helen. Ranger stations and information centres are located at Simpsons Gap and Ormiston Gorge.

The West MacDonnells include the partially completed walking and biking Larapinta Trail. When complete, the trail will comprise 13 sections running the length of the park for 220km. The Simpson Gap Cycle Trail runs across 17km of low hill country from Alice Springs to Simpsons Gap.

How to get there

Vehicle access along the southern side of the West MacDonnells National Park is via the Larapinta and Namatjira drives, west of Alice Springs. There is easy access to all sections of the park from these roads, which are sealed for 135km to Glen Helen Lodge. An unsealed road loops back via Tylers Pass and Hermannsburg on Larapinta Drive. A four-wheel-drive vehicle is not necessary except for the Palm Valley section of the range.

Simpsons Gap National Park tel: (08) 8955–0310

TANAMI TRACK

Cutting through the Tanami Desert is a remote four-wheel-drive dirt track that connects Alice Springs with Halls Creek in Western Australia. The 1057-km route travels through millions of hectares of arid sand dunes, claypans, salt lakes and low, isolated granite hills called whale-backs. The area was largely unexplored by Europeans until early this century when gold was discovered and cattle graziers slowly followed. The original track connected known water sources, but with the demise of stock droving it was re-routed in the mid-1960s and is now a more direct journey across the arid north-western inland area.

Tanami Track: overland beginnings

The Tanami Track begins its north-west journey off the Stuart Highway, 20km north of Alice Springs. There is a bush camp along this first section at Kunoth Bore, with a number of other camp sites located along the way. Initially the track passes through cattle stations, including Amburla Station, which operated one of the last big overland cattle drives in the 1970s from the Kimberleys – 1500 cattle over 1000km. Tilmouth Well Roadhouse is located beside an old stock-watering well near Stuart Bluff Ranges, one of the few rocky ranges around the otherwise flat Tanami landscape.

The Yuendumu Community

The Tanami Track then enters Aboriginal-titled land and passes Limestone Bore before arriving at Yuendumu Aboriginal Community. Yuendumu is a 'closed' Aboriginal town and a permit is required to enter. Formerly a government settlement, the indigenous community received title in 1978 and a council, elected by the community, administers the region. Fuel and other supplies can be obtained at the edge of the settlement without a permit.

Granite tors and fertile mounds

The countryside immediately north of Yuendumu is scattered with granite tors similar, but smaller, to those at Devils Marbles south of Tennant Creek. The landscape around Mount Doreen Station becomes flatter and sandier. The road frequently falls away to below the level of the terrain. After rain it turns into a river and the surrounding grassland, usually full of lizards, becomes a swamp full of frogs. Any washouts remaining after rain can make driving hazardous.

In the region of Refrigerator Well a large number of prominent mounds create eerie shapes on the landscape. These curious forms are termite mounds and provide refuge for the spinifex-eating ant-like insects. In this area there are up to 800 mounds per hectare and the termites are the most abundant and important animal species of the region.

Remote desert country

Heading further north, the track passes to the east of the Granites Gold Mine, where mining activities date back to 1910. The present open-cut mine was established in the early 1990s. None of the mines along the track is open to visitors, nor are supplies available. Not far from here, though, is Rabbit Flat Store, probably Australia's most remote shop. Opened in 1969, the shop lies just north of a sweeping area that drains south to the ephemeral salt lakes, including Lake Mackay. From Rabbit Flat it is only 122km to the Western Australian border. The lonely border crossing is marked only by a few signs beside a small desert wattle.

Into the west

The Tanami Track deteriorates across the border and becomes even more sandy and corrugated. In the sand dune countryside along the banks of the usually dry Sturts Creek is

the Aboriginal community of Billiluna, where supplies can be obtained. Billiluna is about 152km south of Halls Creek. The store marked on some maps at Carranya is now closed. Finally, the sealed Great Northern Highway can be reached about 16km south of Halls Creek.

A cautionary note
Although supplies are available at regular points along the Tanami Track at Tilmouth, Yuendumu, Rabbit Flat and Billiluna, it is essential that all vehicles are well equipped before setting off. The route is regularly travelled and stranded visitors are unlikely to be left for too long without help. However, it is wise to be completely self-sufficient with extra water and emergency supplies of fuel as well as your camping equipment, just in case. Leaving the main track is not permitted, especially if the surrounding land is Aboriginal title. Remember, it is best to travel in convoy with other vehicles, and never leave a broken-down vehicle.

How to get there

There are no organised tours along this track. It is essential that you only travel in a reliable four-wheel-drive vehicle. Most of the route passes through Aboriginal land but a permit is not required if you stay on the track.

ABOVE *It is common to find giant termite mounds scattered across the terrain in the northern region of Australia.*

OPPOSITE *Many remote wilderness tracks were created to connect the vast inland cattle stations with the sealed highways.*

Automobile ANT tel: (08) 8953–1322
Rabbit Flat Store tel: (08) 8956–8744

DON'T MISS...

ADVENTURE EXPERIENCES
One of the truly memorable experiences of Central Australia is to go hot-air ballooning in the consistently clear desert skies. Champagne sunrise flights travel along sections of the magnificent MacDonnell Ranges but a number of operators provide different options. This is one of the best ways to experience the Centre.

Camel safaris are also an ideal way to explore and they range from short rides in Alice Springs to camping safaris into remote parts of the ranges and the desert.
Outback Ballooning tel: (08) 8952–8723
Frontier Camel Tours tel: (08) 8953–0444

OTHER INTERESTING AREAS
The **Overland Telegraph Repeater Station** in Alice Springs gives a fascinating insight into the exploration and settlement of the region and is located just north of the town centre at a delightful site on the banks of the Todd River. It is an easy bike ride from the town and an interesting way to spend a few hours.

The **Royal Flying Doctor Service** has a small museum adjacent to the radio communications centre. A brief visit will offer insight into how the outback is medically provided for.

Conditions in Central Australia are ideal for hot-air ballooning.

Bicycle hire in Alice allows for exploration in and around the town and to some of the nearby parks. It is particularly enjoyable in winter.

Alice Springs is a centre for Aboriginal art. Unless one plans to visit remote Aboriginal communities, this is the best place to purchase art and artefacts. There are many galleries and pricing is competitive.
Overland Telegraph Repeater Station tel: (08) 8951–8211
Melanka Bicycle Hire tel: (08) 8952–2233
Royal Flying Doctor Service tel: (08) 8952–1129

TOP END

Kakadu • Litchfield • Nitmiluk

*T*he Top End, as this region of Australia is known, is an exciting combination of towering escarpment, waterfalls, wetlands, wildlife and stunning scenery. The most comfortable time to visit is during the dry season, from May to September, when the days are balmy and clear, averaging about 30°C. During the Wet it is humid and hot, but visitors are rewarded with dramatic flooded landscapes, abundant wildlife and tropical rains. Travelling at this time of the year can be difficult, but during the Dry the region is very popular. To fully appreciate the countryside catch a scenic flight from Darwin, Katherine or Jabiru.

Travel Tips

There is an international and domestic airport at Darwin with daily flights to the regional airfields at Jabiru and Katherine. Coach services also link Darwin with Jabiru and Katherine.

Rental cars, including four-wheel-drives, and a variety of tours can be arranged from Darwin, Katherine and Jabiru. Road access is via the sealed Stuart and Arnhem highways. A round trip from Darwin, via Kakadu to Nitmiluk, returning through Litchfield, is recommended.

You should avoid swimming in northern waters unless you are certain that saltwater crocodiles are not in residence. Crocodiles can be found in fresh water hundreds of kilometres from the sea.

Always take precautions against mosquitoes and sunburn, and, most importantly, always carry drinking water.

ABOVE LEFT *The plunge pools at Florence Falls are one of the many refreshing swimming holes to be enjoyed at Litchfield National Park.*

OPPOSITE *Kakadu National Park is a beautiful wetland region, particularly at sunset when the park is bathed in gold.*

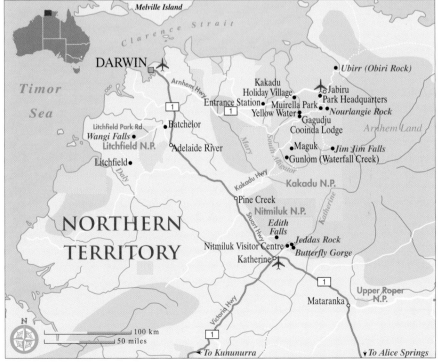

KAKADU NATIONAL PARK

Kakadu is one of the great national parks of the world and was listed as a World Heritage site because of its universal natural and cultural significance. Measuring over 200km in length and 100km wide, Kakadu is about the size of Wales in the United Kingdom and is rich in tropical wildlife and unique landscapes. A powerful and moving place, visitors often feel privileged to have been allowed to visit the park.

Aboriginal people have lived in the Kakadu region for around 55 000 years and their rock paintings, an important feature of the park, date back many thousands of years. Today, Kakadu is controlled by the traditional Aboriginal people who live within the park. The word *kakadu* comes from the local Aboriginal language, Gagudju. The Aboriginal heritage of the region is a major reason for its global significance.

An indigenous heritage

The diversity of Aboriginal culture can be experienced in a variety of ways. There are many walking trails with interpretative information and the visitor centre also provides a wealth of details. At times Aboriginal guides are available to provide further insight into their traditional lifestyle and culture. Ask about these visits and about the Daluk Daluk and Injalak centres at the park's headquarters.

The rock-art galleries of Ubirr and Nourlangie are essential places to visit. Their antiquity, the richness of the images, and the variety of styles used in the creations are a powerful inspiration. The landscape settings of the galleries, especially at Ubirr, enable visitors to gain a sense of the way generations of Aboriginal people have lived. Try to visit these sites at quiet times, particularly early morning, when the experience is enhanced by the tranquillity.

World Heritage wetlands

If Ubirr and Nourlangie are the cultural features of the park, a morning cruise on Yellow Waters is the wildlife highlight. The boat cruises are commercially yet sensitively operated from a base near the Gagudju Cooinda Lodge. The early morning mists, the huge sweeps of swampland and the vast horizons are a natural theatre for a wildlife show unequalled in Australia. Firstly there is the extraordinary array of waterbirds, from jabirus and sea-eagles to teeming flocks of whistle-ducks. But the star attractions are the salt-water crocodiles.

Either basking in the warmth of the early sun or stalking through the lagoons and billabongs, these ancient reptiles are now common in the park. Their numbers have built up following the establishment of protection orders to prevent the crocodiles from becoming extinct after decades of hunting. Visitors have been attacked and even killed by crocodiles, so swimming is safe only in some of the freshwater creeks and waterholes in the south of the park. There are plenty of warning signs at known crocodile habitats. Strictly observe these signs at waterholes, and if in doubt, do not swim.

Walking the terrain

There are over 20 short marked walking trails ranging from a few hundred metres to over 12km to help visitors appreciate the highlights of the park. The principal walks are at Ubirr and Nourlangie. Other recommended walks are at Maguk, especially the Waterfall Creek Walk, and the two walks at Jim Jim Falls. For the more adventurous, multi-day wilderness walks through the remoter regions of the park are a particular challenge.

Wilderness walking is strenuous in the Dry and even more demanding in the Wet. The harsh climate, difficult landscapes, insects and crocodiles are some of the hurdles. The extraordinary landscapes in the tropical wilderness are the reward. The northern sections of the park are the popular areas but, after having visited Ubirr, Nourlangie and Yellow Waters, head to the south for a more reflective time.

Camping

Park permits are required for bush camping and facilities are provided at over a dozen locations through the park. Some parks – like Merl, Gunlon and Muirella – have showers and water. Others have only basic facilities. Most of these areas are closed during the Wet. Several hotels, motels and lodges are available at Jabiru, Cooinda and Kakadu Frontier Village. Visitors should certainly plan to spend some time at the visitor centre, which is at the park headquarters 3km from Jabiru.

How to get there

The main areas of the Kakadu National Park and the visitor centre are located near Jabiru, 250km east of Darwin on the sealed Arnhem Highway. From Pine Creek it is 200km along the Kakadu Highway, which is both sealed and unsealed.

Kakadu National Park
tel: (08) 8979–9101

JABIRU

The jabiru is Australia's only stork and is a common resident of wetlands across the Top End. With its long black neck, bright red legs and massive bill, this stately wetland bird is unlikely to be confused with any other swamp resident. Kakadu National Park is a stronghold of the species and the park's main town is named after the stork.

LITCHFIELD NATIONAL PARK

Often described as the 'accessible Kakadu', Litchfield National Park is one of northern Australia's most scenically diverse parks. Within a relatively contained area there are waterfalls, rock pools, rapids, permanent streams, weathered rock formations and plateaux. Monsoon forests and woodlands harbour a wealth of tropical wildlife. Fields of giant termite mounds evoke a sense of another world. Historical sites include old tin and copper mines and the ruins of simple homes built by pastoralists. Visitors can enjoy safe swimming, bushwalking in interesting landscapes, four-wheel-drive touring, wildlife photography and observation, and camping; all without the need to travel long distances.

Termite homes

Litchfield's termites are world famous because of their homes. Of the thousands of known species in the world of these tiny ant-like insects, only a few make their presence as obvious as the park's two mound-building species. The magnetic or meridian termites build 2-m-high flattened mounds like giant tombstones looming on the seasonally flooded black soil plains. The mounds are aligned north–south to control the temperature of the insects' living chambers. The relative heating and cooling of the two faces of the mound creates an air-conditioning effect for the residents.

A second species, the cathedral-building termite, makes its home on the dry woodland floor. As its name suggests, this

Curiously, and despite its Aboriginal sound, the word *jabiru* is not Australian. The bird takes its name from a similar South American stork where the word *jabiru* is derived from a mix of Amazonian Indian and Portuguese. To avoid confusion with the South American species, some biologists refer to the Australian species as the black-necked stork.

Jabirus, like their well-known European relatives, build huge stick nests – some are platforms up to 2m wide and 1m high. However, unlike European storks, they do not migrate and are not sociable. A pair will usually build its nest away from both people and other storks, high in a tree on the edge of a swamp. The nest may be re-used annually for years. Nest-building and the raising of young is shared by both parents and takes about five months. Pairs may remain together for many years.

During the Wet, the Top End's swamplands are vast, and solitary jabirus stalk fish in the shallow waters. As the Dry advances and the swamps begin to disappear, the storks are forced together into flocks to fish at the remaining waterholes. Large numbers of waterbirds, including herons, geese and jabirus, are found feeding together at this difficult time of the year. As fresh fish become more difficult to find in the muddy bogs, jabirus turn to eating frogs, rodents and even carrion.

species builds huge rounded mounds sometimes exceeding 6m in height. Over 100 other species of termite also share the forests of the Top End. The best viewing areas are along the Litchfield Park Road about 20km from the park entrance.

City of rocks

A large sandstone plateau, which includes the Tabletop Range, makes up the major part of the park. The plateau cascades to the Daly River floodplain, which fringes the western edge of the park. Along this section, from the plateau to the vast plain, waterfalls, plunge pools and pockets of monsoon forest prove to be the main attractions for the park's visitors.

ABOVE *Huge structures built by tiny termites dot the Litchfield landscape. The chambers' positioning regulates their temperature.*

As Litchfield Park Road enters the park it climbs up onto the plateau at the Aida Jump-up. Four kilometres along the plateau a four-wheel-drive track leaves the sealed road and heads south to the Lost City. This strange cluster of rock formations, perched above the plateau edge, provides a wealth of photographic opportunities. Wandering amongst the huge columns it is easy to imagine the location to be a weird Hollywood movie set.

The track may be closed but, depending on the conditions, head down the scarp and join the four-wheel-drive track heading south along the western edge of the park. This southern track winds along the upper reaches of the Reynolds River and eventually leads to the Daly River Road, 40km west of the Dorat Road.

Secluded falls

Wangi Falls are at the end of the sealed section of the entrance road. These falls have the most popular plunge pool for swimming, and basic bush camping facilities are located nearby. Tjaynera Falls, which can only be reached by four-wheel-drive, are located about 7km south of the Greenant Creek picnic area and just off the main southern four-wheel-drive track. Goannas often come to scavenge a feed around the picnic grounds. Eight different species of these large lizards occur in the park.

An array of fascinating underwater life

Litchfield is on the edge of the floodplains and the Reynolds River drains the vast swamplands of the Daly River.

Swimming can be enjoyed in many of the park's plunge pools where a snorkel and pair of goggles can reveal some interesting aquatic life. Over 20 species of native fish inhabit these waters, including rainbow fish, barramundi, grunters and archerfish. The water in these pools and streams is usually so clear that many small fish, frogs and turtles can even be observed from the bank.

Saltwater crocodiles move up the lowland rivers and can be found in small freshwater pools well inland. Check with park staff before swimming or only enter water that is sign-posted as being safe.

Camping

Facilities for bush camping, including a picnic area and toilets, are provided at Wangi Falls, Florence Falls, Buley Rockhole and Tjaynera Falls.

How to get there

Litchfield National Park is 100km south of Darwin. Rental cars and tours are available from Darwin as are scenic flights. Access on sealed roads is via Stuart Highway and Litchfield Park Road. Litchfield Park Road continues as a gravel road through the park and joins sealed Coxs Peninsula Road which returns to Stuart Highway.

Litchfield National Park tel: (08) 8976–0282

NITMILUK NATIONAL PARK

Nitmiluk National Park, previously known as Katherine Gorge, is a vast rocky sandstone plateau punctuated by deep gorges with cool watercourses and rainforest oases. The wet season torrents are drained from the plateau westward and down the Katherine River. Before spilling out onto the floodplains near the town of Katherine, the river snakes for 15km through a series of spectacular gorges. This formation is now known by its Aboriginal name of Nitmiluk.

Ochre-coloured walls, rising 60m or more from the dry season water levels, are testament to the erosive power of the river. Every year during the Wet the surge is unleashed on the gorges. Boating on the river is not recommended at this time of the year as whirlpools are common and waves over 2m high pound the gorge walls. When the sandstone of the Nitmiluk plateau cracks it forms right-angled fissures. Over the aeons,

this has allowed the water to carve the huge gorges that turn sharply along the river path. Many landmarks of the gorge, such as Jeddas Rock and the Narrows, were formed as a direct result of this ancient sandstone cracking.

Exploring the gorges

For most visitors, the main focus at Nitmiluk is exploring the dozen or more river gorges by boat. This can take the form of an organised excursion tour on a large tour craft or a more intimate investigation by canoe. Canoes can be hired for the day or overnight or you can launch your own. Canoe safaris, with overnight camping in the gorge, is a speciality of several local tour operators.

A network of walks

During the Dry, walking and bush camping is another popular choice for exploring Nitmiluk. There is a comprehensive network of tracks connecting the various gorges, as well as long walks taking up to five days and reaching more remote parts of the park. These walks offer the reward of many refreshing swimming spots and great views from the plateau

LEFT *A multi-day canoeing and camping expedition is the best way to explore the famous gorge at Nitmiluk.*

BELOW *A variety of walking treks leads to the top of the Nitmiluk plateau, where the full magnitude of the gorges can be seen.*

to the gorges and floodplains beyond. The shortest walking track is to a lookout above the first gorge. However, although less than 4km long, the Lookout Walk is quite steep. The return walk will take about three hours to complete.

Craggy waterfalls

Although the best-known feature of the park is the gorge, Edith Falls, 60km north of Katherine, is a good stop between Darwin and Katherine for travellers with a bit of time on their hands. A huge deep freshwater pool backed by craggy rock walls makes a picturesque backdrop to the campground. Several short walks provide access to lookouts and smaller swimming holes. An overnight bush camp at Sweetwater Pool is only 5km away and a short day's stroll from Edith Falls. This walk is the start of a five-day trek which, via a series of waterholes and camp sites, connects with the main gorge at the Nitmiluk visitor centre.

Crocodile haven

Freshwater crocodiles, growing up to 2m in length, abound in the gorges at Nitmiluk where they can be seen basking on the sand banks or patrolling for fish. Fortunately, they usually pose no threat to people unless deliberately provoked. Crocodiles nest in the warm sand of some of the beaches in the gorge and rangers sign-post these areas to keep people and crocodiles apart as nesting crocodiles can be aggressive.

Archerfish may also be seen along the water's edge, squirting water at insects that may settle on the streamside vegetation.

Rainforest oases

Most of the vegetation on the plateau is tough and adapted to the dry conditions and frequent fires. By the stream edges, tall paperbark trees with sheets of fibrous bark predominate. Here and there, in protected wet places such as at Butterfly Gorge, pockets of monsoon rainforest can also be found. These damp, dark remnants of wetter times are remarkable oases for people and wildlife alike in an otherwise dry, harsh landscape.

Nitmiluk is a photographer's paradise. During the Dry, the days are clear and the abundant wildlife is concentrated at water sources. The landscapes are diverse and access by water and walking tracks to the gorge edge is easy. A few days spent bush or riverside camping should be well rewarded.

How to get there

The main section of Nitmiluk National Park and the park visitor centre is 30km east of Katherine on the sealed Stuart Highway or 350km south of Darwin. Edith Falls is also reached via the Stuart Highway, 60km north of Katherine. There are daily flights and coaches to Katherine from Darwin and rental cars are available.

Nitmiluk National Park tel: (08) 8972–1886

DON'T MISS...

ADVENTURE EXPERIENCES

Cobourg Peninsula and Gurig National Park are located north of Kakadu and are accessible by air or, in the Dry, by four-wheel-drive track through Kakadu and then through remote wilderness country. Tours include four-wheel-drive camping safaris from Darwin, fly-in camping safaris (Umorrduk) or fly-in luxury resort holidays (Seven Spirit Bay).

Jim Jim Falls in Kakadu National Park is located 60km off the Kakadu Highway at the end of a four-wheel-drive track that is open only in the Dry. A camping area and trails lead to Jim Jim, one of the country's most famous waterfalls.

OTHER INTERESTING AREAS

From Darwin, several interesting tours to Melville Island enable visitors to experience the culture of the Tiwi Islanders.

Territory Wildlife Park, located on the route between Darwin and Litchfield, is one of the best wildlife parks in Australia. Allow at least half a day to explore. In Darwin, try the bright, modern and air-conditioned NT Museum which features Top End wildlife, Aboriginal culture and maritime history. Both of these activities are good in the Wet.

A scenic boat trip is available at Yellow Waters, Kakadu National Park.

Some of the country's most spectacular landscapes in the Top End can be viewed from the air. Try flights over Litchfield from Darwin, or over Kakadu from Jabiru. A round tour by air of Kakadu and Cobourg from Darwin is highly recommended. Aerial tours of Kakadu's waterfalls in the Wet are breathtaking.

Territory Wildlife Park tel: (08) 8988–7200
Northern Territory Museum tel: (08) 8999–8201
Umorrduk Safaris tel: (08) 8948–1306
Seven Spirit Bay tel: (08) 8979–0277

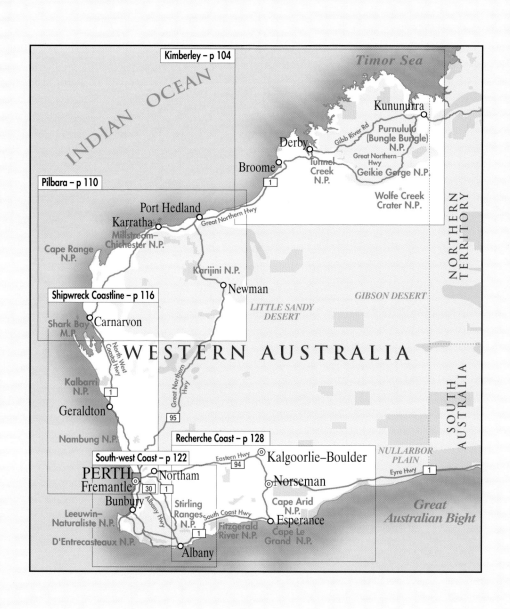

INDIAN OCEAN

Timor Sea

Kimberley – p 104

Kununurra

Purnululu
(Bungle Bungle)
N.P.

Derby

Gibb River Rd

Great Northern
Hwy

Geikie Gorge N.P.

Broome

Tunnel
Creek
N.P.

Wolfe Creek
Crater N.P.

1

Pilbara – p 110

Port Hedland

Great Northern Hwy

Karratha

Millstream–
Chichester N.P.

Cape Range
N.P.

NORTHERN TERRITORY

Karijini N.P.

Newman

GIBSON DESERT

Shipwreck Coastline – p 116

LITTLE SANDY
DESERT

Shark Bay
M.P.

Carnarvon

WESTERN AUSTRALIA

North West
Coastal Hwy

SOUTH AUSTRALIA

Kalbarri
N.P.

1

Great Northern Hwy

Geraldton

95

Nambung N.P.

Recherche Coast – p 128

South-west Coast – p 122

Eastern Hwy

NULLARBOR
PLAIN

Kalgoorlie–Boulder

94

PERTH

Northam

Eyre Hwy

1

Fremantle

30

1

Norseman

Bunbury

Albany Hwy

Stirling
Ranges
N.P.

South Coast Hwy

Cape Arid
N.P.

Great
Australian Bight

Leeuwin–
Naturaliste N.P.

Fitzgerald
River N.P.

Cape Le
Grand N.P.

Esperance

D'Entrecasteaux N.P.

1

Albany

WESTERN AUSTRALIA

KIMBERLEY

Gibb River Road • Purnululu • Geikie Gorge

The Kimberley region in the north of Western Australia is an immense plateau carved by rivers. The area is also cut by two long roads: the unsealed Gibb River Road, originally a cattle route, stretches 722km from Derby to Wyndham; the sealed Great Northern Highway, after its 2200-km run from Perth to Broome, travels 1060km from Broome to Kununurra, and then a further 820km from Kununurra to Darwin. The ideal time to travel is the Dry season, from April to October.

Travel Tips

Kununurra, Wyndham, Derby and Broome all have regional airports with flights to and from Perth and Darwin. There are also a number of small airfields, including one at Purnululu.

PREVIOUS PAGE *Kalbarri's coastline is often rugged, but the mouth of the Murchison offers a tranquil respite.*

ABOVE *The water level in Geikie Gorge rises over 16m during the wet season.*

OPPOSITE *The dry, dusty Gibb River Road passes through the Kimberley region.*

Four-wheel-drives are recommended, and are available for hire at all main centres. As with all remote travelling, be prepared and carry extra supplies in case of car breakdown and long delays. Many areas can be cut off by floodwaters during the Wet when humid conditions make any activity an effort and cyclones are likely.

There are a number of natural hazards in this region. Saltwater crocodiles inhabit most large streams and the ocean, so keep clear of the water's edge. Snakes are active in warm weather so you should always wear boots and long trousers in the bush. Box jellyfish and other marine stingers are a hazard. Generally less dangerous but highly irritating are flies, mosquitoes and sandflies. Stay covered and use insect repellents.

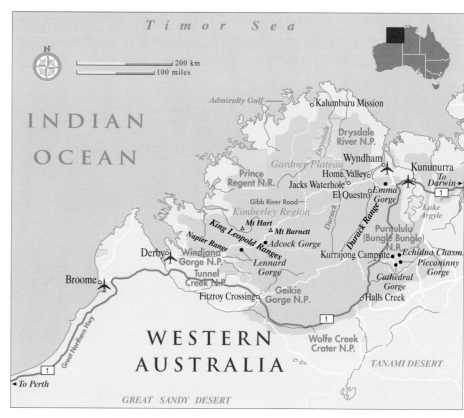

GIBB RIVER ROAD

The Gibb River Road provides access to the Windjana Gorge, the new Mount Hart conservation area and other wilderness regions on the way to Wyndham. For those with plenty of time, a week could be spent on the side-trip north on the Kalumburu Road to the remote Kalumburu Mission or the Drysdale River National Park. During the Wet this area is spectacular, but the road can only be relied upon during the Dry. Sudden downpours during the summer can also leave travellers stranded for months.

A fossilised seabed

Windjana Gorge, a small national park 140km from Derby, is a popular point from which to start any exploration of the Kimberley. The Napier Range, a limestone plateau formed from an ancient coral reef when this area was covered by ocean waters, rises 100m above the flat floodplains of the Lennard River. Over time the river sliced a 3-km-long gorge through the semi-arid plateau, exposing the fossils from the long-since disappeared seabed.

Early in the dry season, before the riverbed dries up, Windjana Gorge is a great place in which to canoe. The towering, layered cliffs and wide river flats are very picturesque. Parrots come to drink at the waterholes that remain during the Dry and tall boab trees are also a prominent feature of the area.

Camping facilities

A marked 4-km walk winds into the gorge from the camping areas. Longer wilderness walks are also possible. The camping area at the open gum forest near the entrance to the gorge is divided into quiet areas – where no portable generators are allowed – and noisy areas. The camp ground is well equipped with toilets and showers. Rangers are based at the gorge during the Dry.

Exploring the Kimberley

Travelling along the Gibb River Road is an adventure, however it is important to remember that the cattle stations along the route are running businesses in a remote and difficult region. Although the country spirit of lending a helping hand is always present, frustration may arise when ill-equipped travellers get into predictable difficulties. This is very remote country and should be explored only by parties who are extremely well prepared and who are travelling in four-wheel-drive vehicles.

From Windjana, the Gibb River Road heads north-east through the Napier and Leopold ranges. Just past Inglis Gap is the turn-off north to Mount Hart Homestead. Eight kilometres further along the Gibb River Road is the southern track which leads to the Lennard Gorge. A new conservation park being developed by the national park services and the local council is changing the access to many of these areas. Because of this it would be wise to check ahead to discover any new routes that might have opened up.

Adcock Gorge and its camp site is located just south of the Gibb River Road, 270km from Derby. An hour's drive further east is Mount Barnett Roadhouse. From the roadhouse it is only a short trip to another delightful gorge, Barnett River Gorge, and its established camping area.

A side-trek to Kalumburu

About 400km from Derby the Kalumburu Road leaves Gibb River Road and heads to the north. This track travels along the Gardner Plateau through vast, remote cattle properties to the Kalumburu Aboriginal community and to the coast along Admiralty Gulf. If you choose to take this side-trip, be aware that supplies are available at Kalumburu, but not on weekends.

Continuing along Gibb River Road, several steep sections are encountered over the next 100km, along with a number of creek crossings. At Jacks Waterhole on the Durack River, 550km from Derby, there are delightful swimming holes. Camp sites and supplies are also available.

To Wyndham

Further on along the Gibb River Road is the Home Valley Homestead and lookout, where the Old Kurunjie Road heads to the north. This rough track runs along the southern edge of the Durack River estuary. It is an alternate shorter but slower route to Wyndham, and passes the famous hollow boab tree once used as a prison cell.

Heading for Wyndham via the Gibb River Road, it passes the entrance to El Questro, which has luxury accommodation and camping at Chambers Gorge. Cabins are also available 10km further east at Emma Gorge. Finally the bitumen Great Northern Road is reached 50km south of Wyndham.

How to get there

The Gibb River Road from Derby to Wyndham extends for 722km and is not accessible in the wet season. The sealed section of the Gibb River Road ends 60km after you leave Derby and is then definitely best suited to four-wheel-drive vehicles. Conventional vehicles can, however, reach Windjana Gorge. From the turn-off on the Gibb River Road, Windjana Gorge National Park is 21km away. Both the Kalumburu and Old Kurunjie roads are suitable only for four-wheel-drive vehicles.

Derby CALM tel: (08) 9193–1411

PURNULULU

Enjoyed from either the air or the ground, Purnululu National Park, once known as the Bungle Bungles, is an impressive place. Its beehive domes (*purnululu* is an Aboriginal word meaning 'sandstone'), hidden gorges and layered formations make it a geological wonderland. The palm-filled gorges and rock pools also make it an oasis in a seemingly forbidding landscape. Further south, Wolfe Creek Crater is a remnant of a meteorite hit. Both parks are difficult to reach, but the rewards when you get there are immense due to their impressive features.

Thousands of round domes divided by deep gorges rise about 200m above the surrounding flat plain, giving the landscape an ethereal quality, especially in late-afternoon sunlight. The solid sandstone range is estimated to be around 360 million years old. Beneath the surface, the rock is an even pale colour but the exterior is banded orange and black. This colouring is created by lichens and silica deposits.

It is believed that Aboriginal people have lived around Purnululu for at least 20 000 years. The first Europeans to enter the area were graziers who moved in at the end of last century and stayed until the park was declared in 1987. Very few visitors came to the park until the mid-1980s, but it is now an area of rapidly increasing popularity.

FRESHWATER CROCODILE

Two species of crocodile occur in Australian waters. One is the relatively harmless freshwater crocodile and the other the very dangerous estuarine, or saltwater, crocodile. Both live in fresh water but only the saltwater crocodile also occurs on ocean beaches and in the open sea. The vernacular names for the two species, 'freshies' and 'salties', could easily lead to fatal misunderstandings as saltwater crocodiles are equally at home in both salt and fresh water.

Freshwater crocodiles can be distinguished from the estuarine species by their long narrow snout, and may inhabit any of the freshwater streams in tropical Australia. Deep permanent pools are their preferred habitat. The freshwater crocodile feeds at night but is often active in the day. Food consists of any small animal: frogs, fish, shrimps, reptiles, birds, and mammals. Prey is grasped by the crocodile's impressive array of sharp teeth. Whilst this reptile does not go out of its way to attack humans, its teeth are formidable weapons and undue provocation could result in a nasty injury. Always take care at the water's edge and never swim unless the waterway has a sign indicating that it is safe.

Freshwater crocodiles lay their eggs in a hole dug in a sand bar. Up to 20 eggs make a clutch and these are usually laid at the end of the dry season, around October or November. In many northern riverside parks at this time of year sections of riverbank known to be used for nesting are marked by rangers with signs. Keeping clear of these areas protects both crocodiles and humans.

There are many locations in northern Australia where 'freshies' are easy to observe, among them Katherine Gorge in Nitmiluk National Park in the Northern Territory, and Geikie Gorge and Lake Argyle in Western Australia. Boat cruises or canoeing create a great opportunity to closely observe these crocodiles in the daytime.

25km in length with the best one being into Piccaninny Gorge. This is wilderness walking at its very best. The crusty exterior of the domes is brittle and climbing on their surface is not allowed.

Wolfe Creek Crater

South of Purnululu is Wolfe Creek Crater, a beautiful clear structure with sharp features. It is highly visible due to the general absence of vegetation. The 800-m-wide, 25-m-deep crater is the largest crater in Australia containing meteorite fragments, and the second largest in the world. There are possibly larger sites in Australia, for example, Gosses Bluff and Lake Acraman, however these are much older and less well-defined, and meteorite fragments have not been found around these locations. Originally Wolfe Creek Crater would have been 200m deep but it has slowly filled with sand over the approximately 2 million years since the impact occurred.

Camping facilities

The rough entry road, which is closed during the Wet, splits near the ranger station. The northern route winds around to Echidna Chasm and Froghole past the basic camp site at Kurrajong. The southern route passes Walardi camp site as it winds around to Piccaninny and Cathedral gorges. A group camp site is located at Bellbird. All the sites have simple facilities and water is scarce. No camping is allowed at Wolfe Creek Crater and only simple day-use facilities are offered there.

Oases for wildlife

Very little grows on the rock surfaces but fan palms cling to the damp watercourses in the narrow gorges. The Osmond Valley supports a patch of rainforest and the surrounding plains are covered in spinifex with the occasional gum tree. Birds are the most obvious of all the region's interesting wildlife. Flocks of budgerigars can be seen coming in for water and many species of eagle and falcon circle overhead. Rare mammals, such as the nail-tail wallaby and narbarlek rock wallaby, occur around the gorges. Euros are likely to be observed either on the rock surfaces or within the gorges.

Exploring the chasms

The northern gorges are narrower and more sheltered and so are quite different to the gorges on the southern side. Short walking trails allow exploration of Cathedral Gorge and Echidna Chasm and it is recommended that both major gorge walks be undertaken. They are only a few kilometres long. Overnight walks into the centre of the ranges explore even more spectacular gorges. These longer walks range up to

How to get there

Turn off the Great Northern Highway for Purnululu 250km south of Kununurra or 110km north of Halls Creek. Access to the park is then about 50km by four-wheel-drive vehicle. Local tours are available from Kununurra with extended-stay tours setting out from Broome, Perth and Darwin. Scenic flights over the park can be arranged at Kununurra or with any of the local helicopter operators.

Wolfe Creek Crater National Park is located 130km south of the Great Northern Highway from a turn-off 16km south of Halls Creek. During the dry season, access is possible in a conventional vehicle.

Kununurra CALM tel: (08) 9192–1036

GEIKIE GORGE NATIONAL PARK

During the Wet the flooded Fitzroy River is a raging torrent that is testament to the massive forces of nature. However, even these forces pale into insignificance when you consider that the river gorges of this region have cut through limestone that was once a coral and alga reef on the floor of a warm ocean. An enormous barrier reef 1000km long and 20km wide extended through parts of what is now the Kimberley region 350 million years ago. The limestone formed as a result of these reefs is exposed at Tunnel Creek, Windjana Gorge and Geikie Gorge. The latter is one of the most popular areas in the north-west and should not be missed, if only for the crocodiles.

Beds of fossils

The rich fossil beds at the gorge are full of evidence of marine life, and the sediment layers are clearly visible in the cliff faces. From the air it is possible to trace the line of the ancient reef across the landscape. The fossil beds and limestone usually stand 50 to 100m above the surrounding plains. With a little imagination it is possible to believe that the sea has only just drained away.

The gorge is lined with tropical paperbark trees and river red gums. Much of the vegetation in the park has to withstand an annual flooding of up to 7m as the river breaks its banks after the gorge water level rises about 16m.

In addition to the conspicuous freshwater crocodiles, freshwater stingrays and sawfish inhabit the gorge waters. They all feed on the dozens of species of fish which include the curious archerfish. Three species of kangaroo live around the gorge and most visitors should be able to observe agile wallabies or euros in the cool of the evening. The elusive rock wallabies are much more difficult to see.

To protect the crocodile habitats and sensitive streamside vegetation both banks of the river are sanctuaries.

Boating and swimming

The only foot access to the edge of the water is along parts of the west bank. The Reef Walk to the western wall of the gorge is an enjoyable 1-km-long track of moderate difficulty.

Geikie Gorge boat tours are operated by the park's service rangers and offer a good-quality experience. Private boats may be launched but certain conditions apply – speak to the rangers in advance.

Swimming is popular and safe despite the freshwater crocodiles. The best spot for swimming is usually at the junction of the Margaret and Fitzroy rivers, where a sand bank develops each year after the wet season. Although there are no camping facilities in the park, there is a range of pleasant picnic areas.

ABOVE *Geikie Gorge is a popular dry season destination and well known for its wildlife, including freshwater crocodiles.*

OPPOSITE *An underground river flows through the Tunnel Creek Cave, making exploration possible only if you are prepared to get wet!*

Underground river at Tunnel Creek
Tunnel Creek is a large national park between Fitzroy Crossing and Windjana Gorge National Park. A stream once flowed across Napier Plateau's limestone surface and eventually cracks on the stream floor allowed water to percolate through. The water then gradually took an easier underground route. The dried creek bed is visible on the top of the plateau, but Tunnel Creek still travels underground through a 750-m-long channel. This area provides excellent material for photographers.

Visitors can walk through the tunnel, which is 15m wide and between 3 and 12m high. Be prepared to get wet from time to time as the track switches back and forth through the river. A torch is handy and swimsuits and sandshoes are the recommended walking gear.

Five species of bat live in the cave system, including flying foxes and ghost bats. Occasionally freshwater crocodiles take up residence in the creek's waterholes. This area is inaccessible in the summer. There are no camping areas and only limited day-use facilities.

How to get there

Geikie Gorge National Park is only 16km from Fitzroy Crossing. Tunnel Creek National Park is 120km west of the Crossing along the turn-off from the Great Western Highway. For travellers from the south, Tunnel Creek can be approached from the Great Northern Highway 40km west of Fitzroy Crossing. The Gibb River Road can then be reached via the back road to Windjana. Access to both these parks is best in a four-wheel-drive vehicle. Many organised tours are available from Broome or Halls Creek.
Geikie Gorge National Park tel: (08) 9191–5121

DON'T MISS...

ADVENTURE EXPERIENCES
Drysdale River National Park is one of the most remote wilderness parks on the continent. Access is difficult, open to four-wheel-drive vehicles only and permitted only in the dry season. Travellers must first contact the national park office. The nearest town is Wyndham (580km away). Tours do not visit this region so special expedition plans need to be made.

Boat charters or cruises of the remote Kimberley coastline are another adventure option. This is the perfect area for diving, exploring wilderness islands, photography, observing crocodiles and other wildlife, and gorge trekking. A large number of boats are based in Broome and also in Derby. Some follow the route from Broome to Darwin. Highly recommended is the huge Prince Regent Nature Reserve, a wilderness area accessible only by boat.

There is a variety of canoeing, rock climbing, horse riding and cycling tours on offer, especially from Kununurra.
Kimberley Tourism tel: (08) 9193–6660
Kununurra CALM tel: (08) 9168–0200
Kununurra Visitor Centre tel: (08) 9168–1177

OTHER INTERESTING AREAS
Broome Bird Observatory is run by the Royal Australian Ornithologist Union to keep track of migratory waders. It is located 25km east of Broome and accommodation is available.

A flight over Purnululu shows the size of the range.

Highly recommended are scenic flights over Purnululu (especially by helicopter) from Kununurra or the Walcott Inlet (spectacular on an outgoing tide as the tide range is 11m) and surrounding coast from Derby. **Ibis Aerial Highway** is a collaboration between the park's service and private tour operators to enable greater access to many remote areas.
Bird Observatory tel: (08) 9193–5600
Kimberley Tourism tel: (08) 9193–6660

THE PILBARA

Karijini • Millstream • Coral Coast

*T*he Pilbara region lies on the Tropic of Capricorn and has pleasant weather year-round, although summers are hot and wet. Winter is the best time to visit with clear, warm days and cool to cold nights. If you are camping though, be prepared for frosts at night. The deep pools of the inland gorges can be surprisingly cold in winter. To visit the most interesting locations use the North West Highway and make sorties inland.

Travel Tips

Carnarvon and Karratha both have regional airports with flights from Perth. Local tours and multi-day safaris are available from Perth with a number of longer safaris travelling through this region. Interstate coach services run along the coast from Perth to Darwin.

Rental cars including four-wheel-drives are available. The major sealed highways are the North West Coastal, which runs along the coast from Perth to Karratha, and the inland Great Northern running from Perth to Port Hedland. It is usually possible to travel in conventional vehicles, but four-wheel-drives can end up being useful.

Mosquitoes can be annoying and do carry diseases, so take precautions by wearing pants and loose clothing with long sleeves, and by using repellents. The sun can be intense, so protect your skin with sunscreens and clothing. Always carry water.

ABOVE LEFT *Most of the roads within the Millstream–Chichester National Park are unsealed, so take extra care when driving on bulldust and at creek crossings.*

OPPOSITE *A trail to the Fortescue Falls, the only permanent waterfall in the Karijini National Park, sets out from a car park on the Dales Lookout Road. The cascade tumbles into Dales Gorge.*

KARIJINI NATIONAL PARK

The Karijini National Park is a large reserve with many attractions spread over a huge area. The ancient landscape is shaped by both large and small geological features, while the permanent waterfalls of the deep gorges and the water-blasted rock surfaces contrast with the harsh red of the exposed chasms. The main information centre is at the junction of the Juna Downs–Yampire Gorge roads, 40km east of Mount Bruce.

Karijini is the second-largest national park in Western Australia. Only the remote Rudall River National Park in the eastern inland deserts is larger. Previously known as the Hamersley Ranges National Park, it reverted to its Aboriginal name in recognition of the estimated 20 000-year occupation of the region by the indigenous population and the region's continuing importance to them. The Aborigines practised traditional fire management over the centuries and this altered the landscape, creating the diverse plant and animal communities of the area.

Iron country
Karijini is a wild terrain of desert mountains, escarpments and wide, dry watercourses. However its fame stems from its sheer-sided chasms and waterfalls. Hundred-metre cliffs drop into cool gorges and all over the landscape, the ancient rocks

have been sculpted into canyons and narrow water channels. The 2.5 billion-year-old bedrocks are rich in iron resulting in the blood-red hue of the gorges and the rust-coloured cliff faces. Many days can be spent on long wilderness walks clambering into the remotest corners of each gorge.

The great botanical variety within the park is due to the diversity of its landforms. Huge tropical paperbark trees called cajeputs grip the rocky floors of the canyons and are often accompanied by figs, various gums and vines.

Huge termite nests tower over 6m in height in the grasslands near the visitor centre. Reptiles including goannas are seen along the roads and many species of snake are common. Euros are a frequent sight and rare rock wallabies have been observed in some of the rocky gorges.

Walk the gorges
Visitors will find plenty to enjoy within the park. Activities range from strolls to scenic lookouts to adventure canyoning. The recommended place to start exploring Karijini is to head for Weano camp site close to Hancock and Weano gorges. There are many possible road approaches to Weano, but it is wise to avoid the 24km of the Yampire Gorge Road as blue asbestos tailings are present in the gorge, and if these are disturbed and inhaled, the dust could compromise your health. From Weano, drives of between 20 and 70km provide access to all the other main gorges such as Hamersley, Fortescue, Kalamina and Joffre.

Bushwalking is the reason many people visit Karijini. Several days can be spent making sorties to the different gorges and exploring each one. Twenty or more marked trails provide access to gorge lookouts and there are also longer two- to three-hour exploratory walks. In addition there are several marked walks at Mount Bruce, including a challenging summit climb of around 9km return.

There are no large pools at Karijini suitable for canoeing such as at Millstream further north. Most pools are small but some, such as at Fortescue Falls, provide an opportunity for a quick refreshing dip. There are six main clusters of spectacular gorges and at three of these – Dale, Yampire and Weano – camping is permitted, but not elsewhere in the park.

Canyon wading at Knox
One of the most challenging and unusual walks is through Knox Canyon. This canyon narrows into a slippery dark fissure, where it is tricky to walk on the highly water-polished

rock surfaces. There are several places where the walk becomes a swim and there is no turning back. Lilos are needed to cross many of the deep pools. Eventually the walkers/swimmers emerge at the junction of the Knox, Wittenoom and Weano gorges, where magnificent cliffs tower over the water-filled ravine. The return trip via Hancock Gorge is also precarious with slippery rock surfaces.

How to get there

There is a small airfield nearby Tom Price but you will need to arrange a rental car from one of the larger coastal towns. Road access is suitable for conventional vehicles, though a four-wheel-drive is useful. By road the national park is located 310km from Roebourne and 285km from Port Hedland. The Great Northern Highway cuts across the western edge of the park.
Karratha CALM tel: (08) 9186–8288

RAINBOW BEE-EATER

Northern and inland Australia is the summer home of the multi-coloured Rainbow Bee-eater (*Merops ornatus*). Often heard before it is seen, this bird is associated with rivers and watercourses and is usually observed in small flocks of up to 30 individual birds, forming a distinctive V-shaped flight pattern. An easily recognisable species with its long curved bill, the Rainbow Bee-eater's plumage is a rich range of intertwined colours: gold, green and pastel blues dominate with heavy black lines on the throat and through its red eyes, hence its name. The blue tail has a curiously elongated pair of central feathers which can grow up to 40cm long for males in fresh breeding plumage. During activity in the nesting burrow these elongated feathers are worn away.

Rainbow Bee-eaters have a very specialised diet. Their main quarry is venomous wasps and bees. Insects are caught on the wing after aerial sorties by the bird from exposed perches, often in dead trees along streams. On its perch, the bird carefully beats the sting from the insect before eating it. Occasionally Rainbow Bee-eaters undertake aerial sorties from the ground.

This species nests in small colonies. Nests are chambers at the end of 1-m-long hollows dug into riverbanks or old quarries. In southern Australia the clutch of around four white eggs is laid before Christmas and the young are on the wing with the parents by February. In northern Australia, however, nesting is earlier or later in order to avoid the wet season.

All the Rainbow Bee-eaters in inland Australia migrate north to New Guinea during the winter. They are joined by most of the birds from northern Australia. Some individual birds remain in the Australian tropics all year round.

MILLSTREAM–CHICHESTER NATIONAL PARK

Hidden amongst the spinifex-clad hills of the Chichester Range are the deep basalt gorges and cool oases of the Millstream, Fortescue and Snake rivers within the Millstream–Chichester National Park. Delightful walks, wildlife watching and swimming in deep rock pools are the secluded highlights. This reserve is split into two main regions – the Millstream in the south and the Chichester Range in the north – both of which are equally appealing. The Chinderwarriner Pool in the Millstream is the most popular area and the shady camping areas and quiet pools on the Fortescue provide tranquil spots for walks and canoeing.

Water in the dry
The rocky inland ranges rise dramatically from the coastal plains south of Karratha and are cut by deep gorges. Most of the escarpment and range country is dominated by desert-dwelling plants such as spinifex and animals like the euro. Pale coolabah trees cluster along the usually dry watercourses and snappy gums dot the dry hills.

Natural underground aquifers produce fresh water which fills a string of pools along what would normally be dry inland rivers. Along the banks of these watercourses are relics from the time when rainforest covered the region. Millstream palms and paperbark trees cluster along the water's edge and water-lilies carpet the pools.

Fortescue: cultural ceremonies
The Fortescue River region is the home of the Yinjibarndi people. The pools were important meeting places and the location for special Aboriginal ceremonies and rituals. Feasting often accompanied these events and the wet gorges yielded abundant supplies of fish and edible roots. This region remains culturally important to the local Aborigines.

Cool pool walks
There are several pleasant short walks that start at the visitor centre at Millstream and wind along the banks of the Chinderwarriner Pool amongst the native and exotic palms. A longer 7-km-return walk leads down to the Crossing Pool and this

route, the Murlunmunyjurna Track, winds through riverine forests and over small wooden footbridges across small pools. Some of the plants of Aboriginal significance are identified along the track.

Chichester Range Camel Trail

For those wanting an energetic 8-km-one-way walk, the Chichester Range Camel Trail is recommended. This walk in the north of the park starts at Mount Herbert and takes about three hours to complete. It follows the original camel supply track operated by Afghans in the 1870s. These cameleers served the needs of remote sheep stations and mines prior to rail and road transport. It was the Afghans who also introduced the date palms that now dominate the landscape around the main pools of the region.

From Mount Herbert it is a downhill walk to McKenzie Pool, the Python Pool and finally the Snake Creek camp site. The heritage walking trail crosses an attractive and rugged section of the Chichester Range and is very exciting for photographers. It is best enjoyed in the early morning. Return transport will need to be arranged prior to setting out.

Snappy Gum Circuit by car

There are several good local drives and the Snappy Gum Circuit is the best. This unsealed 30-km route links the Millstream visitor centre with Crossing Pool, Deep Reach Pool and Cliff Lookout. The route is suitable usually for conventional vehicles and there are no publicly accessible four-wheel-drive tracks within the park. A number of lookouts along the route provide vistas to the coastal plains and Pyramid Hill.

Exploring the pools

Canoes, lilos, or windsurfers are ideal means of exploring the deep rock pools on the Fortescue River. Deep Reach Pool and Crossing Pool are suitable particularly for canoes. Many of the deep pools are suitable for swimming and ladders are provided for safe access where the banks are steep.

Camping facilities

Three separate bush camps are sited in the park and camping is restricted to those areas. In the north of the park there is a basic camp site at Python Pool, and at Snake Creek there are picnic facilities, toilets and a swimming hole. In the south of the park at Millstream there are two camp sites, one at Deep Reach Pool, the other at Crossing Pool. The original homestead at Millstream has now been made the park headquarters and visitor centre. Water is available but visitors should always carry reasonable supplies in this arid region. Some of the picnic areas have gas-fired barbecues.

How to get there

The easiest access is off the North West Coastal Highway past Roebourne to Python Pool in the north of the park and Millstream in the south of the park. Roads are generally suitable for conventional vehicles. Safari tours operate from Perth, but no local tours are available.

Karratha CALM tel: (08) 9186–8288

BELOW *Western Australia is renowned for its wildflower displays; fields of* ptilotus, *or mulla mulla, bloom in the region.*

Ningaloo, a fringing reef

Long and narrow, Ningaloo Reef, Australia's largest fringing reef, hugs the shoreline for around 260km. A shallow sandy lagoon has formed between the reef and shoreline, making Ningaloo a paradise for snorkellers. Over 200 species of coral make up the reef and more than 500 species of fish feed here. Turtles, dugongs and the whale shark – the world's largest fish – also inhabit these waters. Close to the shore, between 300m and 4km away, the lagoon offers tranquil, sheltered swimming to the most inexperienced of divers. The water in the lagoon is always over 30°C, making swimming a year-round delight.

Cape Range's craggy peaks

Cape Range National Park has a wide variety of facilities. The main visitor centre and park headquarters are located at Milyering, just behind the beach about 50km from Exmouth. Cape Range is a dry, harsh, limestone landscape with no sources of fresh water or permanent streams except Yardie Creek. Deep rocky gorges and high plateaux form craggy peaks overlooking the Indian Ocean. Thomas Carter Lookout, on the east of the range, is reached via Charles Knife Road, 20km south of Exmouth.

Nature observation

Bird hides are located at Mangrove Bay at the Cape. Terrestrial wildlife on the dry ranges of the Coral Coast is scarce but interesting. Low, irregular rainfall and poor limy soils contribute to sparse vegetation. Nevertheless 10 species of shrub are unique to the Cape, including the Cape Range grevillea. Rare shrubland birds are also found here. At the beginning of this century pastoralist and ornithologist Thomas Carter discovered two new species of bird in the

CORAL COAST

With its reef, beaches and hot dry weather the Coral Coast is an aquatic playground. Contributing to the sense of wild isolation is the sharp contrast of the high, rugged, uninhabited Cape Range National Park backing the beaches and lagoon. This desert setting is unlike other reef locations around the world and makes for a unique experience.

The Coral Coast sweeps south from North West Cape to the Tropic of Capricorn. Cape Range and Ningaloo Marine Park are linked and together form the Coral Coast, a fascinating region of biological diversity and adventure activities. On the Cape, the reefs and mountains share a beachfront and from the mouth of Yardie Creek the marine park extends a further 150km south.

arid bushland – the spinifex bird and the rufous crowned emu-wren. The spinifex bird and the Cape Range National Park lookout are now named after Thomas Carter.

Walking the Cape
Short walking trails are located at Mandu Mandu and Yardie Creek and are a delightful contrast to beach-based activities. On the eastern side of the park, the Lightfoot Heritage Trail is a 7-km-loop walk, which weaves through the limestone crags of the Cape Range. A second track, the Badjirrajirra Trail, links the Charles Knife and Shothole Canyon roads. This is a one-way walk beginning at Charles Knife. Return transport will need to be arranged.

Getting around
Further south from Cape Range, access to the marine park and reef is possible 24km south of Coral Bay on the Fourteen Mile Road and via a series of four-wheel-drive vehicle tracks to the north of the bay. Located beside the reef, the township of Coral Bay has the best-organised access to the reefs with a variety of boat, diving and four-wheel-drive vehicle tours. Accommodation is also available. Exmouth, at the northern end of the reef, also has similar facilities.

Camping facilities
Bush camping sites are located at more than 10 places along the coast. The two camp sites to the south of Yardie Creek are accessible only by four-wheel-drive, either by the difficult crossing at Yardie Creek or by travelling north from Coral Bay. Camping is permitted on pastoral properties between Cape Range National Park and Coral Bay, but permission must be sought. Boat-launching facilities are located in the park and small craft can be launched from the beach in most places. There are many day-use picnic sites.

How to get there

There is a regional airfield at Learmonth where the RAAF airfield is located. The main road access to the park is north from the North West Coastal Highway at Minilya Road-house to Exmouth, continuing north to the tip of the cape. Access to Ningaloo Marine Park is via Coral Bay or the Cape Range National Park. Park roads are all unsealed and some of the roads in the south are accessible only by four-wheel-drive vehicle. Tours by boat or car are also available from Exmouth.
Exmouth CALM tel: (08) 9949–1676

DON'T MISS...

ADVENTURE EXPERIENCES
The Canning Stock Route from Wiluna to Halls Creek is one of the continent's last remote cross-country four-wheel-drive vehicle tracks. A potentially dangerous route which should only be undertaken by very well-organised and well-equipped expeditions, it consists of 1700km of winding sand track. Now undertaken by many hundreds of vehicles a year, it is a three-week trip that crosses 900 sand dunes and passes 51 wells. The Canning Stock Route connects with the northern end of the Tanami Track near Wolf Crater and was last used for a cattle drive in 1958.

Snorkelling with whale sharks, the ocean's largest fish, at Ningaloo Marine Park is a once-in-a-lifetime experience (April to June). This is also an ideal area for whale watching (July to September) and reef dives.

Turtle watching on warm summer nights, especially at Cowrie Beach, an hour's drive south of Port Hedland, is an experience not to be missed for keen nature watchers. Eggs are laid in nests above the high-tide mark.
Royal Auto Club WA (Canning Stock Route)
 tel: (08) 9421–4000
Exmouth Visitor Bureau tel: (08) 9949–1176
Coral Bay Visitor Centre tel: (08) 9942–5988
Karratha Visitor Bureau tel: (08) 9144–4600

An aerial view of Ningaloo Reef.

OTHER INTERESTING AREAS
Mount Augustus is the world's largest monocline and is double the size of Uluru. It is located almost 500km from Carnarvon, a drive of approximately five hours. A walk off Lyons Road climbs the northern side. A trip to Mount Augustus can be combined with a trip to Kennedy Range National Park and Edithanna Pool (wildlife and swimming).
Mount Augustus Resort tel: (08) 9943–0527

SHIPWRECK COASTLINE

Nambung • Kalbarri • Shark Bay

*N*orth of Perth lie a handful of national parks that contain some of the world's strangest and most intriguing natural features, among them the Pinnacles at Nambung and the stromatolites at Hamelin Bay. There is also a wonderful example of how humans can interact with wildlife at Monkey Mia. In addition, this stretch of coastline is rich in history, having witnessed a number of shipwrecks over the centuries as well as being one of the first regions in Australia to be visited by Europeans.

Travel Tips

Perth has both a domestic and an international airport. There are regional airports at Geraldton, Denham and Carnarvon. A number of organised day

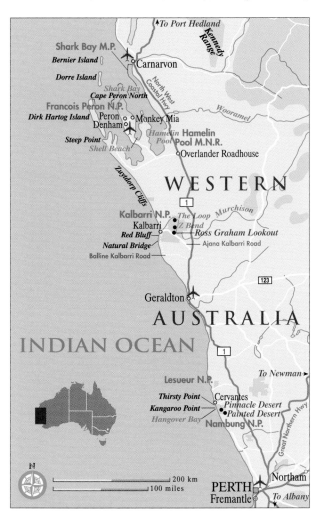

ABOVE *The name of the dramatic Zuytdorp Cliffs is taken from a Dutch vessel shipwrecked here in 1712.*

OPPOSITE *The Pinnacle Desert, a vast expanse of rolling sand dunes, is dotted with bizarre sculpted limestone pillars.*

tours are available from Perth and Geraldton. Longer safaris also set out from Perth and interstate coaches travel through the region.

The Brand and North West Coastal highways from Perth to Geraldton and on through to Carnarvon are sealed, while sealed or good unsealed roads connect the main areas. There are some roads suitable for four-wheel-drive only, particularly in Francois Peron and Lesueur national parks.

Mosquitoes can be annoying and do carry disease, so cover skin with loose clothing and use repellents. Ticks can also be a problem in coastal bushland. Tropical reef nasties like stonefish, cone shells and blue-ringed octopus occur north of Shark Bay. Wear sandshoes when walking on ocean rock platforms and do not handle marine animals.

Summers are hot and winters wet, with warm days and cool nights. Campers should be prepared for frost at night in winter.

NAMBUNG NATIONAL PARK

Nambung National Park is conveniently located just north of Perth and can be visited as a long daytrip or as part of an extended journey north. It is a strange place with huge sand dunes, rich coastal shrublands and white expansive beaches. A particular feature of this national park, and one that has given the area its international fame, are the bizarre statuesque formations of the Pinnacle Desert. Like ancient tortured sentinels, they stand over 5m high in a sea of yellow sand guarding a desert devoid of life.

Variously described as the remnants of an ancient city, nature's graveyard or fossil termite mounds, the Pinnacles are, in fact, geologically transient formations of eroded layers of wind-blown limestone. To fully understand these landscape forms making up the Pinnacle Desert, it is necessary to understand a little of the region's geological past.

An ancient sea

Around half a million years ago, shallow marine seas covered the area and allowed a rich marine life to flourish. The lime sand that built up on the floor of that sea eventually hardened to form the Tamala Limestone. As the sea receded and coastal vegetation slowly covered the coast, acidic surface water percolated through the limestone, leaching some sections and leaving other areas to harden around the deeper roots of the plants. These large hardened columns that developed around the roots remained beneath the surface, surrounded by the leached sand. Arid conditions over the past tens of thousands of years allowed the subterranean structures to be revealed as the loose dry sands eroded away. There is some evidence to suggest that the Pinnacles have been exposed several times and then re-covered by drifting sands. It is clear from radio-carbon dating tests that the formations were exposed for a period of time about 6000 years ago.

One intriguing fact is that there are no Aboriginal stories about the formations. There is also no evidence of Aboriginal occupation of the area. In addition, early European explorers made no mention of the existence of an area that would surely have aroused their curiosity, and knowledge of the Pinnacles did not spread until the middle of the current century. This raises the interesting proposition that the Pinnacles have been uncovered this time round only as recently as the last 50 years or thereabouts.

Exploring the Pinnacles

The Pinnacle formations can be explored on a 500-m-loop walk. On this track it is possible to view the variety of the bizarre shapes up close as well as enjoy views over the Pinnacle Desert to the coast beyond. A drive of several kilometres along the one-way loop road also winds its way amongst the formations.

Nocturnal wanderers

Much of the wildlife of Nambung is nocturnal. Over 100 species of bird inhabit the park and emus are frequently observed. Western grey kangaroos are sometimes active on cool days. The warm days, however, bring out many species of snake and lizard – stumpy tail and dragon lizards are often seen crossing the sandy park tracks.

Eroding power

The west-flowing Nambung River fails to reach the sea – instead it dissipates into the sand in a series of pools on the edge of the Pinnacle Desert. Several other eroded landscapes in the park are known for their strange formations including the Painted Desert, covered in white and red sands and grey limestone, west of the Pinnacles. The high white Quindalup sand dunes immediately behind the beach are constantly being reformed by the actions of wind and rain.

Coastal plants

Gleaming white beaches provide opportunities for many activities including beachcombing and snorkelling. Bush-walkers in the coastal heathlands will be rewarded with the proliferation of flowering shrubs such as myrtles and banksias in the winter and spring months. Aptly named Thirsty Point, which is just north of the park at the local town of Cervantes, it is a reminder of the need to carry water on any walks.

Camping facilities

There is a small bush camp site with limited facilities within the park and picnic facilities at a variety of sites along the coast, including Hangover Bay and Kangaroo Point.

How to get there

Nambung National Park is an easy 250-km drive north from Perth on the Brand Highway and then along a sealed road to Cervantes. Park tracks are unsealed but fine for conventional vehicles. There are also four-wheel-drive vehicle tracks along parts of the adjacent coast. Many day-tour options are available from Perth and Geraldton.

Geraldton Visitor Centre tel: (08) 9921–3999
Cervantes CALM tel: (08) 9652–7043
Pinnacles Tours tel: (08) 9221–5411

KALBARRI NATIONAL PARK

Famous for the 80-km-long Murchison River Gorge, the Kalbarri National Park is a large coastal zone for adventurers and has plenty of areas to enjoy. Bushwalking, abseiling, canyoning and whitewater canoeing are all potential highlights of a visit. The park also caters for those with less strenuous tastes.

Colourful ocean cliffs are separated from the inland river gorge by undulating sand plains. Shallow soils overlying the sandstone bedrock support 300 species of flowering plant, which in turn support several hundred bird species. The most conspicuous wildlife are emus, red kangaroos, grey kangaroos and euros. Rock wallabies inhabit the gorge, however they are unlikely to be seen. Most terrestrial mammals in the park are nocturnal. The high cliff lookouts along the coast are excellent locations for observing sea eagles, whales, dolphins and sea lions.

Murchison River Gorge

Many short and some longer walks provide visitors with access to some rugged and remote landscapes. The gorge and the ocean cliffs are the most popular focal points for walkers. A comfortable day walk at the Loop captures the full beauty of the Murchison River Gorge; the Around The Loop Walk

STROMATOLITES

Strange bulbous 1-m-high structures grow in a few shallow saline bays and lakes located in Western Australia. Easily overlooked or mistaken for rocks until their soft surface reveals their biological nature, these strange life forms are a direct link to the earliest life on earth.

Stromatolites are structures built by tiny micro-organisms called cyanobacteria. Growth rates are extremely slow – a rate of 1mm a year has been measured. Structures 1m high would have taken thousands of years to build. In some places the stromatolites are separate structures, in others they have merged together forming solid mats.

Fossil stromatolites have been found in the Pilbara and date back three and a half billion years. They are the earliest evidence of living creatures on earth, and the fossil structures have revealed information about the earth's status millions of years ago. For example, scientists have been able to calculate from the annual growth rings of stromatolites that about 850 years ago, the earth's year was 435 days long. At this time, a day would have been only about 20 hours long.

Living stromatolites are found also in shallow pools in the US, Bahamas and the Persian Gulf. However, in Western Australia

the stromatolite locations number more than anywhere else in the world. These organisms are found near Perth in pools at Lake Thetis, Lake Richmond and on Rottnest Island. The first-living stromatolites discovered – and probably the most famous – are in Hamelin Pool, part of the World Heritage area at Shark Bay. Here it is possible to walk beside structures that are over 2000 years old. Boardwalks have been built to help visitors get closer to the stromatolites without damaging them.

ABOVE *Gantheaume Bay is an inlet within the Kalbarri National Park. Its waters are perfect for fishing.*

their own. These are hazardous activities and should only be attempted after seeking local advice. The gorge, particularly the Z Bend, is also a popular location for rock climbing and abseiling enthusiasts.

Coastal strolls

South of Kalbarri town, the Balline Road skirts along the coast. From here, unsealed tracks wind down and out to the high ocean cliffs at many points, including Mushroom Rock, Red Bluff, Eagle Gorge and Natural Bridge. A marked loop trail links Mushroom Rock and Rainbow Valley. Here features of botanic and geological interest are highlighted along the route. It is a leisurely two-hour stroll.

Short walks also lead from the car parks at Port Alley and Red Bluff. Further south the longer Coastal Trail connects Eagle Gorge to Natural Bridge. This three-hour, one-way walk takes in some delightful but windy seascapes. At Eagle Gorge another short walking track into the gorge also leads onto a lovely ocean beach. Care is required when exploring the ocean cliffs as rock ledges near the water along the Kalbarri coast are infamous for their freak waves, which from time to time claim human lives.

firstly follows the gorge rim via several lookouts and then descends to the river. A feature of this walk is the Natural Arch which superbly frames the upstream view of the river. At Z Bend there is a 500-m walk to an overhanging lookout. This is a dramatic if somewhat dangerous spot.

Longer trekking

Murchison Gorge has around 80km of bushwalking trails. The best section is from Ross Graham Lookout to the Loop, a distance of 40km. This walk takes about four days and will mean camping out in the gorge. There are many spots where water crossings are required. Walkers need to be experienced, prepared to get wet and careful to protect themselves against heat exhaustion as the gorge intensifies the hot dry weather.

Park officials recommend that this walk only be tackled by groups of at least five people. This is the smallest number capable of self-sufficient activity in an emergency.

Several shorter two-day gorge walks are created by taking breaks at the Z Bend. There are no facilities in the gorge and the trail is not marked. At the four access points and lookouts, picnic areas and toilets are provided.

Adventure water sports

Usually a series of isolated pools, the river becomes a torrent after heavy rains and gorge walks are impossible. Adventure pursuits, like whitewater canoeing and rafting, come into

Accommodation facilities

Just inside the park, adjacent to Kalbarri on the Ajana Road, is the park information centre and ranger station. No facilities are available in the park for overnight camping. Wilderness walkers can camp away from roads and tracks, while the town of Kalbarri provides a full range of services including accommodation and park tours. A scenic flight over the gorge and then along the coastal cliffs is a wonderful way to complete a visit to this national park.

How to get there

Kalbarri National Park is 100km north of Geraldton along the North West Coastal Highway. The road to the coastal town of Kalbarri passes through the park. Access to the park from the south is also possible along the coast. There are day tours from Geraldton and Kalbarri. Light aircraft fly scheduled services to Kalbarri from Perth.

Kalbarri Visitor Centre tel: (08) 9937–1104
Geraldton Visitor Centre tel: (08) 9921–3999

SHARK BAY

Shark Bay is an excellent place to observe marine wildlife and to enjoy aquatic activities. A complete holiday destination in itself, it is also the perfect place to spend a couple of days before travelling on to other areas in the state.

Shark Bay was World Heritage-listed in 1991 and is the site of a myriad natural wonders. Ancient living fossils, stromatolites, carpet the shallow pools of Hamelin Bay while at Monkey Mia dolphins swim in to shore to be hand-fed. Dugongs feed in Shark Bay's protected waters and several tiny mammals, including the banded hare-wallaby, are found only on the bay's offshore islands. In addition, the exceptional natural beauty of the bay, the treacherous Zuytdorp Cliffs and Cape Peron form a majestic setting for this display of globally significant biological features.

Shark Bay's protected waters

All the waters within Shark Bay are protected as some form of marine reserve. The northern tip of the Peron Peninsula is a national park and Dorre and Bernier islands are nature reserves. The best centres for activities are Denham, Monkey Mia or, if camping with a four-wheel-drive, Francois Peron National Park. Shark Bay is ideal for observing nature, walking on wide, protected beaches, snorkelling or swimming. A sea kayak, sailing boat or small outboard-motor boat allows the best access to the wide bays and inlets. Shark Bay can be subject to stormy conditions and boats should be well equipped with safety gear such as flares and life jackets.

A dolphin haven

The bay is home to large populations of dolphins, dugongs and green turtles. Bottlenose dolphins live in pods of up to 20 individuals. Every day since the early 1960s dolphins have been hand-fed fish near the jetty at Monkey Mia. Several are known to be third-generation visitors. The feeding activity is supervised by wildlife rangers, who are on duty every day to ensure safety for both people and dolphins. It is a rare example of direct contact between wild mammals and humans and appears to give both species pleasure.

Dugongs: docile creatures

Ten per cent of the world's population of dugongs lives in the warm waters of Shark Bay. Thousands of these docile marine mammals find refuge here and feed on the world's largest area of sea-grass. Almost 3m long and weighing up to 300kg, it is hard to imagine that this creature was the cause of the mermaid myths. Herds are regularly seen at the surface as they come up to breathe. They are sometimes curious around boats but, being slow swimmers, can be injured by outboard motors. It is therefore important, when boating, to travel slowly and turn engines off in the presence of these dugongs.

ABOVE *Visitors to Monkey Mia share a rare opportunity for contact with wild dolphins. The sea mammals have been visiting the shores of this region daily for the last 30 years.*

A haven for threatened species

Over 6000 marine turtles also live in the bay. Most are green turtles which nest on the adjacent islands in the summer months. Rare terrestrial wildlife such as thick-billed grasswrens are found on the Peron Peninsula. Banded hare-wallabies and barred bandicoots also used to occur on the mainland, but have been displaced by cats, foxes and rabbits. Many of these species now live exclusively on islands such as those in Shark Bay. Access to these islands is strictly controlled.

In an exciting practical experiment, Peron Peninsula has been fenced off at the narrow neck at Shell Beach and exotic pests have been removed. It may one day be possible to reintroduce endangered mammals to this protected area.

Walks and a car heritage trail

From the Overlander Roadhouse on the North West Coastal Highway, a car heritage trail begins and leads into Monkey Mia. Brochures detailing the trail are available at the roadhouse or visitor centre.

A short marked walking trail is located at the Peron homestead north of Denham. From Monkey Mia is a 3-km walking trail that features a bird hide, as well as Aboriginal shelter caves and a quiet beach.

Remote tracks at Steep Point, the continent's most westerly projection, and in Francois Peron National Park are suitable only for four-wheel-drive vehicles.

Camping facilities

In Francois Peron, three camp sites on the water's edge – Big Lagoon, Gregories and Herald Bight – are accessible along the four-wheel-drive tracks. Limited facilities are provided at the sites but visitors must be self-sufficient with water. At the historic homestead a soak in the unique artesian hot tub is highly recommended.

How to get there

By road, head along the sealed Brand and North West Coastal highways to the Overland Roadhouse 700km north of Perth or 280km north of Geraldton. The road into Shark Bay is sealed as far as the town of Denham, but is unsealed if you turn off to Useless Loop. Tracks for four-wheel-drives only head to Steep Point and Francois Peron National Park on the western peninsula of Shark Bay. There is a local air service to Denham.

Denham CALM tel: (08) 9948–1208

DON'T MISS...

ADVENTURE EXPERIENCES

Two outback roads connect Perth to Uluru: the northern so-called Gunbarrel Highway via Wiluna (2290km) and the southern Tjukaruru Road via Leonora (2090km). The southern route, although remote, is generally passable in a well-equipped four-wheel-drive vehicle. The more difficult track, the Gunbarrel Highway, needs very careful planning. Vehicles should travel at the very least in pairs and carry enough supplies for a minimum of 800km of travel.

Starting from Perth or Alice Springs, a loop linking the Gunbarrel, Canning Stock Route and Tanami Track is the ultimate four-wheel-drive vehicle desert adventure.

From Kalbarri there are excursions to Murchison Gorge where you can learn abseiling at the Z Bend and other vertical sections of the gorge, or simply take in the rugged atmosphere.

Royal Auto Club WA (Gunbarrel) tel: (08) 9421–4000
Geraldton CALM tel: (08) 9921–5955
Kalbarri Visitor Centre tel: (08) 9937–1104
Kalbarri Abseiling tel: (08) 9937–1618

OTHER INTERESTING AREAS

Lesueur National Park, about 8km north of Jurien, which is just north of Nambung National Park, has been set aside for its diversity of flowering shrubs, birds and reptiles. Access to the

Spectacular views on the rugged Kalbarri coastline.

park is by four-wheel-drive vehicle only. No camping is allowed. Tick and insect repellents are highly recommended.

The Wildflower Way from Dalwallinu to Mullewa north of Perth passes through mainly wheat farms. However, the agricultural land is dotted with small bushland reserves based around granite outcrops which in winter and spring are ablaze with wildflowers. Watch out for Petrudor Rocks and Buntine Reserve.

Cervantes CALM tel: (08) 9652–7043
Dalwallinu Visitor Centre tel: (08) 9661–1001

SOUTH-WEST COAST

Stirling Range • D'Entrecasteaux Coast • Leeuwin Coast

*U*sing Perth as a base, many round trips are possible into the south-western region of Western Australia. Try heading south to Albany and circling back along the coastal roads. A recommended trip, taking three to four days, would be a southern loop centred on Albany and Margaret River. This is a compact region by Australian standards with many main roads connecting to the wilderness areas.

Travel Tips

The south-west is a popular area for Perth residents so it would be best to avoid visiting during weekends and school holidays. There is a domestic and international airport at Perth and a regional one at Albany. Many day and overnight tours and safaris are available from Perth and the larger regional centres.

Conventional vehicles are suitable as the roads are usually sealed and driving has no particular hazards. The Albany Highway from Perth is 410km and is the longest distance in the region. There are two coastal routes south of Perth to Bunbury while the South Coast Highway links to Recherche Coast and the Nullarbor.

Generally summers are warm and pleasant, sometimes with cool nights. Inland summers are progressively hotter and drier. Winter is wet and can be windy and cold. Local weather is strongly influenced by the ocean and can vary considerably.

ABOVE LEFT *Green Pool located in William Bay National Park is a tranquil inlet.*

OPPOSITE *The Stirling Range is a botanic wonderland of wildflowers and forests.*

Map locations: To Geraldton, Northam, Eastern Hwy, PERTH, Fremantle, Mandurah, Albany Hwy, Murray, WESTERN AUSTRALIA, 20, 120, 1, 30, Bunker Bay, Bunbury, Cape Naturaliste, Yallingup, Yallingup Cave, Canal Rocks, 10, Leeuwin–Naturaliste N.P., Gracetown, Bussell Hwy, Margaret River, Hwy, To Esperance, Canto's Field, Brockman, Donnelly, South Coast Hwy, Giants Adventure Cave, Scott N.P., Manjimup, Cranbrook, Stirling Ranges N.P., Cosy Corner, Mt Hassle, Mt Trio, Bluff Knoll, Augusta, Pemberton, Toolyelup Peak, Stirling Range, Moingup Springs, 1, Cape Leeuwin, Frankland, Parongurup N.P., Black Point, Fernhook Falls, 102, Stirling Range, Rangers, Northcliffe, Deep, Valley of the Giants, Devils Slide, Castle Rock, D'Entrecasteaux N.P., Broke Inlet, Walpole, Denmark, Many Peaks, Windy Harbour, Crystal Springs, Albany, Mandalay Beach, Nornalup Inlet, William Bay N.P., Shelley Beach, Torndirrup N.P., Walpole–Nornalup N.P., West Cape Howe N.P., Conspicuous Cliff, SOUTHERN OCEAN, 100 km, 50 miles

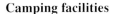

STIRLING RANGE

The Stirling Range is 65km long and is conserved within the Stirling Range National Park. High rocky peaks with sheer cliffs and cold mountain weather are its hallmarks. A striking contrast to the surrounding undulating countryside, the craggy Stirling Range is a haven for wilderness walkers who enjoy a challenge. The rugged peaks are also known for their brilliant displays of spring wildflowers.

With a complex geological history, the billion-year-old twisted rocks of the Stirling Range rise to form a series of more than a dozen peaks of over 750m in height (Bluff Knoll is the highest, rising to just over 1000m). These peaks, close to the sea, are the only areas in the state to see the occasional fall of light snow. Cold, wet conditions can descend quickly at any time of the year but particularly between June and August.

Flourishing flora

In the deeper gullies patches of jarrah, wandoo and marri trees flourish. From August to November the area's heaths and shrublands break out into a colourful floral display. Some species, such as smokebushes, coneflowers, mountain peas and hoveas, compete for colour supremacy. More than 1000 flowering species are recorded in the park and 60 are found only on the range. The darwinias, or mountain bells, are a feature of the park and 10 species of these delicate flowers are known, with only one also occurring elsewhere in the world.

Wildlife: heard but not seen

Wildlife is usually difficult to see but birds feed noisily in the thickets. Parrots, wrens, honeyeaters and whistlers are all common. Mammals such as wallabies, grey kangaroos and quokkas are also prevalent, but rarely seen. Honey possums compete with the honeyeaters for pollen and nectar. Emus are sometimes seen striding across the roads and clearings.

Steep summit walks

Steep and spectacular walks are a speciality of the Stirling Range but even the short walks can take some time. Summit walks to Bluff Knoll, Toolbrunup Peak, Mount Trio and Mount Hassell are less than 6km, but take around three hours to complete. However, the views are magnificent and longer walks, such as the east Pillenorup Track and the Yungermere Crescent, are great ways to explore the park. The sheer cliffs of the peaks are also popular with rock climbers.

A number of link tracks provide a variety of return walks. Overnight walks are popular. It is wise to inform park staff of your plans. On longer walks always carry water and wear long trousers as protection from the prickly undergrowth. Walkers should be prepared for sudden changes in weather.

Exploring by car

Along the northern boundary of the park is the Salt River Road. Using this road, together with the park's internal roads and the Formby South Road back to the Chester Pass Road, a round trip of around 70km can be enjoyed. There are many lookouts and picnic areas along the Stirling Range Drive. Day facilities are located at the car park below Bluff Knoll.

Porongurup National Park: granite domes

South of the Stirling Range National Park, and just to the west of the Chester Pass Road, is Porongurup National Park, characterised by its granite domes and karri forests. At the end of Bolganup Road are several loop walks to granite formations with names like Devils Slide. Marked trails take from an hour to three hours to complete. At Castle Rock, the closest park entry point to Chester Pass Road, there is a summit walk of around 3km return, which takes about two hours. A steel walkway crosses the highest boulders on the summit.

Camping facilities

Moingup Springs is the only camp ground in the Stirling Range National Park and has basic facilities. Just outside to the north of the park is the Stirling Range Caravan Park, which has more camping facilities. Visitor information is available at Moingup and at the northern park entrance where there is also a day picnic area.

A park ranger station is located on Bolganup Road in the Porongurup National Park. The steep Angwin Scenic Drive links the ranger station with Woodlands Road and from here it is south to Albany. There are no camping facilities in the park, however there are many short walks and picnic spots.

How to get there

The main access is via Chester Pass Road, which runs 86km north of Albany and through the park. There are also sealed roads from Cranbrook and Kendernup, which join onto the unsealed Red Gum Pass Road at the western end of the park. The unsealed Stirling Range Drive runs along the mountain range linking the eastern and western ends.

Stirling Range National Park tel: (08) 9827–9230

HONEY POSSUM

Of the two dozen or so species of nocturnal possums and gliders occurring across the continent, the honey possum is unique. Its long snout, long thin tail, reduced number of teeth and brush-tipped tongue make it unlike any of its possum cousins. In addition, its diet is confined exclusively to honey and pollen as opposed to the more generalised diets of other possum species. Adult honey possums are no bigger than a domestic mouse. Males and females are a similar size except that males have longer tails and females are heavier.

Found in the coastal heathlands of the south-west corner of Western Australia, honey possums find daytime shelter in birds' nests or grasstree stumps. In the evenings or on overcast days they move through the undergrowth searching out flowering banksias and grevilleas, aided by their strong sense of smell. Grasping the branches with their hands and feet (this species' claws are almost non-existent) they can climb several metres into the thick shrubs to reach pollen-laden flowers. Their long probing snout and specialised tongue enables them to reach deep into the flowers in much the same way as birds like honeyeaters do. This small marsupial is important for the pollination of the flowers of many heathland plants. Most of the habitat of these unique possums is protected in national parks and reserves.

Honey possums are capable of a type of torpor or form of hibernation. In cold weather, groups of honey possums huddle together to stay warm. The breeding season extends throughout most of the year and a litter of two or three is typical. The young remain in their mother's pouch for about two months. Juveniles reach adult size in their first year.

D'ENTRECASTEAUX COAST

From the limestone and granite headlands near Augusta to the famous granite coast at Albany, this is a region where rocky headlands meet the stormy Southern Ocean. Along the 300-km coastline there are six coastal parks: Scott, D'Entrecasteaux, Walpole–Nornalup, William Bay, West Cape Howe, and finally, Torndirrup. There are also a number of small coastal nature reserves and adjoining national parks further inland.

Many more forests and parks lie inland from the coastal parks and offer multiple activity options: heritage trails, bush camping, canoeing and river swimming. The granite coast and hinterland could act as the base for a lengthy holiday.

Tranquil Scott National Park

Scott National Park is a small park just across the inlet from Augusta. Little known, the park is accessed by four-wheel-drive track from the Brockman Highway east of Alexandra Bridge. Found here are stands of tall jarrah, marri and karri forests, and wide swamplands which make exploring by boat a pleasure. There are no park facilities and bush camping is for those in search of the ultimate bush solitude.

D'Entrecasteaux: dunes and cliffs

Further east, D'Entrecasteaux is a park of pristine beaches, swamps, shifting dunes, heathlands, and spectacular coastal cliffs. There are only two formed road accesses to the beach, one at Windy Harbour and the other at Broke Inlet, both south of Northcliffe. All the other beach access tracks are for four-wheel-drive vehicle only. The park has no formal camping facilities but many beach camp sites. Many walking tracks and day-time picnic spots are also available. Rainfall averages 1300mm per annum, the highest in the state, and most of it falls in winter. Six short streams drain the park, and are excellent for canoeing.

Walpole–Nornalup: inlets and rivers

South of the town of Walpole lies the Walpole–Nornalup Park. Forests, inlets and rivers frame a beautiful coastline set with dozens of beaches and headlands. There are unsealed roads to the beaches at Conspicuous Cliff and Mandalay Beach.

ABOVE *The small bay at William Bay National Park provides safe waterways for swimming, sailing and canoeing.*

BELOW *Seascapes of granite headlands and white beaches create a dramatic coastline at Torndirrup National Park.*

Canoeing on the Frankland River, Deep River and Nornalup Inlet provides a chance to observe the local waterbirds.

Bush camp sites are located at Fernhook Falls in the forest north of the park and at Crystal Springs near the road to Mandalay Beach. Bush camping is permitted in the state forests. There are a number of marked forestry drives, including the road to the Valley of the Giants. Here, a nature trail and picnic ground have been established near the rare red tingle woods.

Protected William Bay

William Bay National Park is a beautiful small park 15km west of Denmark on the South Coast Highway. At Green Pool, granite boulders and rocky shelfs enclose a small bay. Largely protected from the open ocean, the beach is an ideal place for swimming and snorkelling during the summer and autumn months. There are no camping facilities in the park but an information station is located near its entrance.

Granite cliffs of West Cape Howe

West Cape Howe National Park's granite terrain faces the full onslaught of the Southern Ocean. Wide beaches and rocky

headlands backed by heaths, lakes and forests are part of the impressive range of habitats within its boundaries. The high cliffs make the park popular for rock climbing, while Shelley Beach Lookout is internationally known as a hang-gliding venue.

Access to the coast by conventional vehicle is possible at Shelley Beach, 30km west of Albany. Walkers and four-wheel-drive vehicles can reach the coast at several other points. Unmarked bush walks, coastal exploring and swimming are all popular activities. There are no camping facilities.

Torndirrup: dramatic headlands

Torndirrup National Park is just across the bay from Princess Royal Harbour at Albany. Granite headlands exposed to the Southern Ocean swell and geological formations like the Gap, Bald Head, Salmon Holes and Blowholes create dramatic seascapes. Rock climbers find many challenges and photographers are surrounded by endless natural subjects.

There are marked walks to most of the park's southern points but the longest and best walks lead to the eastern point of the park at Bald Head. This is a challenging trek of over 10km return. There is a ranger station in the park and lookouts, but few other facilities.

How to get there

Take the Vasse Highway east from Busselton to Pemberton or the South Western Highway from Manjimup to Walpole and Denmark. The South Coast Highway travels east from Denmark to Albany. These sealed highways are generally close to the coast. There are also unsealed roads south and east of Northcliffe.

Pemberton CALM tel: (08) 9776–1200
Albany CALM tel: (08) 9841–7133

ABOVE *Jewel Cave near Augusta is one of the most spectacular caves in the south-west and is open for tours daily.*

ABOVE RIGHT *Cape Naturaliste marks the northern end of the long and narrow Leeuwin–Naturaliste National Park.*

LEEUWIN COAST

Once two separate parks, virtually the entire 120-km stretch of coast between Cape Leeuwin and Cape Naturaliste is now a long, thin national park. Squarely facing the full brunt of the westerly roll where the Indian Ocean meets the Southern Ocean, this is also known as the Limestone Coast. Leeuwin–Naturaliste National Park is principally a summer park with a focus on ocean activities and caves. The relatively open camping grounds provide little protection from winter storms, but are ideal places for swimming and diving.

Exploring the limestone caves

The Leeuwin coast consists of wide beaches and dune fields juxtaposed with rocky headlands. Over 300 limestone caves are scattered along its length, ranging in size from potholes to caves 14km long. Many caves in the region are significant for their scientific revelations, including the fossil remains of extinct animals such as marsupial lions, and evidence of human habitation. There are guided tours of the Jewel Cave, near Augusta, two caves near Conto's Field and the Yallingup Cave adjacent to Caves House and Yallingup. Permits are issued by the park authorities for visits, either on guided tours or for adventure trips at the Giants and Calgardup caves.

A karri forest

Behind the beach dunes is a limestone-capped plateau carpeted with low heaths and peppermint tree shrublands. Rare pineapple bushes and bottlebrushes are found in patches amongst the more common shark-toothed wattles. Jarrah gums – giants elsewhere – grow as stunted shrubs on the shallow soils. Karri trees in the Boranup forest are only 100 years old and are over 50m tall, standing testimony to the regenerative powers of karri (this area was clear-felled last century and has now regenerated). This species is also known for the pink colouring of the freshly shed bark in autumn.

Leeuwin's animals and birds

Nocturnal mammals such as grey kangaroos, ringtail possums and honey possums are common in the park. In the karris of the Boranup forest, near the camp sites, bandicoots and possums often occur. Over 200 bird species are recognised in the park, including tropicbirds and sea eagles. A tiny rare snail is found only in this area beside small freshwater soaks in the deeper gullies.

Seasonal whale migrations

Each July and then again in October, humpback whales and southern right whales pass the coast on their annual migrations. The best locations for whale watching are the two capes, Gracetown and Cowaramup, and the Sugarloaf car park. Whaling for humpbacks was common until it was banned in 1963 when the whale numbers dropped from about 15 000 to only 600. Recent surveys suggest the numbers passing the Leeuwin coast are now around 30 a day, making the estimated population about 4000 whales.

Diving on shipwrecks

Early this century and late last century about 14 known ships were wrecked on the Leeuwin coast. Four of them are in Hamelin Bay and an underwater dive trail has been established to view these historic wrecks. One of the ships, the British *Agincourt* which went down in 1883, lies only 200m offshore.

Walking the coast

Short walking trails meander up to the old Ellenbrook Homestead, the lighthouse at Cape Leeuwin and to the headland at Canal Rocks. Bunker Bay has a series of 3-km-long trails linking the lighthouse and the bay. This is a great location to spot migrating whales. Tracks to some of the more remote beaches are suitable only for four-wheel-drive vehicles because of the rough limestone blocks that protrude from the ground and which can easily damage cars.

Camping facilities

Facilities in the park are scattered over a large area. There are camp sites at Boranup, Point Road and Conto's Field. The latter is a prize-winning site set amongst peppermint woodlands. The camp sites are all south of the Margaret River and north of Karridale. Access is from Caves Road. There are many picnic areas along the coast and beaches at which to swim and surf.

How to get there

Leeuwin–Naturaliste National Park is 250km south of Perth via the South Western and Bussell highways. Many westerly routes to the park are off Caves Road between Busselton and Augusta. The largest areas are around Karridale. Various tours are on offer from Perth, Margaret River and other regional towns. The National Park's office is at Margaret River about halfway between Vasse and Karridale on the Bussell Highway.

Margaret River CALM tel: (08) 9757–2322
Margaret River Visitor Centre tel: (08) 9757–2911

DON'T MISS...

ADVENTURE EXPERIENCES

The upper reaches of the Avon, Murray, Blackwood and Deep rivers all have excellent white water. More sedate canoeing and camping on the lower reaches of each of these rivers and the Warren is also possible.

Hang-gliding at West Cape Howe near Denmark is the best in the state. Participants launch from Shelley Beach Lookout and fly over the coastal cliffs for hours (the record is eight hours), to finally land on Shelley Beach.

Adventure caving is possible near Leeuwin–Naturaliste National Park in the Brides, Giants or Calgardup caves.

WA Tourist Centre tel: (08) 9483–1111
Canoe Association tel: (08) 9322–2999
Denmark Visitor Centre tel: (08) 9848–2055
Busselton CALM tel: (08) 9752–1677

OTHER INTERESTING AREAS

Lane Poole Reserve, located an hour and a half south of Perth via Pinjarra, is a recreation reserve in the northern jarrah forests. Canoeing on the Murray River, walks in the tall forests and the camp grounds along the river are all part of its appeal. The area is, however, very wet in winter.

A hang-glider soars above the blue waters at West Cape Howe.

Yalgorup National Park is a series of beaches and coastal lakes 130km south of Perth. Wildlife watching and bushwalking are possible, but there are no camping facilities.

The **Dryandra State Forest** around the town of Narrogin is an important dry forest area for many rare animals including numbats. Accommodation is available in cabins but there are no camping facilities.

Dwellingup CALM tel: (08) 9538–1078
Harvey CALM tel: (08) 9729–1505
Narrogin CALM tel: (08) 9881–1113
Dryandra Cabins tel: (08) 9883–6020

RECHERCHE COAST

Cape Arid • Cape Le Grand •

Fitzgerald River

The popular route between Perth and South Australia is inland through Kalgoorlie (not many travellers take the South Coast Highway through Bunbury, Margaret River, Albany and Esperance, but they inevitably miss a region of vast open beaches that are usually deserted). The Recherche Coast is a great wilderness area for isolated camping and trekking.

Travel Tips

There is a major international and domestic airport at Perth and regional ones are located at Albany and Esperance. Organised tours are available from Albany and interstate coaches serve some stops along the Eyre Highway.

The main highways to the region are the South Coast Highway from Albany to Esperance, the Coolgardie–Esperance Highway running north–south, and the Eyre Highway from Norseman to the South Australian border. Conventional vehicles travel the long distances comfortably, however many local roads are very rough and suitable only for four-wheel-drive vehicles. At any time, but especially at night, animals can wander onto the road so avoid night driving.

Most of the year the weather is pleasant. Winters are wet but there is less winter rain occurring the further east you travel towards the Nullarbor Plain. Beaches are potentially dangerous with strong tidal rips. Be cautious and swim in calmer inlets or fresh water where-ever it occurs.

ABOVE RIGHT *Fitzgerald National Park faces the Southern Ocean's fury.*

OPPOSITE *Cape Barren geese are found only on islands and windswept headlands across southern Australia.*

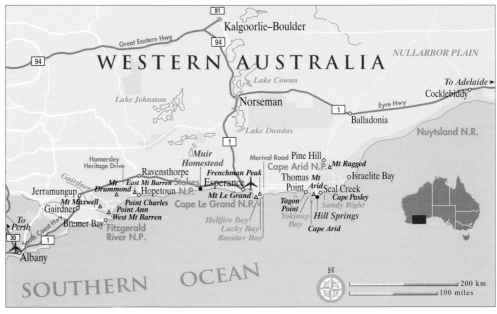

CAPE ARID NATIONAL PARK

The low granite hills of the Cape Arid National Park roll inland to the Russell Range, which crosses the northern corner of the park. With the Nuytsland Nature Reserve to the east, Cape Arid forms an almost continuous area of nature conservation from the Duke of Orleans Bay to the South Australian border, a distance of over 700km. Best known for its beautiful beaches and crystal seascapes, the park is a remote location for the determined traveller.

The vegetation of the park has evolved from the need to conserve water. Typical coastal heaths are replaced with woodlands in the north, dominated by an understorey of salt-bush and bluebush. Scattered throughout the park are pockets of granite rocks which collect small amounts of water for tiny communities of plants that thrive on water.

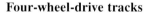

Shy birds of the heath
Brush wallabies are seen regularly, especially at night. Many other mammals are also nocturnal, therefore rarely observed. An unusual resident of the park is the world's most primitive ant, which was discovered in 1930. This species is common on Mount Ragged. Also along the coast lives Australia's only goose, the Cape Barren. Feeding mainly on grasses, this bird was close to extinction in the 1960s but is well re-established now along the arid and remote southern coastline of the country.

Another unusual bird found in the park is the secretive ground parrot. While now rare in the eastern states, places like Cape Arid are a stronghold for the species. Its mournful whistles are often heard at dusk in the thick heaths. Occasionally a bird will break from cover and drop, quail-like, back into the undergrowth.

Nature trails
Four marked trails are provided for visitors to explore the main habitats and features of the region. The Len Otte Nature Trail is around 1km long and provides a brief introduction to the park's plants and landforms. From the Tagon Camp there is a 7-km-return coastal walk which traverses rough coastal headlands. This walk is an ideal winter whale-watching location.

The Boolenlup Lake is a saline soak, which can easily be reached off the 4km-return walking track from Tagon Road. From the car park on the Balladonia Road the summit of Mount Ragged can be reached in a three-hour-return hike. It is a strenuous climb up to the peak, however breathtaking views are afforded across the park to Sandy Bight and Yokinup Bay. Longer unmarked walks are possible, especially along the coast.

Walkers need to remember to regularly clean boots of soil and mud as they move through the park to limit the spread of any plant diseases.

Grazing pioneers
Information is available from the rangers at the Thomas River camp ground. Two historic locations have special information bays: one adjacent to Mount Arid, the other at the Pine Hill Homestead site on the northern extremity of the park. Grazing was pioneered in the region in the 1870s and the ruins of the first buildings can now be seen at Pine Creek. One of the first settlers, William Ponton, is buried near the ruins of Hill Springs Homestead situated on the edge of Mount Arid.

Four-wheel-drive tracks
The park is crossed by a number of four-wheel-drive vehicle tracks. The Gore Road connects the Mount Ragged area to Israelite Bay in the east of the park. A return trip can be made along the Old Telegraph Track. It is important to be conscious of not spreading plant diseases by keeping tyres and vehicle underbodies clear of soil and mud.

Camping facilities
Several camping areas are located in Cape Arid National Park. For those in conventional vehicles the sites at Seal Creek, Jorndee Creek and Thomas River on Point Arid are all accessible. These coastal sites have basic facilities. The Mount Ragged camp site in the centre of the park is accessible only to four-wheel-drive. Firewood is scarce in the park and the use of gas stoves is recommended. Water is also scarce and visitors should bring ample supplies. The nearest towns for provisions are Condingup and Esperance.

How to get there

Cape Arid National Park is 120km east of Esperance on the Merivale or Fisheries roads. Balladonia lies about 100km from the Eyre Highway via a four-wheel-drive track. To get to Israelite Bay, take the Telegraph Line Track east across the park. A four-wheel-drive vehicle is recommended for most of the park's roads.
Cape Arid National Park tel: (08) 9075–0055

CAPE LE GRAND

Cape Le Grand has an attractive coastline of small bays, islets and beaches. It is a national park of wild coastal scenery, rugged granite peaks and sweeping heathland. Behind the beaches lies a plateau covered in swamps, heathland and freshwater pools. Stokes National Park is a less frequented park with fewer facilities, but it is an ideal place for quiet reflection or observing nature undisturbed.

The best times to enjoy these coastal parks is in the spring and summer since the warm weather is followed by cool wet winters – and the peak flowering time for the heathland shrubs is during the spring.

The western peaks of the park, including Mount Le Grand and Frenchman Peak, are rounded exposures of the underlying granite outcrops. Those lying below sea level are hollowed with caves and tunnels. To the north and east of the peaks the park is largely a flat sandy plain.

RED WATTLEBIRD

The south-west of Western Australia is famous for its coastal heathlands, which provide a rich food source for pollen- and nectar-eating wildlife. Of all the wildlife species that inhabit these heaths, the dozens of colourful and noisy honeyeaters are some of the most obvious.

The largest of Australia's honeyeaters are the wattlebirds. These conspicuous birds get their common name from the coloured lobes that hang from their cheeks. Western Australia's two species are the red and the little wattlebird.

The red wattlebird has round red lobes hanging from below the eye. Its black-and-white-striped plumage, heavy bill and raucous harsh calls make it an obvious heathland resident. The belly of this species is washed in yellow. The little wattlebird is a smaller but otherwise similar honeyeater which shares the western heathlands with its larger cousin. The little wattlebird does not have lobes or a yellow wash.

Outside the breeding season noisy flocks of up to 100 red wattlebirds move through the heaths exploiting concentrations of pollen and nectar. In many places, there are regular migration routes. In addition to pollen, wattlebirds also eat the insects that are attracted to the flowers. Frequently they use exposed perches from which to make aerial sorties to catch flying insects. When breeding, usually during winter and spring, the flocks disperse and pairs establish small territories. These are aggressively defended against any species which might try to exploit the wattlebirds' source of food. The scruffy cup-shaped nest usually contains two or three eggs and is located in the thin outer branches of a tree or tall shrub. The young are fed in the nest for around two weeks during which time they are fed exclusively on insects.

Botanic spoils for the furtive wildlife

The heathland of flowering plants was one of the first sites for European botanists in Australia. Banksias, lambertias, ground orchids, silver tea trees and stackhousias combine to form a brilliant spring floral display.

Honey possums are common in the park but are rarely seen. Dependent on the rich supply of pollen and nectar from the flowers, they play an important role in the pollination of many plant species. Tammar wallabies and rock wallabies are present but are also rarely seen. The offshore islands have colonies of sea lions and fur seals. Honey-eating birds are plentiful. Several species of parrot, including the delicate rock parrot, are residents of the park.

The French names for the landscape features were given in 1792 by Admiral Joseph-Antoine d'Entrecasteaux, commander of the ships *La Recherche* and *L'Esperance*. Le Grand was an officer on the *L'Esperance*, which was forced inshore in bad weather. At the time, D'Entrecasteaux was seeking another French sailor, Admiral LaPerouse, who had been lost in the region four years earlier.

ABOVE   *Dolphins sometimes frolic in the southern waters near Esperance Bay at Cape Le Grand National Park.*

TOP   *The islands of the Archipelago de Recherche can be seen from the idyllic West Beach near Esperance.*

Coastal walks and Frenchman Peak

From Le Grand Beach to Rossiter Bay stretches a scenic coastal walking track, about 15km one way. Granite headlands are a feature of the walk, which also loops down to some of the park's most picturesque white sand beaches. The track can be broken into four shorter sections. The gentle climb to the summit of the curiously shaped Frenchman Peak takes about two hours from the car park.

Stokes National Park

To the west of Esperance, 80km along the South Coast Highway, is the coastal Stokes National Park. Long beaches and rocky headlands backed by heathland and sand dunes are characteristic of this park. The Stokes Inlet provides a refuge for a wide range of waterfowl and shorebirds which has made birdwatching a very popular activity in the park. However, the edge of the swamps is a favoured place for tiger snakes.

The protected waters of the inlet are ideal for boating and canoeing and enable one to closely approach waterbirds. A 1-km-loop heritage track runs along the cliff edge overlooking the inlet.

Surrounding the inlet is a low forest comprising swamp yate trees and paperbarks. A strange tiny gum tree, the bell-fruited mallee, grows along the edge of the swamplands. This tree never reaches more than 1m in height and has magnificent yellow flowers in autumn. Mallees – special dwarfed gum trees with multiple stems and a shrubby growth habit – frequently have disproportionately large flowers.

Camping facilities

Excellent camping facilities are located at Lucky Bay and Le Grange Beach. Camp sites, showers, toilets and picnic facilities are provided. There are a number of other picnic sites, including Hellfire and Rossiter bays. Boats can be safely launched at Lucky Bay and Cape Le Grand Beach although the beach sand is treacherous and vehicles can become easily bogged down.

Stokes National Park has two camping grounds at Stokes Inlet. There are also bush camp sites at the end of a four-wheel-drive track at Skippy Rock and one at Fanny Cove, south of the historic Moir Homestead.

How to get there

From Esperance the park is 40km on the sealed Merivale and Cape Le Grange roads. Rossiter Bay is situated off the Cape Le Grand Road. Also located further east are Dunns Rock and Saddleback roads. Most park roads are sealed or well formed except Hellfire Bay Track. Tours are available from Esperance.

Stokes is approached by a good unsealed road from the South Coast Highway.

Cape Le Grand National Park tel: (08) 9075–9022

131

FITZGERALD RIVER NATIONAL PARK

One of the largest national parks in the state, this important region has a high level of botanical diversity and, as such, was declared an international UNESCO Biosphere Reserve. With about 20 per cent of the state's plant species within its boundaries, this park is one of the most significant botanical reserves in the country. Close to 1800 different species have been identified with 75 species being unique to the park. Unusual species include the royal hakea, the Western Australian tea tree and the southern plains banksia. The annual spring flowering is spectacular in Fitzgerald River National Park, however flowering does occur year-round.

Facing Point Charles Bay and rising to high points at West Mount Barren and Mount Drummond, most of Fitzgerald River National Park is sheltered from the main force of the westerly prevailing weather. The park is a series of steep ranges rolling down to isolated beaches. Wide rivers spill into the ocean through broad inlets. Popular activities include wildlife observation, bushwalking, canoeing and bush camping. The beaches are inviting, however heavy rips are common and many of the surf beaches are very dangerous.

Halting disease
In an attempt to stop the spread of soil-borne disease organisms, which are devastating forests and shrublands throughout Western Australia, the movement of vehicles is restricted to the eastern and western ends of the park. Soil transported on the wheels and underbodies of vehicles or on footwear can harbour these organisms, so by limiting vehicle and foot traffic the spread of the disease can be controlled. For this reason access restrictions sometimes apply on park roads and tracks, particularly in wet months.

A wealth of wildlife
Almost 200 bird species occur in the park, including rare birds such as the ground parrot, bristlebird and western whipbird. Twenty species of mammal, over 40 species of reptile and a dozen frog species make their home in the park. Whale watching is rewarding from August to November each year as the southern right whales come close inshore to calf.

Wilderness trails
Long-distance wilderness walks are possible in many parts of the park. There are also shorter climbs, such as West Mount Barren summit (which takes about two hours) and East Mount Barren summit (about three hours). The Point

ABOVE *Quoin Head in Fitzgerald River National Park forms part of the World Biosphere Reserve and is dotted with vegetation found nowhere else in the state.*

Ann Heritage Trail should only take about an hour. To prevent the spread of plant disease, walkers are restricted from climbing above the 150-m altitude mark on several peaks in the Mid Mount Barren area.

Exploring the terrain

From the east, the scenic Hamersley Drive leaves the South Coast Highway at the West River Road and provides access to the coast at seven separate beaches. This heritage trail also has four-wheel-drive tracks leading off it to get to Whalebone Beach and Quoin Head. Roadside park interpretive signs are located near the main park entrances.

An access point from the west is off the South Coast Highway 20km west of Jerramungup. From here the Pabelup Drive sweeps around Mount Maxwell and links with Point Ann Road and the track to West Mount Barren. A four-wheel-drive vehicle track leaves Pabelup Drive and heads to Point Charles and Fitzgerald Inlet and Beach. Access from the west is also possible via Gairdner on the Devils Creek Road.

Camping facilities

While there is no formal visitor centre in the Fitzgerald River National Park, the rangers welcome the chance to assist and advise visitors. The rangers' residences are located adjacent to the entrance to the park on the Hopetoun Road, near Jerramungup on the South Coast Highway, and near the Gairdner River Crossing, located close to the western edge of the park.

Camp sites are located at eight coastal sites and half of these can be reached in conventional vehicles. The more remote camping sites are located at Whalebone Beach, Quoin Head, Fitzgerald Inlet and St Mary Inlet. At some of these camp sites free gas stoves are provided to reduce the impact of indiscriminate firewood collection.

How to get there

Fitzgerald River National Park is located between the towns of Bremer Bay and Hopetoun, 420km south-east of Perth. The unsealed Devils Creek, Quiss, West River and Moir roads all head off from the South Coast Highway between the towns of Gairdner and Ravensthorpe. Four-wheel-drive vehicles are recommended but some points in the park are accessible to conventional vehicles, and even small buses and caravans can gain access. Rangers can advise visitors on the best locations to explore.

Fitzgerald River National Park tel: (08) 9835–5043

DON'T MISS...

ADVENTURE EXPERIENCES

Charter a boat or yacht to the Archipelago de Recherche, a perfect spot for seal watching, whale watching in winter, and diving. Several boats and dive schools operate out of Albany and Esperance, and offer day or multi-day charters to visitors wanting to watch the whales.

Drive across the Nullarbor Plain beside the Transcontinental Railway line, the world's longest straight stretch of track. Head north to Kalgoorlie and then head east. A four-wheel-drive vehicle is highly recommended. Get advice from the WA automobile club or railway staff in Kalgoorlie.

Albany Visitor Centre tel: (08) 9841–1088
Esperance Visitor Centre tel: (08) 9071–2330

OTHER INTERESTING AREAS

Eucla National Park is a small Western Australian park that abuts the South Australian border. There are spectacular views, reached by four-wheel-drive vehicle, at Wilson Bluff, a high limestone cliff. Many rare and unusual plants inhabit Eucla's sand dunes. Nearby is the abandoned Eucla Telegraph Station, almost engulfed by sand. Drive down onto Roe Plains to the derelict telegraph station supply jetty which is the place for a cautious swim. This area has no facilities.

The Old Telegraph Station, Eucla, is nearly covered by sand.

South of Cocklebiddy and above Twilight Cove, **Eyre Bird Observatory** with its resident wardens is a place to study the local wildlife, particularly birds. Reasonable accommodation is available but access is by four-wheel-drive vehicle. The observatory is located in an old telegraph station. Operated by the Royal Australian Ornithologist Union as a public education facility, it offers bird-study courses.

Eyre Bird Observatory tel: (08) 9039–3450
Eucla/Esperance tel: (08) 9071–3733

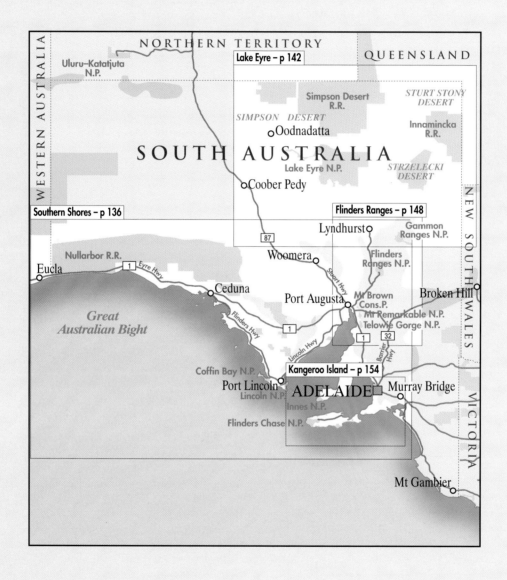

NORTHERN TERRITORY

QUEENSLAND

WESTERN AUSTRALIA

Uluru–Katatjuta N.P.

Lake Eyre – p 142

Simpson Desert R.R.

STURT STONY DESERT

SIMPSON DESERT

Oodnadatta

Innamincka R.R.

SOUTH AUSTRALIA

Lake Eyre N.P.

STRZELECKI DESERT

Coober Pedy

NEW SOUTH WALES

Southern Shores – p 136

Flinders Ranges – p 148

Lyndhurst

Gammon Ranges N.P.

87

Nullarbor R.R.

Woomera

Flinders Ranges N.P.

Eucla

1   Eyre Hwy

Ceduna

Port Augusta

Mt Brown Cons.P.

Broken Hill

Great Australian Bight

Flinders Hwy

1

Mt Remarkable N.P.
Telowie Gorge N.P.

1   32

Coffin Bay N.P.

Lincoln Hwy

Kangeroo Island – p 154

Barrier Hwy

Port Lincoln

Lincoln N.P.

ADELAIDE

Murray Bridge

Innes N.P.

Flinders Chase N.P.

VICTORIA

Mt Gambier

SOUTH AUSTRALIA

SOUTHERN SHORES

Nullarbor Plain • Lincoln • Innes

*A*ll the wilderness areas along the southern shores between Adelaide and Western Australia are off the major tourist routes and away from major centres of population, therefore they are not usually too busy. The coastline provides some of the most interesting scenery in the country. The Nullarbor region is always dry and has more pleasant weather in winter. The summers are very hot. Lincoln and Innes national parks can be cold and rainy in winter and unsuitable for camping.

Travel Tips

The nearest major airport is at Adelaide. Regional airports are at Port Lincoln, Whyalla and Ceduna. Flying from Adelaide is a viable option for a visit to Ceduna or Port Lincoln – or both.

Rental cars, including four-wheel-drive, are available at airports. The Princes Highway from Adelaide links up with two local sealed roads from Port Wakefield to Yorketown and then to Innes National Park. Take the Princes Highway to Port Augusta and either the Lincoln Highway to Port Lincoln or Eyre Highway to Nullarbor Plain before going to Perth. Distances between features of interest are long with dry country farmland in between. If you plan to drive, stay for a few days in the places of interest. Wildlife wandering onto the road can be a problem on the Eyre Highway. Avoid night driving.

PREVIOUS PAGE *The Southern Ocean pounds South Australia's Cape Carnot at the end of Whalers Way.*

ABOVE RIGHT *The Great Australian Bight is lined with dramatic sheer cliffs.*

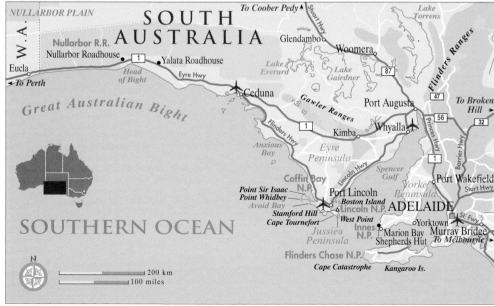

LEFT *The Nullarbor Plain evokes a powerful and eerie mood due to its vast, empty terrain.*

BELOW *Due to wildlife, driving on the Eyre Highway at night can be very hazardous.*

Nullarbor's limestone plains

Originally laid down as sediment on the floor of an ancient sea, the limestones that now form the Nullarbor have risen in one huge block. No tilting of the earth's crust or other forces have caused cracks or upwelling to occur. Since limestone is porous, rain falling on the plain seeps immediately underground and no surface watercourses have formed. In fact, the most active land formation on the plains has occurred beneath the ground where the softer layers of limestone have been worn away by underground rivers. Underground caves and streams form a surprising presence in this seemingly featureless place.

The caves of the plain are not sculpted into the fantastic formations generally characteristic of limestone caves. This is due to the lack of rain and the resulting absence of a flow of erosive water from above. However, the caves are extensive and contain cathedral-sized chambers, rivers and large lakes. Sinkholes are common across the top, where the roofs of the caves have collapsed. Unfortunately none of the caves or sinkholes is open to the public, but special permission may be given for research expeditions.

The lack of water in the limestone soil makes it impossible for trees to survive. The vegetation of the plain is restricted to a low cover of the drought-resistant saltbush and blue-bush. Stunted black she-oaks and mallee gum trees can be found along the edge of the plain.

Dwellings below

Allen's Cave was the site of an Aboriginal occupation 34 000 years ago and contains important Aboriginal art. Dozens of other caves display evidence of indigenous occupation, including stencil sites and stone artefacts. Mummified bodies of animals, preserved in the limestone after they fell into the sinkholes, have provided a wealth of information. Tasmanian tigers have not been seen on the mainland in modern times, but their remains have been found in the caves. It is estimated that they lived on the Nullarbor 4600 years ago and perhaps disappeared with the arrival of dingoes.

Hardy wildlife residents

The wildlife on the Nullarbor is restricted, but watching breeding herds of southern right whales close to the shore is an inspiring sight. Desert dwellers include dingoes which stalk

NULLARBOR PLAIN

The word Nullarbor sounds strangely Aboriginal, but this vast treeless plain's name comes from two Latin words meaning 'no trees'. The relentless flatness of the red plains is testimony to the hardness of its limestone surface and the lack of major geological activity for over 20 million years. At the Great Australian Bight the plains drop suddenly to the ocean and the best of the Nullarbor is easily accessible along the Eyre Highway linking east and west. It is definitely worth spending a night or two at the Nullarbor on the way across the conti-nent, as the landscape is unlike any other.

The Nullarbor National Park is nearly 200km long, beginning just west of the Nullarbor Roadhouse and running to the Western Australian border. The Nullarbor Plain is located mostly in South Australia but it does extend into Western Australia. The park does not include the Head of the Bight, a bay located adjacent to Aboriginal land between the Yalata and Nullarbor roadhouses. This is the northernmost area of the Great Australian Bight and has the best whale-watching areas.

the plains and red kangaroos, the world's largest marsupial. The southern hairy-nosed wombat digs under the limestone to find protection from the drying heat, and the low saltbushes conceal birds, including quail-thrushes and blue bonnet parrots. These hardy animals find just enough water to survive.

Precarious cliff walks

Most walks in the park are short and connect to the lookouts over the Bight. Take care along the cliff edges since limestone is soft and crumbly and the cliff tops are almost always windy.

Camping facilities

Facilities in the park include basic camp grounds, lookouts and picnic areas. There are five marked lookouts at the end of short tracks off the highway: the first of these is about 50km into the park. They are then spaced apart every 20 to 30km. Tracks suitable only for four-wheel-drive run north through the park, but watch out for sinkholes. The old unsealed Eyre Highway runs parallel with the new sealed road, about 10km inland.

How to get there

The only access to this region is by road, the Eyre Highway. You can travel in your own vehicle or by interstate coach. Note that most coaches travel the best section, from Nullarbor Roadhouse to Eucla, at night. If on a coach in winter, break the journey for 24 hours and go whale watching at Yalata or Nullarbor.

Port Augusta National Park and Wildlife Service
tel: (08) 8642–3880

LINCOLN NATIONAL PARK

Lincoln National Park, at the eastern foot of the Eyre Peninsula, is a coastal region with sheltered bays and inlets, and a history strongly connected to Matthew Flinders, an early European explorer. Flinders left many reminders of his coastal voyage in 1802. Memory Cove and Cape Catastrophe near the southern tip of the park have special significance. Here, in rough surf, eight of his ship's crew were killed when a small boat capsized. The drowned men are commemorated in the names of the park's main offshore islands.

Lincoln and the nearby Coffin Bay National Park, located on the west tip of the Eyre Peninsula, contain rich picturesque coastal environments. These parks protect a wilderness region that has not been significantly altered by human activity since first sighted by Flinders. The attractive seascapes, usually clear skies and dry weather of the region make these parks worth the long detour from the usual routes travelled by visitors.

Jussieu Peninsula: breakaway cliffs

Most of Jussieu Peninsula is contained in Lincoln National Park. The peninsula has a narrow neck south of Port Lincoln, which opens out into a large park with a long and sometimes precipitous coastline. The hard granite, which forms the ocean-facing eastern cliffs, is also the reason for the many small offshore islands.

SOUTHERN HAIRY-NOSED WOMBAT

Australia has three species of wombat: the common wombat, occurring in the forest country of eastern Australia, which has no hair on its nose; the extremely rare northern hairy-nosed wombat which now survives in only one tiny inland park in Queensland; and the southern hairy-nosed wombat, occurring on the Nullarbor Plain and a few other spots in central South Australia.

Being a desert dweller, the southern hairy-nosed wombat is active mainly at night. During the day it takes refuge in deep burrows where it can preserve the moisture it obtains from the dry grasses on which it feeds. Up to 10 individuals – males and females – may share a warren. The female's large rear-opening pouch is home to a single young for up to nine months following birth. Young wombats do not mature for three years. This desert wombat has a slow reproductive rate, which becomes inactive if conditions become too difficult – a survival strategy until conditions improve.

Major interstate highways cross the home ranges of the species in two places: the Sturt Highway west of Blanchetown crosses the Brookfield Conservation Park, an important wombat reserve, and the Eyre Highway crosses wombat country west of Ceduna. Road signs warn of wombats on the road at night, so take care when driving as these creatures may look slow but they can travel at up to 40kph in short bursts.

Colourful birds and shrubs

The park's soil is shallow and supports a low shrubland of mallee gum trees. Guinea flowers, native cherry and a variety of wattles make up the understorey plants. An interesting assemblage of birds is found in Lincoln National Park with desert, heath and coastal species mixing together in a colourful array. In the mallee are the large black, yellow and green Port Lincoln parrots while the unusual coastal rock parrot searches for food on the dunes and ospreys soar over bays filled with dolphins and seals. Grey kangaroos graze in the clearings.

Bushwalking

Conventional vehicles can reach most areas in the north of the park. There is a long, sandy, four-wheel-drive track which winds through the south of the park to Memory Cove via Wanna Beach and Jussieu Bay. This is an ideal place for lonely beaches and a wilderness walk to Cape Catastrophe.

Stamford Hill provides the best opportunity for a short bush walk. Look out for the monument Flinders placed on the summit to honour his lost colleagues. The view over the park, bay and islands is superb. Many other longer walks are possible, especially around West Point and Cape Tournefort.

Camping facilities

Bush camping is permitted in Lincoln National Park adjacent to the beach in a dozen places, from Memory Cove to Woodcutters Beach. Most camping areas are centred on Spalding Cove and Cape Donnington. Taylors Landing is a camp site with modest facilities and can be used as a walking access point to low cliffs and remote beaches such as Shag Cove. Camping on the leeward side of the Cape is preferred in stormy weather as the seaward camp sites at Maclaren Point and on the Cape are dramatic but best during fair weather. In summer there is often a shortage of fresh water.

Sheltered beaches are plentiful but swimmers should be aware of the presence of large numbers of huge sharks attracted by the nearby sea lion colonies.

Coffin Bay: a wilderness park

Coffin Bay National Park is a large coastal wilderness park, 50km west of Port Lincoln and 2km west of Coffin Bay village. Flinders named this delightful bay after one of his expedition's financiers, Sir Isaac Coffin. Much of the park is accessible only by four-wheel-drive vehicle.

A sandy four-wheel-drive track crosses the narrow neck of the main peninsula and reaches camping areas at Sensation Beach and Point Sir Isaac. Parts of this track travel along Seven Mile Beach which is only passable at low tide. There are three other beach camping sites along the track. The park is short of fresh water in summer.

Bushwalking and wildlife observation are popular. Marked nature trails are located in three different habitats. Point Avoid is, despite its name, worth a visit as there are numerous lookouts and marked walks. A camping area is located at Avoid Bay. Wilderness walks are recommended especially to Whidbey Beach and Point. The park has a resident ranger and information is available at the entry station.

How to get there

From Port Augusta travel on the Lincoln Highway, or from Ceduna on the Flinders Highway. Regular flights and coaches depart from Adelaide to Port Lincoln.

Port Lincoln National Park and Wildlife Service
tel: (08) 8688–3177

BELOW *Granite boulders lie scattered across Cape Donnington at the northern tip of Lincoln National Park.*

INNES NATIONAL PARK

Shaped like a large foot, the Yorke Peninsula forms the middle one of three, all of which provide South Australia with its magnificent variety of seascapes. Travelling south through the wheat and barley farms and sheep paddocks of Yorke, it is hard to believe that a natural wilderness is to be found at land's end. But a few kilometres after Marion Bay the farmland stops and Innes National Park begins. Just inside the park and after Stenhouse Bay, the Pondalowie Road crosses a low hill and the full rugged beauty of the park and coastline is spread out ahead. Innes National Park is the largest area of natural bushland on the peninsula.

Granite headlands, rugged cliffs, white beaches and saline lakes are the park's main features. The high points at Cape Spencer, West Cape and Royston Head roll back to a flatter landscape in the centre of the peninsula. The western coast north of Ethel Beach is a maze of sand dunes, some stable, some shifting. Some dunes reach over 20m in height.

Rare birdlife in the scrublands

Mallee scrubland, which is very dense in places, dominates the landscape. Around Inneston there are patches of open grassland with scattered native pines and she-oaks. The headlands are covered with a low heath sometimes reaching 1m high and flowers are prolific in the spring and summer.

Rare mallee and coastal birds are the wildlife highlights of the area. Mound-building malleefowl, the secretive western whipbird, ospreys and rock parrots all attract international visitors. The best places to observe malleefowl are south of Marion Lake. A good vantage point is the 5-km walking track from Inneston to Stenhouse Bay. Whipbirds can be heard and, if you are lucky, seen in the coastal heathland. Good observation spots include the dune fields to the west of Browns Beach Road.

Wildlife at Innes

Grey kangaroos are common in the park, as is the amazing pygmy possum. At dusk this little creature may be seen feeding on blossoms in the flowering heathlands. Common and bottlenose dolphins are frequent visitors to the waters around the park. Dragon lizards are often seen and shingle-back lizards and western blue tongues may be encountered. Snakes are seldom observed, however one species known to be a park resident is the highly venomous black tiger snake.

ABOVE *At the foot of the coastal cliffs in the Innes National Park lies the wreck of the ship* Ethel, *a Norwegian vessel that struck a reef on its way to pick up grain in Adelaide in 1904.*

A treacherous coastal history

Sealing, gypsum-mining and timber-cutting industries have all been part of the history of Innes National Park. Over the years the treacherous coast has been the scene for stories of bravery and sorrow in many shipwrecks. Evidence of four wrecks can still be found in the waters around the park. Two wrecks, the *Ethel* and the *Ferret*, wrecked 16 years apart, lie side by side at the northern end of Ethel Beach.

Walking and cycling trails

Walking, swimming and wildlife observation are the most popular activities in the park. The fire trails through the park's interior allow visitors to combine walking and wildlife watching. The 9-km one-way track from Inneston Lake to Spider Lake passes through many different habitats before reaching the northern edge of the park and open farmland. Shorter walks near the coast include the 2-km walk to Royston Head and the 500-m walk to West Cape Lighthouse.

There are several good walks in the heathland between the Gap and Cape Spencer. From the Gap there is a tricky and steep track down to Howling Cave Beach. A 5-km one-way walking track skirts the rear of huge sand dunes connecting Browns Beach to Gym Beach. At Gym Beach there is a camp site immediately within the park boundary although the main beach is just outside. Many of the park's trails are suitable for cycling.

Camping facilities

Innes has 10 basic camping areas, with the most popular ones on Pondalowie Bay. This delightful bay with its 1-km-long beach and offshore islands has the best surf on the peninsula and is well-frequented by surfers. If this area is busy, try the camp sites at the northern end of Browns Beach Road at Shepherds Hut or Browns Beach. These have the advantage of being near to Dolphin and Shell Beach which are the safer beaches in the park for less-confident ocean swimmers.

How to get there

This area is conveniently reached by the sealed road which runs from Adelaide via Port Wakefred and Yorketown. Local bus services are available and conventional vehicles are suitable for use within the park.

Innes National Park tel: (08) 8854–4040

DON'T MISS...

ADVENTURE EXPERIENCES

Between June and October southern right whales can be observed coming inshore to breed. Travellers in their own vehicle should try one of five lookouts west of Nullarbor; the best is Head of Bight Lookout 12km off the highway from the Nullarbor Roadhouse. Permits are necessary to cross the Aboriginal land from Yalata to the coast. These as well as useful information can be obtained at Yalata or Nullarbor Roadhouse. Organised tours from Ceduna and Adelaide include boat and plane trips or four-wheel-drive safari.

Charter fishing boats at Port Lincoln allow visitors to watch white pointer sharks underwater. The observation cage is lowered into the ocean behind the boat and sharks are attracted with food. Viewers have an air line to the boat. There are day and overnight trips for up to six people. This is the ultimate thrill and a great opportunity for underwater photography.

Ceduna Visitor Centre tel: (08) 8625–2780
Calypso Star Charter tel: (08) 8364–4428

OTHER INTERESTING AREAS

Gawler Ranges, north of Kimba, comprise a huge granite monolith and rugged outback desert ranges. They can be explored by four-wheel-drive or as part of an organised multi-day safari from Whyalla or Port Lincoln. There is also a back route to Glendambo via Lake Everard and Kingoonya.

Murphy's Haystacks are peculiar landmark rock formations.

There are also many curiously shaped granite boulders throughout the Eyre Peninsula, for example, **Murphy's Haystacks** at Streaky Bay.

Daily boat cruises are offered from **Port Lincoln** to fur seal colonies and underwater tuna-viewing platforms.

It is possible to hire a fully equipped Gypsy wagon (slow-moving travel driven by one-horse power!) to travel along the beaches of southern Yorke Peninsula.

Port Lincoln Visitor Centre tel: (08) 8682–4688
Gawler Ranges Safaris tel: (08) 8680–2020
Gypsy Waggons tel: (08) 8852–4455

LAKE EYRE

Simpson Desert • Innamincka • Oodnadatta

*T*he dry and forbidding inland desert in the north-east corner of South Australia is a magnet for those seeking the true wilderness. The best way to sample the region is by travelling on three remote tracks circling Lake Eyre. From April to October, days are balmy and nights cool. Summer days are very hot, with temperatures soaring to over 40°C.

Travel Tips

The nearest major airport is at Adelaide with regional airfields at Coober Pedy and Roxby Downs. Safari tours to the inland desert regions set off from Adelaide. The Ghan train service travels regularly from Adelaide to Alice Springs via Port Augusta and nearby Coober Pedy.

By road, the Princes Highway will take you to Port Augusta (336km) and the Stuart leads to Coober Pedy and Alice Springs. There are sealed roads between Woomera and Roxby Downs (76km), and Port Augusta and Lyndhurst (300km). All other roads are unsealed and suitable only for four-wheel-drive. Dust on roads can be a serious problem so drive cautiously and pack valuable items in sealed containers. Roads are often badly corrugated or damaged by washouts and flooding. A steady road speed is often the best approach. Take particular care at watercourses. Oodnadatta Track can often be safely tackled in conventional vehicles, but for most other unsealed routes this is not recommended.

Always carry a sufficient supply of water. If you have problems with your car, do not leave the vehicle as it will provide you with shelter and is much more likely to be spotted by rescuers. Stock or wildlife can be on the road at any time so avoid night driving if at all possible.

ABOVE RIGHT *The Simpson Desert is covered with hundreds of red sand dunes.*

OPPOSITE LEFT *The Birdsville Pub is where locals gather to tell tall stories and true adventures about the Simpson Desert.*

OPPOSITE RIGHT *Because of sand dune gullies, a flag should be tied to your car's aerial to alert other vehicles to your presence.*

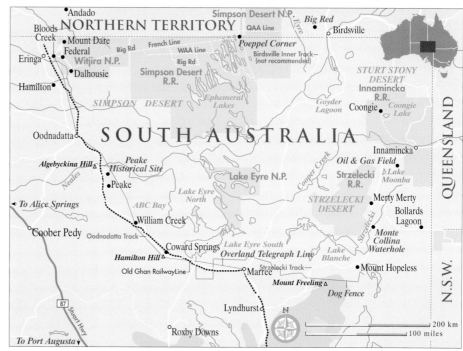

SIMPSON DESERT

Crossing the Simpson Desert, lying north of Lake Eyre, has become synonymous with remote adventure travel. Although it has become easier in the last few decades with the building of better routes, the increased reliability of cars, and electronic navigational and emergency aids, the desert is still an arid and unforgiving environment.

The Simpson Desert straddles the corners of three states and is the largest parallel-sand-dune desert in the world. A four-wheel-drive crossing takes several days of careful negotiation over hundreds of dunes. The camp sites are remote, however in this vast emptiness the night skies are breathtaking. Access to the area is by permit only and a Desert Pass is issued by the park service.

Winding east to Witjira
Starting at Oodnadatta, the last good supply base, the first 160km to Eringa is on an unsealed track. It was once possible to cut through from Hamilton to Dalhousie via Pedirka, but the cost of maintaining this road forced the owners of the station to close the route. From Eringa the route is due east.

After crossing the Old Ghan Line and the route of the Old Telegraph Line, the track enters Witjira National Park at Bloods Creek. There are many camp sites throughout the park. Whitewood trees dot the alluvial plains and red mulga and coolibah grow along the creek lines. Bloods Creek was the starting point for the first recorded crossing of the Simpson Desert. In 1936, Ted Colson and an unnamed Aboriginal guide with a team of 12 camels took 12 days to make the crossing to Birdsville.

Mount Dare
From Bloods Creek a 30-km detour is possible to Mount Dare Station. From there you can travel on to Andado and the Aboriginal community at Finke in the Northern Territory. Otherwise, return to the Simpson Track at the ruins of the Federal Homestead.

Accommodation, camping sites and supplies are all available at Mount Dare. Here you can also take a swim in the thermal hot springs and visit the various interesting homestead ruins. The landscape of the floodplains of the lower Finke River is very different to the sand-dune country of the desert crossing ahead.

Dalhousie's natural springs
Returning to the easterly route, internationally famous and intriguing springs are located at Dalhousie. These permanent waters are upwellings from the desert's subterranean waters. The springs occur along a band of desert between Dalhousie and Marree. Dalhousie is a good place to camp before setting out from Witjira National Park and heading across the Simpson Desert.

Choosing a route
One hundred kilometres from Dalhousie on the Rig Road, now regularly crossing the north–south parallel sand dunes, the first route choice for crossing the desert needs to be made. There are three main routes: you can continue along the Rig Road (600km to Birdsville), take the French Line (320km) or the WAA Line (370km).

The Rig Road was built for seismic trucks on geological explorations and is the easiest route. It passes through the south of the desert. The French Line is often thought of as being the hardest and least interesting. The WAA line is still a challenge and thought by many to be the optimum route for the very well-equipped vehicle. The detailed four-wheel-drive map supplied by the park's service with the Desert Pass will explain the merits of each route. Information about track conditions from local sources must also be considered.

Poeppel Corner: a meeting of borders

Whichever route across the desert is taken, it is possible to visit Poeppel Corner where the three state borders meet. The QAA track then becomes the final leg of the crossing, across the Queensland stretch of the Simpson Desert National Park.

The track crosses Eyre Creek, a delightful tree-lined spot at which to camp, 56km before Birdsville. Gradually the distance between the dunes increases to up to several kilometres. The final dune to cross – the Big Red, claimed to be the biggest dune on the crossing – is located between Eyre Creek and Birdsville. The tiny town of Birdsville is the end of the line. It has one hotel only which supplies fuel, food and accommodation.

How to get there

This is wilderness desert country suitable for four-wheel-drive and is only for those who are fully prepared and entirely self-sufficient. Travelling east to west is recommended, starting at Oodnadatta and finishing at Birdsville, a distance of 712km or more depending on the route taken. Visitors have the option of taking organised safaris.

Hawker National Park and Wildlife Service
tel: (08) 8648–4244

INNAMINCKA

Getting to Innamincka is half the challenge. Exploring the Innamincka Regional Reserve and the Strzelecki Desert makes up the balance. Although it is very unlikely that travellers on a main inland route, like the Strzelecki Track, would find themselves in a life-threatening situation today, the desert is an unforgiving place. Being well prepared for the unexpected is the rule.

The track was originally developed as a route for stock, but its use for this purpose waned in the 1950s. Oil and gas have kept the region open and this is now being boosted by increasing numbers of visitors. The area is to be avoided after rain since roads become impassable.

Gibber plains

The last main supply base heading north from Port Augusta is Lyndhurst at the junction of the Strzelecki Track and the road to the Oodnadatta Track. From here the Strzelecki skirts the extremities of the Flinders Ranges. There is a turn-off to the Mount Freeling talc mines before the Dog Fence is crossed, 92km from Lyndhurst. The country here consists of endless rolling gibber plains.

Mount Hopeless

The next significant feature is Mount Hopeless. Located on the northern tip of the Flinders Ranges it has been an important landmark for thousands of years. The track heads north and 180km from Lyndhurst, there is an intersection with the Moolawatana Track from the northern Flinders Ranges.

BANDED STILT

A strange wading bird of the inland and southern saline swamps, the Banded Stilt is an avian oddity. It was known to science for over 100 years before the first breeding colony was discovered. Even today it has only been recorded breeding on less than 20 separate occasions. Breeding colonies may number in the hundreds of thousands of birds.

Although superficially resembling a stilt, this species has some curiously flamingo-like characteristics. Typical of a stilt are its long pink legs and long straight bill. The plumage is mainly white but breeding adults have a chestnut band across the breast. The wings are black. Like flamingos, Banded Stilts breed and feed in huge colonies, and the chicks are plainly coloured. The chicks of other waders have a camouflaged pattern.

Banded Stilts are not uncommon. In parts of southern Australia, non-breeding concentrations of thousands of birds flock together on salt lakes in the summer months. The birds feed together on tiny shrimps and other crustaceans in salt lakes, salt marshes and mudflats. To catch their prey, banded stilts either wade or swim in shallow water, probing under the water with their long bills.

With the approach of winter, most banded stilts move inland to the Western Australian goldfields region or the salt lakes of northern South Australia. After winter rains, they settle on any temporarily flooded salt lake. One very important area, if it has water, is Lake Eyre. Brine shrimps, the stilts' favourite foods, hatch in billions in the warm salty water. If the food supply lasts and suitable islands are created by the flooding, the stilts may breed. There are many remote inland locations where they may regularly breed but the event goes unnoticed due to the lack of observers.

ABOVE *The gravel-topped Strzelecki Track is usually in good condition, however it can deteriorate quickly after rainfall.*

Bollards Lagoon to the New South Wales and Queensland borders.

The route to Innamincka continues north from Merty Merty, still following the creek line. For about 60km the track is much less distinct. Finally the Innamincka Regional Reserve is reached and the last 45km into the town is an easy run on a well-formed, unsealed track. Supplies are available in Innamincka.

Cooper Creek

Innamincka is located on the banks of the usually dry Cooper Creek. This complex river system drains large areas of western Queensland into Lake Eyre. Its last major flow was in 1974 and it was at this time that the highest floods in living history were recorded along the river. These massive inundations caused Lake Eyre to fill to levels not previously reached for over a thousand years.

Camping at Monte Collina Waterhole

The Strzelecki Track then enters the Strzelecki Regional Reserve and arrives at the first good camp site. At Monte Collina Waterhole on the edge of the Strzelecki Creek there are many camp sites amongst the trees on the riverbank. Fifteen kilometres downstream from this point the creek flows into the normally dry Lake Blanche.

The road to Innamincka

The landscape is now dominated by red sand dunes and the track heads north to run parallel with the main alignment of the dunes. There is another good camp site on the edge of the creek 50km north of Monte Collina. Soon after this the track crosses Strzelecki Creek and there are two alternate routes north. The road to Innamincka via the Moomba oil and gas field is well maintained and in good condition. It is the fastest but longest route. There are no supplies in Moomba and the mine does not welcome visitors.

The original track to Merty Merty, south of Innamincka, can be very rough but it is the recommended route. It is very slow and a four-wheel-drive vehicle is definitely required. Many sections of the track run on the usually dry creek bed. At the Merty Merty Homestead another track, known as Strzelecki Crossing, heads south to Cameron Corner. This route stretches exactly 100km across the sand dunes via

Coongie salt lakes

About 104km from Innamincka, on a narrow, one-way sandy track, is a remote camping destination in the Strzelecki Desert on the shores of the Coongie salt lakes. The largest, Lake Coongie, often has water which is still present many years after rain. The extensive camp grounds around the lake are pleasant and canoeing is permitted. The lake is a haven for birds and fish.

Next stop Birdsville, Queensland

From Innamincka there is an isolated and tricky four-wheel-drive route directly to Birdsville via Walkers Crossing. Vehicles on this track should have Royal Flying Doctor radios and full emergency back-up equipment. Two easier tracks into Queensland are to the west via Nappa Merrie to Nockatunga and Thargomindah, or north via Cordillo Downs and eventually to Birdsville.

How to get there

The unsealed Strzelecki Track, starting at Lyndhurst and finishing at Innamincka, is 456km long. It then connects through to the Burke and Wills Bridge and on to Thargomindah in Queensland. The track is usually in a reasonable condition for conventional vehicles, but most tracks in the Strzelecki Desert around Innamincka are four-wheel-drive territory only.

Innamincka National Park and Wildlife Service
tel: (08) 8675–9909

OODNADATTA TRACK

Once, the Oodnadatta Track was the only route inland and followed the original route established by the Overland Telegraph Line in 1871. It was followed by the Central Australian Railway – the Old Ghan Line – in 1890. Over the years the track and the rail line were constantly cut off by floodwaters until, in the 1970s, the new sealed Stuart Highway was established on the current flood-free alignment, well to the west. The railway now follows this new route.

The original rail line was finally abandoned in 1982 and the towns and facilities that had developed around the camel trains, the old railway and dusty track for over 100 years became deserted. However, these old towns are now being rediscovered by a new breed of cross-country travellers who appreciate the slower pace, the more diverse desert landscapes and the cultural significance of the Oodnadatta Track.

North to Lake Eyre

Stock up with plenty of supplies at Marree, then head north out of town in a good vehicle. Those in a four-wheel-drive immediately have the option to head 94km to the edge of Lake Eyre North along a station road to Muloorina. It travels north through the Dog Fence (dingo fence) and on to Prescott Point on the edge of the Goyder Channel. This channel links the two sections of Lake Eyre. Water has only flowed between the two lakes on three occasions this century, south in 1950 and 1974, and north in 1984. Camping is permitted on the station (check at Muloorina Homestead). Return via the same route.

Salty desert springs

Heading north-west, the Oodnadatta Track follows the Old Telegraph and Old Ghan lines. A series of deserted towns is passed before skirting the western end of Lake Eyre South. At Hamilton Hill, just short of Coward Springs, is the southern turn-off to the Bubbler and Blanche Springs. These extraordinarily out-of-place desert springs bubble salty water to the surface from the underground artesian systems. The mounds around the water are the accumulations of salts that have been deposited over time.

A climb to the summit of Mount Hamilton near Coward Springs is worth the exercise. At the springs, 129km north of Marree, there is a shady roadside camp site.

ABOVE *The inland regions are dotted with the ruins of failed enterprises, like the crumbling Coward Springs homestead.*

William Creek, a supply stop
The township of William Creek, 204km north of Marree, is your first opportunity to re-stock with provisions. Before you reach William Creek there is the only other accessible route to Lake Eyre. The four-wheel-drive track leads to ABC Bay and is a 120-km round trip back to Oodnadatta. From William Creek the Oodnadatta Track separates from the Telegraph Line route and heads north-west, parallel with the boundary of the Woomera Rocket Range.

Abandoned telegraph sites
The Peake Historic Site is also worth a detour. Only 15km off the Oodnadatta Track and about 83km south of Oodnadatta this cluster of restored telegraph station buildings was originally abandoned in 1891. The track crosses Neales Creek next to the old Algebuckina Railbridge. The waterhole by the creek is a popular camp site. Neales Creek swings around and is encountered again a few kilometres outside of Oodnadatta. There are good camp sites along the banks of the usually dry creek bed.

Desert junction
Oodnadatta is a busy desert town of several hundred people. All supplies can be acquired here. From the town there are several choices for further travel. For those heading to Uluru and Alice Springs without a lot of time, the quickest route is via Marla. It is an easy 200km of good unsealed road. For those with more time to get to Alice or who want to explore the Simpson Desert or Mount Dare, continue north from Oodnadatta for a distance of 244km on a less well-maintained road.

A word of caution
Those wishing to light camp fires at night are best advised to collect firewood from areas well away from the popular camp sites. There is an increasing shortage of wood in these areas. Always remember the old bush rule of leaving areas cleaner than you found them.

Road conditions described here are for dry weather only. After rain, the track can become a quagmire and travellers can be stranded for days. Be prepared for long delays in these circumstances.

How to get there
The unsealed Oodnadatta Track runs for 407km from Marree to Oodnadatta. Extensions to the north run 209km to Marla on the Stuart Highway or the 284km to Finke. In dry conditions the main track can be tackled in conventional vehicles, but a four-wheel-drive would be useful. Excursions to Lake Eyre and other side-tracks are only possible with a four-wheel-drive. The Oodnadatta Track is a good introduction to crossing the Simpson Desert.
Pink Roadhouse Oodnadatta tel: (08) 8670–7822

DON'T MISS...

ADVENTURE EXPERIENCES
A four-wheel-drive safari to the edge of Lake Eyre is a desert wilderness adventure. Lake Eyre is the lowest point of Australia (16m below sea level) and a sixth of the continent's water drains into this lake. It is also the largest salt lake in the world. Best explored by four-wheel-drive, Lake Eyre South is accessible along the Oodnadatta Track. Lake Eyre North (the main lake) is accessible via two separate four-wheel-drive tracks: 94km north of Marree and 64km east of William Creek.

Two- to five-week camel safaris venture into some of the most remote desert regions, including Lake Torrens, Simpson Desert, Sturts Stony Desert, and the northern Flinders Ranges. Tours depart from northern towns or Adelaide. There are no summer departures and it is advisable to book well ahead.
Port Augusta Visitor Centre tel: (08) 8641–0793
Outback Camel Company tel: (08) 8543–2280

OTHER INTERESTING AREAS
Wadlata Outback Centre in Port Augusta provides hands-on multimedia and high-tech electronic displays which enable you

Lake Eyre is a vast inland lake that is usually dry.

to experience the hardships and challenges of exploring the outback. This is a great spot to prepare for a trip north or west from Port Augusta as there is an information centre with lots of practical advice.

Coober Pedy opal mines have a range of tours. At **Woomera Rocket Range** there is a display of the British, American and Australian rockets and missiles tested in the desert since 1947.
Wadlata Information Phone tel: (08) 8641–0793
Coober Pedy Visitor Centre tel: (08) 8672–5298
Woomera Missile Park tel: (08) 8673–7042

THE FLINDERS RANGES

Gammon Ranges • Wilpena Pound •

Mount Remarkable

*T*he Flinders Ranges, north of Adelaide, comprise a dry mountainous region with landscapes as diverse as the white salt shores of Lake Frome and the arid vegetated peaks of Mount McKinlay. From Adelaide the whole region can be explored in a leisurely three-day to a week-long return trip from south to north on the eastern side. As an alternative, a long day trip would be to travel up and down the sealed road between Adelaide and Lyndhurst.

Travel Tips

A major domestic airport is situated at Adelaide. Bus and safari tours are also readily available as the Flinders Ranges is a popular location with holidaymakers. Trains travel to Port Pirie and Port Augusta.

The Princes Highway north of Port Pirie and Gladstone goes to Wilmington Road, which travels to the southern sections of the ranges. The central section, Wilpena Pound, is best approached from Port Augusta and Hawker. For the northern section the visitor has a choice of either the unsealed road from Copley, south of Lyndhurst, or the unsealed road from Wilpena via Wirrealpa to Balcanoona.

The weather becomes progressively drier and hotter the further north you travel, therefore the northern areas are best explored in the winter months although the popular areas can become very busy. The southern areas are enjoyable most of the year. Summer temperatures in the north regularly reach 35°C plus. In winter, nights are very cold. Flash floods can cause havoc on roads so take care at creeks. Always carry extra supplies in case you break down in an isolated area.

ABOVE *Alligator Gorge is one of the most spectacular chasms in Mount Remarkable National Park. Lying in the north of the park, the gorge's sheer quartzite walls were carved by the Alligator River.*

OPPOSITE *The yellow-footed rock wallaby has adapted well to its semi-arid environment and lives in colonies of up to 100 individuals.*

GAMMON RANGES NATIONAL PARK

Much of the Flinders Ranges is protected within the Gammon Ranges National Park and the large private wildlife sanctuary at Arkaroola. The sanctuary stretches in the north to where the ranges finally peter out into the inland deserts at Mount Hopeless. This northern section of the Flinders Ranges is a region of significant cultural value and has a landscape that provides powerful inspiration.

The Gammon Ranges are what is known by geologists as 'all slopes terrain', meaning that there is no flat land. Every inch is sloping in one direc-tion or another. Vegetation changes with altitude and moisture, ranging from mulga and gum woodland through mallee shrubland to native pines and grassland. The desert influence is steadily creeping into this region, however, making the plant species more typically arid.

Profuse birdlife and rare wallabies
The rock pools in the park attract thousands of finches, pigeons, and parrots, which need to drink daily. They are joined by marauding birds of prey such as goshawks, brown falcons and peregrines.

One of the most delightful Australian native animals – the yellow-footed rock wallaby – makes its home amongst the gorges of the ranges. Now common only in the northern Flinders Ranges, elsewhere it is either rare or extinct. The wallaby seeks shelter in the rocky cliffs surrounding the gorges during hot weather. The rock pools or soaks are therefore important central points in its territory. Euros share the gorge country with their smaller cousins and red kangaroos are common on the adjacent plains.

Historical landmarks
In addition to the many areas of great Aboriginal significance, there are other cultural relics of an historic kind. Mining, pastoral and exploration history is recorded in the names and structures left about the landscape.

The unique round Bolla Bollana smelter and brick kiln in the north of the national park was built in 1873 for smelting ore from local copper mines. The buildings in the park at Balcanoona are fine examples of early pastoral architecture. Grindells Hut is an outstation built a day's horse ride from the main homestead. The hut is located on the four-wheel-drive track at the western end of Weetootla Gorge and is available for overnight accommodation.

Exploring the range
To fully absorb the outback spirit of this rugged country, bushwalking is a recommended activity. A 15-km walk from Italowie to Grindells Hut should take about eight hours. A variety of walks up Weetootla Gorge, which includes the Grindells Hut route, range from 6 to 18km. For those with a four-wheel-drive vehicle, a cross-park track of around 50km

connects Balcanoona to Yankaninna. It explores spectacular desert mountain country and provides access to many bush camping sites. There are several possible routes and it is worth checking track conditions with park staff.

'Boomerang crack hill'
Chambers Gorge, located 50km south of Balcanoona, is known to the local Aboriginal people as Wadna Yaldha Vambata or 'boomerang crack hill' which describes how they believe the gorge was formed. Cliff faces tower over the Mount Chambers Creek. On these walls are Aboriginal engravings depicting animal tracks, lizards, and circular and linear designs; the engravings are large and are claimed to be the continent's best examples of this art style. Photographers should visit just before midday, when the light is best.

Radioactive springs
Paralana Hot Springs, the green oasis 26km north of Arkaroola, has an interesting history. Official signs warn of the radioactivity of the near-boiling water. Containing radon, the spring water is the result of a deep geyser-like process that may have been active for millions of years. In the 1920s these thermal springs were promoted as a special health cure for all sorts of conditions!

Accommodation and facilities

There are no formal camping facilities in the Gammon Ranges but basic sites are found at Italowie and Weetootla gorges, and Arcoona Creek on the western side of the park. The park headquarters are located at Balcanoona. The village at Arkaroola offers accommodation and has an information centre and a range of tours.

How to get there

From Copley it is 92km via an unsealed road across the main range to Balcanoona. From Wilpena Pound, the main unsealed road via Martins Well and Wirrealpa is about 210km. From Lyndhurst an unsealed road runs for 260km around the northern edges of the ranges to Moolawatana and Balcanoona. A 150-km circuit road runs around the park via Arkaroola and Umberatana, returning to Balcanoona.
Gammon Ranges National Park tel: (08) 8648–4829

EDICARRA FOSSILS

Evidence of the oldest and most abundant groups of animals ever discovered is on the surface of the low Edicarra Hills on the western edge of the Flinders Ranges. Fossil evidence from these rocky ranges confirms the presence of multicellular animals on the earth 650 million years ago. All older fossil sites record the existence of only single-celled life forms. Consequently Edicarra is one of the most important sites known to science. In 1946, a geologist surveying the copper- and silver-rich Edicarra Hills made this remarkable discovery.

Marine animals as we know them today used to live on the floor of an ancient, shallow, warm sea that once covered the region. They include worms, starfish, anemones, trilobites, primitive corals, jellyfish and creatures for which there are no modern counterparts. Some were very large by today's standards, growing to over 1m in length. There is no evidence of spines or other protection, since at that time predators had not evolved. The bodies of these animals were mainly composed of water and for this reason would not normally have made good fossils. However, there is evidence of a huge storm having suddenly flooded the sea floor with millions of tonnes of sand which trapped the soft-bodied animals and even preserved their tracks. Over the millennia these impressions turned to rock.

The small geological reserve which now protects this fossil site is 15km east of Lake Torrens, and 20km west of the Beltana Roadhouse. The reserve is surrounded by private land and entry to it must be sought from the South Australian Museum. The region is dotted with old mines and mine shafts which are of interest but also very dangerous. The South Australian Museum in Adelaide has a spectacular collection of Edicarra fossil specimens on public display.

WILPENA POUND

Wilpena Pound is a major landscape feature of the Flinders Ranges National Park, a region which boasts so many fascinating sights that the visitor can become 'scenery drunk'. Located in the centre of the ranges, this park could easily turn a planned overnight stop into a week-long stay.

A billion years ago the Flinders Ranges had their beginnings in a deep undersea trough caused by titanic expansions and contractions of the earth's crust. Consequently the rocks of this park are some of the oldest in the world. Wilpena is a huge amphitheatre lined by 300-m-high cliffs and surrounded by great bluffs that loom over the approach road from Hawker.

Flinders' fertile gorges

Stretching north from Wilpena Pound the main range stretches north from Mount Abrupt to Mount Hayward and is cut in three places by the Edeowie, Bunyeroo and Brachina gorges. The deep pools in the gorges are lined with river red gums, which make a green splash on an otherwise ochre-red landscape. From the air it is a remarkable vista. A wide, flat plain separates the more fertile western section of the park from the drier Bunker Range and Wilkawillana Gorge in the east. The main northern road to Blinman passes through the centre of the park, past the park headquarters at Oraparinna, with roads leading off it to the pound and the gorges.

Wedge-tailed eagles roam the skies and babblers tumble through the native pines. Cockatoos and crested pigeons gather in the river red gums above the gorge pools for their evening drink. The desert wildlife is everywhere and their colours often contrast with the ochre landscape. Mornings come alive with the rising sun and the choruses of whistlers, robins, thrushes and honeyeaters.

Nature walks

Many walks, both long and short, are possible. The Old Homestead in the centre of Wilpena Pound can be reached after a two-hour stroll (part of the Heysen Trail) from the Wilpena camp ground. In the same

ABOVE *The scenery from the trail to St Mary Peak, the highest point in the Flinders Ranges National Park, is well worth the hike.*

LEFT *The Wilcolo Creek winds across the floor of Wilpena Pound, creating cool picnic spots within the arid landscape.*

area a short nature trail which identifies the main plants of the region is located off the Ohlssen Bagge Track. Aboriginal paintings and an occupation shelter are located at the end of the two-hour walk to Arkaroo Rock off the Hawker Road, just south of the park entrance.

Surprisingly, walks in the park are potentially dangerous in both wet and dry weather. Dehydration is a problem on hot, dry days so you should always carry sufficient water. After rain, both the gorges and cliff tops are slippery. Be prepared for wet, very hot and very cold weather and always inform someone of your intended routes.

Dramatic views at St Mary Peak
The walk to St Mary Peak on the lip of Wilpena Pound is ranked by some as one of the top 20 hikes in the country. The full-day trek to the peak from the Wilpena camp ground can be done as an 18-km round trip, returning via Cooina Camp and the Old Homestead, or it can be completed by retracing the outward route.

Rocky and steep in places, this walk is for the fit and agile. Climbers are rewarded with magnificent views over powerful and dramatic landforms allowing them to fully appreciate the ancient origins of the rugged ranges. The longer walk to Edeowie Gorge is not as strenuous as the Peak Walk and is recommended. The Bunyeroo Gorge is a little off the beaten track and the two-hour walk follows the usually dry creek bed.

Camping facilities
There are many wonderful camp sites in the park and it is hard to recommend one above another. The first overnight stop should be at either Wilpena or Brachina Gorge, but other spots such as at Wilkawillana, Trezona, Youngcoona and Bunyeroo should also be considered. Oraparinna and Wilpena have visitor stations, and there are picnic areas, water points and toilets throughout the park. Hikers can camp away from roads and tracks. Resort facilities are located at Wilpena Lodge.

How to get there

Wilpena Pound is in the Flinders Ranges National Park, which has four principal access points. The main entrance is 50km north of Hawker on a sealed road. There are also entrances from the Lyndhurst Road 71km north of Hawker, from Blinman off the Lyndhurst Road at Parachilna and from half-way along the Martins Well to Wirrealpa Road in the east.
Flinders Ranges National Park tel: (08) 8648–0017

MOUNT REMARKABLE

The southern Flinders Ranges are more than a rugged desert springboard to the arid wilderness areas of the centre. They are rich in remote mountain walks that reveal the beauty of the land. This slightly wetter southern area of the ranges contains four mountainous reserves, important for their role in conservation and well-known for the great bushwalking they offer. The long-distance Heysen Trail crosses all four parks.

A park for bushwalkers

Mount Remarkable National Park is ideal for bushwalkers. In addition to the Heysen Trail which crosses the Mount Remarkable section and loops back to the main park north of Alligator Gorge, there are eight shorter marked trails designed to cater for all tastes.

The walks that start from near the park headquarters at the Mambray Creek picnic and camping area are Sugar Gum Lookout, a comfortable 4-km walk along Mambray Creek to a modest peak with fine views over the park; Daveys Gully Nature trail, a 3-km loop track introducing visitors to a range of habitats in the park; Mount Cavern Trail, a strenuous 11-km, all-day expedition exploring the ridge tops of Black Range; the Blue Gum Flat at the northern end of the park; and the Alligator Gorge Trail, a short but dramatic walk through the most unusual gorge in the ranges.

To Mount Remarkable's summit

In the separate eastern section of this national park, Mount Remarkable rises to almost 1000m. There is no vehicle access to this section of the park but there are several walking routes to the summit. Two approaches are from the town of Melrose or on the Heysen Trail from just north of the town. Alternatively, a longer and more gentle approach can be made from Spring Creek Mine, also using the Heysen Trail, starting 15km north of Melrose. Bush camping is allowed near the summit.

Dramatic gorge

Telowie Gorge Conservation Park is small but dramatic. The 3-km-long Nukuna Nature Trail leaves the car park and enters the gorge lined with gums and native pines. Here rock pools attract parrots and honeyeaters. Euros and yellow-footed rock wallabies may be seen. The gorge is around 10km long and a day could happily be spent exploring its length. Narrow sections, sometimes filled with water, can be carefully negotiated by clambering along the rock faces.

ABOVE *Mount Remarkable rises sharply from the surrounding rolling farmlands west of the village of Melrose.*

Camping and picnicking is permitted adjacent to the car park but not in the gorge itself. Camping is also permitted in the adjacent and much larger Wirrabara State Forest, most of which comprises native vegetation. Good vehicle access is possible via Wirrabara. The main forest road links north to the Germein Gorge Road. There are many long and interesting walks in the state forest and maps of the trails are available at the forestry office which is located 10km to the west of Wirrabara.

Mount Brown Conservation Park

A short section of the Heysen Trail lies in the Mount Brown Conservation Park, 14km south of Quorn. The park's major feature is the forest-topped mountain after which the park is named. Having parked near the usually dry Waukarie Falls, it is a 1-km walk down the creek bed to a natural soak, water tank and bush camp site. From here a loop track of 15km runs up the ridge to Mount Brown and returns via the ridge overlooking Willochra Plains. Alternatively, the return trip can retrace the outward journey, reducing the walk to 12km.

This park is of particular interest to walkers with an interest in geology or botany. The mountain and park are named after Robert Brown, the botanist on Matthew Flinders' 1802 expedition, who collected plant specimens from the summit.

Dutchman's Stern: a day stopover

Dutchman's Stern Conservation Park, 9km north of Quorn, has a range of great day walks and picnic areas. It is a good lunch spot on the way through Quorn. There are no camp sites but the old homestead and shearers' quarters are available for overnight accommodation. The nearest car camp site is located 16km north of the park in the delightful Warrens Gorge.

Two bushwalks in the 3532-ha conservation park are recommended. The Bluff Summit Walk is a three-hour, steep climb to the park's highest peak and the Valley Walk winds south along the main range providing access to three lookouts. A number of plants and animals do not occur further north of this range.

How to get there

Mount Remarkable National Park can be reached from the Princes Highway, 20km north of Port Germein, from Melrose in the west or from Wilmington in the north. Mount Brown and Dutchman's Stern are south and north of Quorn respectively. The entrance to Telowie Gorge is 12km north of Napperby.

Port Germein National Park and Wildlife Service tel: (08) 8634–7068

Homestead at Dutchman's tel: (08) 8648–6277

DON'T MISS...

ADVENTURE EXPERIENCES

Heysen Trail is a 1500-km walk that begins south of Adelaide at Cape Jervis and currently finishes in the Flinders Ranges National Park. It is named after a South Australian landscape artist famous for his watercolours. The trail includes the summit of Mount Remarkable and Wilpena Pound. There are maps of individual sections and many two- and three-day sections make memorable mountain hikes. The trail is closed in summer due to the heat and risk of bush fire.

Horseback trail riding is possible in the Flinders Ranges National Park and in other parts of the ranges and are an excellent way to enjoy the scenery. Some are multi-day camping safaris. Certain companies also offer horse-riding safaris in other parts of South Australia, in particular around the Coorong Lakes region.

Exploring the central Gammon Ranges National Park on foot or by four-wheel-drive ranks as one of the region's best wilderness adventures.

Heysen Trail, State Information Centre tel: (08) 8204–1900
Horse riding, Outback Bush Adventures tel: (08) 8528–2132
Gammon Ranges National Park tel: (08) 8648–4829
Port Augusta Visitor Centre tel: (08) 8641–0793

Aroona Hut is a ruin that can be reached via the Heysen Trail.

OTHER INTERESTING AREAS

Yourambulla Caves are 15km to the south of Hawker and display excellent examples of Aboriginal rock paintings. Three caves are open to visitors. The main gallery is high on the ridge and is a 15-minute walk from the car park, which is a scenic picnic stop. Steel stairs climb to the cave. The paintings here are mainly in black pigment and depict linear designs and animal tracks.

Quorn Visitor Centre tel: (08) 8648–6031

KANGAROO ISLAND

Flinders Chase • Southern Parks •

North Coast

*K*angaroo Island is Australia's best-kept wildlife secret. The island is a paradise as a result of its 6000-year isolation from the mainland and the fact that its wildlife has evolved differently. Kangaroo Island was once home to a distinctive dwarf emu and continues to have a unique form of grey kangaroo. The island also has no dingoes, foxes or rabbits, but does suffer from predatory feral cats. All these circumstances have contributed to a remarkably tame and varied wildlife population.

Travel Tips

Kangaroo Island is larger than it looks (145km long), so plan to spend at least three nights there. Those with limited time should fly from Adelaide, the nearest major airport, spending the day there before flying back the same night. A regional airport is located on the island at Kingscote. Both Kingscote and Adelaide offer organised tours.

It is possible to travel to the island by ferry and return the same day, but this leaves very little time to explore. The daily ferry sails from Cape Jervis, 112km south of Adelaide. Driving is slow on the island's narrow roads and wildlife often wanders across the paths. Sealed roads connect the main centres but some minor roads may be sand tracks. A four-wheel-drive vehicle is not necessary.

Weather is temperate and affected by the sea conditions. Winter can be cool and wet. There is usually good weather for the rest of the year but be prepared for a cold storm, even in summer.

ABOVE RIGHT *Sea lions on Kangaroo Island have become accustomed to sharing their beach with humans.*

OPPOSITE *Quaint cottages in wild coastal settings make wonderful accommodation.*

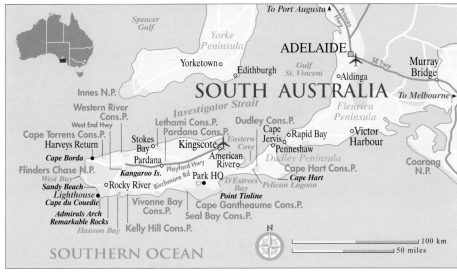

154

FLINDERS CHASE NATIONAL PARK

Abundant tame wildlife, remote coastal walks and impressive rock formations contribute to the wide appeal of the Flinders Chase National Park. Its natural beauty was recognised in 1919, when the area became one of South Australia's first parks. It remains the largest park on Kangaroo Island.

Craggy headlands punctuated with long white beaches dominate the coastal scenery. A plateau behind the cliffs is mostly covered with mallee and gum woodland. Many deep ravines with permanent streams run their short length to the sea, breaking through the cliffs to the beaches to form charming estuaries. The deep wet gullies are lined with tall sugar gums and a tangle of banksias and wattles.

Remarkable Rocks
Kangaroo Island's most impressive granite outcrops occur at Kirkpatrick Point. The Remarkable Rocks are a pile of tors that have been sculpted by the wind and are set on a huge granite dome. They can be seen clearly from Weirs Lookout near the Cape du Couedic lighthouse.

A steep track descends below the lighthouse to one of the most photographed points on Kangaroo Island. Admirals Arch is a natural limestone cave carved out by the ocean from the calcrete capping of the plateau and hard granite bedrock below. New Zealand fur seals breed around the cliff base and can be seen frolicking in the surging seas or resting on the sloping granite shoreline.

An abundance of wildlife
In addition to the conspicuous grey kangaroos, after which the island was named, there are many other species of wildlife that are encountered regularly in the 'Chase'. Platypus were introduced to the park and may be seen in Rocky River.

Koalas were also introduced to the island and are now plentiful in the manna gums around Rocky River. Tamar wallabies are common on grassy clearings, especially at dawn and dusk. Many rare birds inhabit the forests of the park, including glossy black cockatoos and the western whipbird. Not so shy are the ospreys and sea eagles, often observed soaring over the ocean cliffs.

Ravine des Casoars: a walk to the sea
In 1801 the French explorer Thomas Nicolas Baudin identified, incorrectly, the now extinct local emus as cassowaries and also named a valley close to Cape Borda as Ravine des Casoars, a name it still bears. The valley gives its name to one of the most pleasant walks in the park. The steep and rough trail of 7-km return starts at the end of a short driving track off Playford Highway. The beach and coastal scenery is well worth the walk – check times and arrange to arrive on the beach at around low tide so that you can explore the limestone sea caves. A torch is a handy item of equipment to carry. Back at Cape Borda are spectacular coastal views and Harveys Return camping area, which has basic facilities.

Trek to West Bay
A 22-km drive to West Bay from Rocky River takes visitors to the westernmost point of the island. On the way are two short walks of less than 2km each, which lead to Sandy Beach and Cascades Beach. Both of these walks pass through rich heathland filled with birds and provide a myriad opportunities for photography. A third track also leading to the coast follows the course of Breakneck River. This walk is 6-km return and passes through tall sugar gum forests before emerging onto a broad sandy beach.

Living in a lighthouse

Some of the history of the Chase is prominently displayed in the two old lighthouses at Cape Borda and Cape du Couedic. Both have now been converted for automatic operation and today the lighthouse cottages have a new role to play as modest accommodation.

Camping and facilities

The main facilities are at Rocky River, where there is a visitor centre, a camping ground and toilets. Here the wildlife is so tame, particularly the emus, kangaroos and Cape Barren geese, that special pens have had to be built for human visitors to enable them to prepare their picnics inside the fenced enclosures without the continuous attention of hungry beaks and muzzles. Rocky River is one of the few places in the Chase that is not dominated by the heavy pounding of the surf, a hallmark of this coastal park.

How to get there

Flinders Chase National Park is located at the western end of the island, about 102km from Kingscote. Take either the sealed Playford Highway to the West End Highway and head south, or the slower sealed Birchmore Road and unsealed South Coast Road. The park visitor centre is at Rocky River.
Flinders Chase National Park tel: (08) 8483–7235

SOUTHERN PARKS

The parks in the southern region of Kangaroo Island offer a very different aspect of nature. At Seal Bay Conservation Park, sea lions loaf on the beach and are not fazed by people walking amongst them. At Kelly Hill Conservation Park, walks among the ground foliage reveal the plants and animals that have made the park their habitat, and also introduce visitors to the caves that dominate the underground landscape.

Close encounters with seals

It is rare for humans to have an inspirational contact with wild animals, but at Seal Bay the walk amongst the sea lions will touch nearly everyone who ventures there. At the bay people can enjoy the open beach, sand dunes, wild Southern Ocean, and untamed sea lions. This Australian sea lion colony is unique in that they don't seem to mind the presence of people, whereas in other places colonies of the same species are disturbed by human approaches. Sea lions are capable of giving sharp bites, so never approach them too closely.

This colony represents about 10 per cent of the world's breeding population of Australian sea lions. The species now breeds only in Western Australian and South Australian waters. Last century sealing eliminated the Bass Strait colonies and threatened to send the species into extinction. There are now about 500 sea lions at Seal Bay and they

ECHIDNA

Although common throughout Australia, echidnas are usually rarely seen. Kangaroo Island is, however, one place where the casual observer is likely to see one of these mammalian curiosities. Their trusting nature on the island may be connected to the fact that Aborigines have not lived on Kangaroo Island in modern times. Elsewhere in Australia Aborigines regard echidnas as good food.

Together with the platypus, echidnas are the only mammals to lay eggs. The female lays a single egg into her pouch and carries it for 10 days before it hatches. The young echidna stays in the pouch and suckles milk for about three months. By the end of this time, with its short spines now well developed, the youngster leaves the pouch.

Echidnas are usually active when the temperature is neither too hot nor too cold. They are therefore normally nocturnal in the inland deserts. In southern Australia during the warmer months they are often observed feeding at dawn and dusk. During the winter months it is not uncommon to see echidnas out and about in the middle of the day.

Termites and ants form the diet of this specialised mammal. The echidna tears open the insects' nest, prodding its long snout into the centre, and then uses its sticky tongue to gather up the creatures and swallow them whole (echidnas have no teeth).

Their powerful digging ability enables them to escape from danger by disappearing quickly into the earth. They can also roll up into a tight ball leaving only their hard pointed spines and tough claws exposed. Adult echidnas may occasionally fall prey to dingoes but loss of habitat, being killed on roads, and being hunted appear to be their main threats. Youngsters are prone to predation by goannas.

appear secure. Each year around 200 pups are produced, but not all survive. The ocean harbours the white pointer shark, which is the sea lions' main predator.

Visitor access to Seal Bay is controlled to ensure a limited number of people on the beach at any one time. Access is 9km from the South Coast Road and only permitted to the centre of the beach as there are seal nurseries at both ends which must not be disturbed. Stairs and seating platforms ensure the dunes are protected from erosion. Seal Bay is for day visits only and no overnight facilities are provided.

Escaping crowds at Vivonne Bay
After heading west from Seal Bay for about 13km, there is a turn-off to Vivonne Bay. The coast and dunes south of the village that form the Vivonne Bay Conservation Park are little-visited, wild and lonely stretches of coastline. Point Ellen at the eastern end affords great views.

Kelly Hill's limestone caves
Thirty-eight kilometres west of Seal Bay lies Kelly Hill Conservation Park. It boasts, as its prime attraction, extensive and impressive limestone caves. Local legend has it that the caves were discovered in 1880 when a stockman fell with his horse, Kelly, into a sinkhole. The stockman escaped out of the cave, but when he returned to rescue his horse the animal had disappeared, never to be seen again.

The caves are around 130 000 years old. Some are open to the public with guided tours scheduled daily. After climbing a small forested hill, the entrance to the main cave is straight down a set of steep stairs. The caves are well lit and display ornate calcite formations. Rangers run adventure caving tours in addition to regular tours. Ring ahead well in advance to get more information about these expeditions.

Forest wildlife
The forests of Kelly Park are unusually tall and damp. Nearer the coast, mallee shrubland dominates and there is a swampland and large freshwater lagoon. Clearings provide places for kangaroos and wallabies to graze. At night the clearings are home to the stone curlews whose haunting calls resonate through the forest.

Activities in Kelly Park
A 9-km walking track via the lagoon links the park headquarters to the idyllic beach at Hanson Bay. Take the unsealed road down the western boundary of the park. It is a great swimming and canoeing spot, but watch out for the white pointer sharks!

Camping is permitted near the caves, and picnic facilities are available in the delightful tall forests. The kangaroos and wallabies have become accustomed to people and can be a little too friendly around the picnic tables.

How to get there

Kelly Hill, Seal Bay and Vivonne conservation parks are accessed from Kingscote via the sealed Birchmore Road or the unsealed South Coast Road. Conventional vehicles are suitable. Kelly Hill and Seal Bay have visitor centres and information booths. There are a number of guided tours from Kingscote.
Kelly Hill Caves tel: (08) 8483–7231

BELOW *The Kelly Hill Cave system is a subterranean wonderland with many small but delicately sculpted caves. Apart from the usual calcite formations, they are also home to unusual helictites.*

ABOVE *The north coast near Harvey Lookout is protected from the rough open sea so this area is popular for boating and diving.*

LEFT *The Southern Ocean pounds the rounded granite coast at Admirals Arch at the tip of Cape du Couedic.*

NORTH COAST

To experience the island's wildlife it is not necessary to confine exploration to the major parks. Kangaroo Island has many small reserves along the north coast and in the west. These areas are dramatic in their own way and are often quieter, especially during the holiday period over summer.

Wild cliffs of Cape Torrens
For wilderness walking and wildlife observation the Cape Torrens Conservation Park is a rugged northern stretch of cliffs, accessible via the Jump-off Road off the Playford Highway, 12km past the West End Highway turn-off. Roads may be closed in winter. Within the park the only means of transport is on foot. The cliffs soar to over 200m in height and are amongst the highest in South Australia. Camping is not permitted at Cape Torrens.

Birdwatching
Western River Conservation Park is another remote area suitable for wildlife observation and wilderness walking. Access is via Colmans Road off the Playford Highway, 2km past the West End Highway turn-off. The park's cliffs and small beaches boast some of the island's best birdwatching areas. Camping is not permitted.

Swimming and cliff-top walks
Adjacent to Lathami Conservation Park is the Stokes Bay camping area. Situated at the end of the unsealed Stokes Bay Road, or Bark Hut Road, off the Playford Highway the area offers safe swimming and cliff-top walks. The conservation park has a variety of coastal vegetation and is an important region for rare birds.

Nearby, the Parndana Conservation Park is small but rich in wildlife. Located at the end of an unsealed dirt track off the Playford Highway 6km east of Parndana, there are no facilities and access is by foot only.

Cape Gantheaume: whales and bushwalks
Cape Gantheaume Conservation Park is an enormous wilderness area and Kangaroo Island's second-biggest park. It is only accessible by foot. Multi-day bush walks are a feature of this area and the 18-km coastal walk to Cape Gantheaume is the most popular. The park headquarters are located off Seagers Road, which is off the South Coast Road. Bush camping is permitted and the start of the Cape Walk is near Point Tinline at the southern end of D'Estrees Bay. Southern right whales breed in this bay during the winter months.

Wildlife watching
Two small conservation parks are found on the Dudley Peninsula: Dudley and Cape Hart. Cape Hart is a coastal park where horse riding is popular, while Dudley is located near Brown Beach, off the East–West Road. Camping is permitted in the latter and both are good wildlife observation locations.

Pelican Lagoon: a waterbird haven
Pelican Lagoon Conservation Park is named for the pelican colony that resided here at the time of Matthew Flinders' journey of discovery in 1802. Flinders noted: 'Alas, for the pelicans! Their golden age is past; but it has much exceeded in duration that of man'. Prophetic words, since pelicans have not nested on Pelican Lagoon's islands for over 100 years. However, it is still an extremely important estuary and wetland area for waterbirds.

This park, partly islands and partly mainland, is at the Eastern Cove head and is reached by foot or boat from Sapphiretown. There are no park facilities and entry permits are required from the park service.

Penguins nest in burrows around the island cliff tops and, remarkably, find safe homes in Kingscote and Penneshaw. Rangers conduct guided tours of penguin rookeries each evening. Penguins are often seen feeding in the inshore waters or from the ferry during crossings to Cape Jervis.

How to get there

The north coast area includes the whole of the Dudley Peninsula and the north coast. Sealed roads cross the island from the ferry terminal at Penneshaw to American River and Kingscote. The area is also accessed by the sealed Playford Highway. The most interesting areas are on short unsealed roads and in some areas a four-wheel-drive vehicle is useful.
Kingscote National Park and Wildlife Service
tel: (08) 8482–2381

DON'T MISS...

ADVENTURE EXPERIENCES
Diving the cold, clear waters of Kangaroo Island is a very different experience to diving the warm tropical waters of North Queensland and the Great Barrier Reef. The raw beauty of the Kangaroo Island coastline and its abundant marine animals make this a dive location to remember. Swimming with seals at Cape Gantheaume is a highlight of some dive programs. First-time dive courses are on offer as well as expeditions for the experienced diver. A choice of operators provide a variety of tour and accommodation packages. Some operators also include canoeing and abseiling for non-dive-time activities. A three- or four-day dive program can be arranged to include tours of the main terrestrial features of Kangaroo Island.

Tandem sky diving is popular every weekend in Adelaide's clear skies. A brief introduction to sky diving will have you on a tandem jump within hours. Freefalls are from over 1500m (5000ft) and the views of the Fleurieu Peninsula, gulf and Lake Alexandrina are superb.
Adventureland Diving tel: (08) 8483–1072
South Australia SkyDiving tel: (08) 8388–9444

A lighthouse is perched on Cape du Couedic.

OTHER INTERESTING AREAS
Ten lighthouse-keeper cottages and historic houses, located in some of the most spectacular coastal settings, are available at modest cost for overnight accommodation. This is one of the best ways to really experience Kangaroo Island. Cottages are at **Cape Borda**, **Cape du Couedic** and **Cape Willoughby** (lighthouse tours are also available). There are more cottages at **Rocky River** near the Flinders Chase Park Headquarters.
Flinders Chase National Park tel: (08) 8483–7235

VICTORIA

SUNSET COUNTRY

Hattah Lakes • Wyperfeld •

Grampians (Gariwerd)

*T*he western region of Victoria is mainly flat, dry agricultural land. The Murray River creates a natural northern border to the state and at times, when rainfall is sufficient, provides the water that fills the usually dry Hattah Lakes and those at Wyperfeld. The Grampians (Gariwerd) National Park is a rugged range filled with botanical wonders.

Travel Tips

A regional airport is located at Mildura. There are very few organised or adventure tours to this area and little public transport except between major towns. The area is serviced by interstate coach routes between Sydney and Melbourne or Adelaide.

Road access from Melbourne is via Ballarat or Bendigo. Access to northern areas from Adelaide or Sydney is through Mildura. Conventional vehicles are sufficient but some desert tracks and parts of the Grampians (Gariwerd) require a four-wheel-drive. The area is best experienced by car and foot in the desert areas, and elsewhere by foot.

Between Wodonga and Swan Hill and to the north of Murray Valley Highway, there are 15 highly recommended car camping areas in picturesque state forests along the river. Try the Barmah (east of Echuca), Cobram and Gunbower state forests. If, en route from Melbourne to the Grampians you have a little time to spare, take the Great Ocean Road and camp in Otway National Park.

Northern Victoria is very dry and hot in the day, and frosty at night. The south has cold, wet, coastal storms. Be prepared for mosquitoes at night and bees in spring.

PREVIOUS PAGE *Victoria's most renowned feature is its rugged and wild southern coastline, which has claimed many ships over the centuries.*

ABOVE *The Balconies at the Grampians (Gariwerd) National Park offer extensive views of the folded sandstone range and rolling agricultural lands that make up the Sunset Country.*

OPPOSITE *A houseboat on the Murray River provides a relaxing way to enjoy river life and observe the diverse riparian wildlife.*

Contrasting vegetation

Magnificent stands of river red gums and black box dominate the riverside vegetation. These mighty trees contrast with the stunted plants that occupy the areas further away from water. Beyond the floodplains, the roots of the mallee shrubland hold together the rolling red sand dunes. Here a ground cover of porcupine grass provides an impenetrable home for a variety of desert birds and reptiles. Scattered here and there across the grassy plains are woodlands of cypress pine.

Wildlife at the lakes

The lakes are a magnet for waterbirds, including pelicans, ducks and black swans. Other wildlife is also drawn to the supply of water, including parrots, rainbow birds and tortoises. Some wildlife is more typical of drier regions, such as the prolific emu and western grey kangaroo. Hattah is also one of the few places in Victoria where the red kangaroo makes its home.

HATTAH LAKES

The serene Hattah Lakes stretch along the banks of the Murray River and fill completely with water only when the river floods. This watery oasis forms a pleasant contrast to the vast arid, flat country of northern Victoria, where the local annual average rainfall is only 28cm and the highest point is less than 50m above sea level.

Two adjacent parks, Hattah–Kulkyne National Park and Murray–Kulkyne Park, provide interesting areas to explore.

Over 20 natural overflow lakes are scattered throughout these two parks. When the Murray River floods, the Chalka Creek fills with water which then flows into the series of overflow lakes. The first lake to fill is Lockie, followed by Mournpall and Hattah. The last in line are Nip Nip and Bitterang, hence these are almost always dry. Some lakes fill regularly and then dry out quickly, such as Lake Lockie. Other lakes hold water for much longer periods of time. Lake Mournpall, the most permanent lake, takes seven years to dry out after being filled, while Lake Hattah holds water for three years.

The lakes are often muddy or shallow depending on how long ago the last flood occurred, and so swimming is not always possible or recommended. There are suitable swimming areas along the river. There is also a shortage of fresh drinking water and the lake water should not be drunk.

Park activities

Highlights for visitors to Hattah–Kulkyne include canoeing on Chalka Creek and the lakes, and bushwalking. Wildlife observation is popular and nature photography is rewarding, especially along the river and lake edges.

There are many bush tracks in the parks. Some are open only for walkers, but others were created for vehicles. The choice of tracks allow visitors to cover a range of distances of up to 10km. The best walks are those from Lake Hattah and those that circle the adjacent lakes. Short marked nature trails provide interesting insights into the red gum, cypress and mallee landscapes.

Marked nature drives

Kulkyne Nature Drive is a 50-km, signposted drive that leads north through the centre of the Hattah–Kulkyne National Park and returns along the Murray River. A shorter loop drive provides a more detailed introduction to the park's landscapes. This drive starts near the rangers' residences and winds between Lake Hattah and Lake Arawak. Many common species of plant and an Aboriginal canoe tree are identified by numbered markers. Both these marked drives are recommended. After rare rainfall, unsealed tracks can become slippery and unpassable for vehicles. The park staff at the visitor centre can advise on the condition of tracks and provide guide brochures.

Exploring the forests

The less frequented state forests along the Murray River west of Merbein and around Robinvale are great for exploring. Basic riverside camping facilities are located at Wallpolla Island State Forest on the Murray, north of Kulnine off the Sturt Highway west of Mildura, and at Passage Camp State Forest near Boundary Bend.

Camping facilities

Simple camping facilities with fireplaces and toilets are provided at Lake Mournpall and Lake Hattah at the Hattah–Kulkyne National Park. The shortage of water means there are no showers. Bush camping is permitted amongst the red gums along the river in Murray–Kulkyne Park, although there are no facilities.

How to get there

Hattah–Kulkyne National Park is 470km from Melbourne on the Calder Highway. The main entrance at Hattah is off the Calder, 35km north of Ouyen and 69km south of Mildura. The visitor centre is 4km east of Hattah. Access to Murray–Kulkyne Park is via the River Road south of Colignan, which is 14km east of Calder Highway.

Hattah Lakes National Park tel: (03) 5029–3253

WYPERFELD

Like the Hattah Lakes in the north, Wyperfeld National Park centres on a string of overflow lakes: Wonga, Lake Agnes and Lake Brambruk. For the park's lakes to fill, the Wimmera River must first fill two large lakes to the south, Hindmarsh and Albacutya. In this arid climate there is rarely enough rain for the Wimmera River to flood and Wyperfeld's lakes are usually dry. This century the Wyperfeld overflow lakes have filled only in 1918, 1956 and 1975.

Mallee shrublands

Wyperfeld has a renowned diversity of landscapes and wildlife. The park is a patchwork of cypress pine woodland, riverine gum forest and heathland. The biological feature is the huge expanse of mallee – a term used to describe a dwarf gum with multiple stems. There are many species of gum that have this peculiar growth form. Most of the continent's mallee shrubland has been cleared for wheat growing and the Wyperfeld mallee is the last stronghold for many plants, birds and reptiles. Mallee requires fire to maintain its biological diversity so Wyperfeld is burnt regularly to create plots of shrubland of different ages.

Mallee dwellers

While emus and western grey kangaroos are common and very conspicuous, it is the more elusive wildlife of the mallee that draws biologists from around the world. Perhaps the most famous mallee dweller is the rare mound-building malleefowl.

PINK-EARED DUCK

Pink-eared ducks are the most delicately shaped and marked of all Australia's waterfowl. The chocolate-brown zebra stripes are diagnostic, as is the over-sized shovel-shaped bill. The duck's eyes are set in a field of chocolate-brown, high-lighted by a fine white line. This species of duck gets its name from a tiny pink spot behind the eyes. Both males and females have similar plumage. They make a distinctive continuous chirring sound when they call.

This small duck is an Australian nomad. Flocks of birds move from the breeding wetlands of the southern inland and disperse widely when not breeding. Pink-eared ducks are frequently encountered in the shallow-water lakes and billabongs of northern Victoria. Particularly when not breeding, they may be encountered in any shallow, warm lake in inland Australia. Pink-eareds leave the water rarely and never dive except if moulting or injured. They sometimes loaf at the water's edge or perch on exposed tree branches with other ducks such as grey and chestnut teal.

Pink-eared ducks feed on microscopic plankton which occurs in abundance, floating in the waters of swamps and lakes. Their enormous bill, which is dipped into the water up to the ducks' eyes, is used to sieve the tiny plants and animals from the warm shallows. Birds feed often in small flocks while they paddle across the surface. The whole group filters the surface water as it moves.

Breeding occurs around the big inland lakes and along riverbanks immediately after flooding – this is the time when food is most abundant. Huge concentrations of pink-eared ducks breed together in wet years, but breeding is rare in dry years. Nests are made in tree hollows, in bushes or even on fence posts standing in the water. When the adult leaves the nest, the eggs are concealed in a large ball of grey down. Around five to six eggs are laid.

LEFT A scenic view of the Murray–Sunset National Park with dry Lake Crosbie in the background. Camping facilities on the shores of the lake are available to travellers.

BELOW The mound-building malleefowl is becoming increasingly rare, but can still be found at the Wyperfeld National Park. These birds, as their name suggests, build mounds of rotting vegetation in which to incubate their eggs.

This ground-living bird incubates its eggs in large piles of carefully tended rotting leaves. The male manages the heap, checking the temperature with its tongue. The 10 to 20 eggs require an incubation temperature of 33°C. Many tonnes of decomposing mulch are moved daily in the male's efforts to check and maintain the nest at this temperature.

Hundreds of active mounds are scattered throughout the park. Deserted old mounds persist for decades in the dry climate and can be seen on some of the nature walks. The turkey-sized malleefowl is more difficult to observe.

Shrubland walks

The Lake Brambruk and Tyakil nature walks at Black Flat Lake cross the park's main features and are highly recommended. They are each about 6km in length. There are other marked walks of similar or greater length as well as many that penetrate deep into the arid shrublands. Bush-walkers are rewarded with a sense of isolation and the opportunity to closely study the rarer desert wildlife.

Camping facilities

A large camping area with good facilities is located in Wyperfeld near the visitor centre at Flagstaff Hill. A basic camping facility is also located at Casuarina at the northern park entry on the road from Patchewollock.

Lake Albacutya

Adjoining the southern boundary of Wyperfeld is Lake Albacutya Park. This small park provides camping and recreational activities focused on the lake. Part of the Wimmera River overflow system, the lake last filled in 1974. It was dry by 1983. There are three main camp sites in the park, which is popular for a variety of water-based activities when the lake is full. Hunting is permitted, so avoid the duck open season, which is usually in autumn.

Murray–Sunset: red-hued lakes

The new Murray–Sunset National Park, which includes the area previously known as Pink Lakes State Park, is located north of Wyperfeld. The park's original name stemmed from the red hue of the salt lakes, created by red pigments secreted by algae. Some of the lakes were once used for commercial salt production and evidence of this now abandoned practice is still present.

Murray–Sunset has pleasant basic camping facilities on the southern shore of the dry Lake Crosbie. There are many enjoyable walks in the riverine forests around the salt lakes of Kenyon (four hours), Crosbie (three hours), Becking (two hours) and Hardy (30 minutes).

Big Desert: hardy walking

The Big Desert Wilderness Park is one of Victoria's few large wilderness areas. Access is on foot only via the rough four-wheel-drive track from the Murray to the Yanac River north of Nhill. There is a basic camp site at Broken Bucket Reserve 30km north of Yanac. Walkers must be self-sufficient and equipped for survival in desert conditions.

How to get there

Wyperfeld National Park is west of Hopetoun and can be reached via the Henty Highway. The main entrance to this national park is via Yaapeet. Albacutya Park is also reached from Hopetoun via Rainbow and Albacutya. Murray–Sunset National Park is between the Mallee, Sturt and Calder highways. The main park entrance is via Underbool but four-wheel-drive access is possible from all sides.

Murray–Sunset National Park tel: (03) 5029–3253
Wyperfeld National Park tel: (03) 5395–7221

GRAMPIANS (GARIWERD) NATIONAL PARK

The Grampians (Gariwerd) National Park is a rugged sandstone range that emerges dramatically from the surrounding undulating western Victorian agricultural lands. The vistas to the adjacent farmlands are an ever-present reminder of the tensions between wilderness conservation and the conversion of these areas for other purposes.

The Grampian Ranges are oriented north–south and the southern end is only 100km from the sea. As a result the park tends to have a drier north and a wetter south. During inclement weather look for activities or camp sites in the north of the park where the weather is inclined to be kinder.

LEFT *The Grampians (Gariwerd) National Park covers a region where volcanoes once erupted, and the MacKenzie Falls now cascade down an ancient volcanic rock wall.*

BELOW *The road through Halls Gap in the Grampians region provides wonderful access to this area of easy walks, swimming, camping, wilderness treks and rock climbing.*

The area's Aboriginal heritage is ever present. Since 1990 all the park's features have reverted to their Aboriginal names. Often the new official names are a combination of both the Aboriginal and European names, hence the present two-part name. Given the park's largely unspoilt natural beauty, its Aboriginal heritage and spectacular wildflower displays, it is surprising that this park was only created as recently as 1984.

Aboriginal art sites
The Grampians is an area of great Aboriginal cultural significance. Over 80 per cent of Victoria's Aboriginal art sites are here. The Billimina Shelter is perhaps the best known and most well preserved. Located less than 1km from the Buandik picnic area, the art site – depicting initiation themes, kangaroos, emus, and hunters – can be found in an area of rugged cliff lines and rocky overhangs. The climb to the site is steep but highly recommended as the area has a great deal of power and symbolism.

The colours of spring
Spring is undoubtedly the best time to visit the Grampians. Not only is the weather at its best but the mountains are famous for the spring flowering of native plants. More than 1000 species of plant have been recorded in the area, an unusually high number for such a contained region. Twenty species are found only in this park and a third of all Victoria's plant species have been recorded here. In addition to over 100 orchids, other flowering species include wattles, boronia, grevilleas and tea trees.

Most of the wildlife is elusive. Despite the fact that koalas are common, visitors will find that they are very difficult to spot.

Dramatic bushwalks
Bushwalking is the only way to really appreciate the park's

dramatic scenery. Almost 200km of formed walking tracks cross the park. The short walks to Sundial Peak, the Balconies (from Reid Lookout), and MacKenzie Falls are recommended. The pick of the longer walks is the 10-km Wonderland Loop from the Halls Gap camp ground. There are many rough unsealed driving tracks which are suitable only for four-wheel-drive vehicles. After heavy rain these tracks may be closed.

Water sports
There are many places to swim. The best known are at Lake Bellfield, south of Halls Gap; Lake Fyans, just outside the park; and the beaches on the northern shore of Lake Lonsdale. However, for those who swim for the experience, the best spots are the rock pools scattered throughout the park. Many are in very inaccessible places, which only adds to their appeal. Boating on Lake Bellfield is restricted to electric, sail or manual-powered craft, making canoeing a pleasure.

Camping facilities
The Grampians has over a dozen basic camping areas accessible by car. The most scenic and most recommended are Stapylton and Troopers Creek in the northern ranges, Burrunj Range and Kalymna Falls in the centre, and Wannon

Crossing in the south. Bush camping is permitted anywhere in the park except in the Wonderland Range and adjacent to the water reservoirs.

Mount Eccles: volcanic crater
South of the Grampians (Gariwerd) National Park and 42km south of Hamilton is the small but interesting Mount Eccles National Park. The mountain is a volcanic cone which last erupted 7000 years ago – this was also one of Australia's last eruptions. The crater has a deep lake and many well-preserved volcanic features, including lava canals. A nature walk goes around the crater rim and there is a simple camp site with basic facilities.

How to get there

The Grampians are located 260km west of Melbourne in an area bounded by the towns of Hamilton, Horsham and Ararat. Many sealed and unsealed roads travel off the Western, Glenelg and Henty highways. An alternative entrance to the park is from Dunkeld. The main visitor centre is at Halls Gap, which is 26km from Stawell.
Grampians (Gariwerd) National Park tel: (03) 5356–4381
Mount Eccles National Park tel: (03) 5576–1014

DON'T MISS...

ADVENTURE EXPERIENCES
Mount Arapiles west of Horsham is one of Australia's premier climbing crags. There are also a large number of rock climbing venues in the Grampian (Gariwerd) Ranges. The hardest climbs are in the south of the park. All the cliffs are composed of particularly rough-textured sandstone, and some are over 100m high. Regular tours for various levels of experience leave from Halls Creek.

Little Desert National Park is a wilderness desert park which can be accessed only with a four-wheel-drive. It lies between Horsham and the South Australian border, and to the south of the Western Highway. There are many north–south routes through the park.

The best shore-based whale watching venue in Australia is at Logans Beach near Warrnambool. Every winter, calving southern right whales are observed easily from the elevated dune-top platforms that have been erected. Boat trips and diving are also on offer from Warrnambool.
Grampians (Gariwerd) National Park tel: (03) 5356–4381
Little Desert National Park tel: (03) 5389–1204
Base Camp and Beyond (climbing) tel: (03) 5356–4300
Horsham Visitor Centre tel: (03) 5382–1853
Warrnambool Visitor Information tel: (03) 5564–9837

Reid Lookout in the Sierra Range affords extensive views of the Grampians.

OTHER INTERESTING AREAS
The **Great South West Walk** is a comfortable 10-day, marked 200-km trail, centred on Lower Glenelg National Park. This walk winds through tall gum forests, coastal parks and along river gorges, making it a delight for bushwalkers.

Lower Glenelg National Park also contains the impressive 35-km-long and 50-m-deep **Glenelg River Gorge**. This is an ideal location for calm-water canoeing with overnight camps. Canoes are available for hire in Nelson. The limestone **Princess Margaret Rose Caves** are also worth a visit.
Lower Glenelg National Park tel: (08) 8738–4051

VICTORIAN ALPS

Wonnangatta • Bogong • Snowy River

*T*he Alpine National Park is the largest park in Victoria. *Stretching along the Great Dividing Range, it combines a number of previously separate parks – Wonnangatta–Moroka, Bogong, Dartmouth and Cobberas–Tingaringy. The area incorporates a vast 250-km-long mountainous region from Eildon State Park, 50km east of Melbourne, to Kosciuszko National Park in New South Wales.*

All but one of the alpine resorts are outside the national parks and managed by the Alpine Resorts Commission. The facilities at Mount Buffalo are managed by a private operator. There are many options for exploring by canoe or on foot, but the region is best explored by vehicle. The weather can be cold and wet, with snow in summer or winter.

Travel Tips

The closest major airport is at Melbourne. The main access towns are Mansfield, Bright, Corryong, and Omeo. Buses serve the resorts in winter and some organised tours are available from Melbourne. The Hume Highway from Melbourne provides several access points to the ranges' northern side, as does the Princes Highway from the south. During summer the roads from Kosciuszko provide an alternative route. As well as the major routes for conventional vehicles there are many minor and four-wheel-drive roads. Some roads are closed each winter as a result of inclement weather conditions, including the Dargo Road and the Mansfield to Licola Road.

ABOVE *Many of the remote bush tracks through the Alpine National Park are suitable only for four-wheel-drive.*

OPPOSITE *Mount Buffalo's dramatic landscape is well suited to the pursuit of various active outdoor activities.*

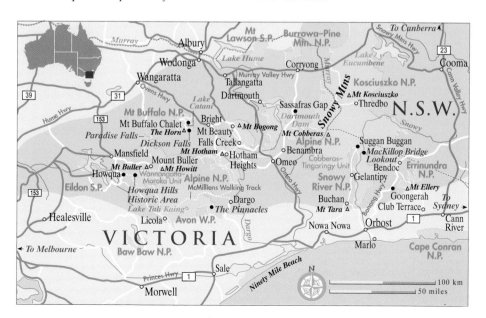

WONNANGATTA

The Wonnangatta region includes a large southern section of the Alpine National Park and many historic areas, smaller national parks, wilderness parks, and state forests. It is well worth exploring and includes the Mount Buller Resort near Mansfield.

The Wonnangatta section also has some of the state's highest peaks. Wonnangatta Valley is an area of gorges, rough tracks and camp sites. A four-wheel-drive vehicle is essential and many roads are closed in winter.

This region is a walker's paradise. There are marked walks at Moroka Gorge, Paradise Falls and The Pinnacles. The Alpine Walking Track crosses the park and this leg of the track is recommended. Starting at Howqua Hills camping area the route climbs to the highest peaks, Mount Howitt and Mount Speculation, and then crosses to Hotham Resort, a distance of around 65km. The Alpine National Park has five basic camp grounds and there is one camp site at Lake Tarli Karng. Resort facilities are available at Mount Buller.

Historic goldmines
Grant Historic Site is an area steeped in mining history and has riverside camp sites at Grant and Howittville. Gold was discovered in the 1860s and thousands of diggers set up temporary towns along the valleys of the Crooked and Wonnangatta rivers. Reminders of those frantic days still remain in the form of ruins, old mines and orchards. Some tracks require a four-wheel-drive vehicle – one spectacular route is the Wombat Spur Track north of Grant Historic Site, linking with the Blue Rag Track and then heading on to Mount Hotham.

Avon River wilderness walks
The Avon Wilderness Park can only be accessed on foot from Licola or along forestry tracks north of Briagolong. There are no facilities in the park. Wilderness walking along the Avon River is possible with connecting routes to the McWilliams Walking Track in the Alpine National Park.

Mount Buffalo's granite cliffs
The Horn, a massive granite tor, dominates the high plateau that forms Mount Buffalo National Park. This vast highland is circled by soaring cliffs, some reaching over 400m in height. The explorers Hume and Hovell gave the area its name since, from a distance, they thought the plateau resembled a buffalo.

Like the high country all along the Great Dividing Range, the crevices of the granite peaks are the summer home of bogong moths. This once provided a reason for Aborigines to visit the plateau for feasting and, with the abundance of food, made it possible for large numbers of people to gather for special ceremonies.

At the turn of the century the plateau became a park and The Chalet, a spacious old-style hotel, was built in the grand tradition of the day.

Mount Buffalo is a naturalist's and an adventurer's playground. Almost 100km of walking tracks can be explored in the summer months and the snow gums and alpine flowers are the great attraction. Sub-alpine heaths cover the plateau and gum forests extend around its edge. Marked walks range from short strolls to full-day hikes.

The Gorge Track is one of the longer and most popular walks and extends to the edge of the plateau at Eagle Point

and Dickson Falls. A circuit walk across 10km of the plateau is recommended. Pulpit Rock, near to The Chalet and creating an overhang at the cliff edge, provides a wonderful panorama over the Ovens Valley.

Sporting activities

Canoeing and swimming on Lake Catani are refreshing activities on warm days. In summer, horse riding is permitted in the park. Horses can be hired at The Chalet.

Mount Buffalo is one of the state's best-known rock climbing venues and hang-gliders often launch from the cliff-tops. In the winter Mount Buffalo offers cross-country and down-hill skiing.

Accommodation and facilities

A visitor centre is located near the camp ground at the lake. Facilities are excellent and include showers. Accommodation is available year-round in the park. Access from the lowland valley at Bright is via a steep but sealed road which is also open year-round.

How to get there

From Wangaratta, travel via the Ovens Highway and from Mansfield via the Maroondah Highway. Further south is Avon Wilderness Park with road access from Licola, and Grant Historic Site with access from Dargo.
Bright NR and Environment tel: (03) 5755–1577

BOGONG

Mount Bogong, the highest peak in Victoria, dominates an alpine landscape carpeted with wildflowers in the summer and blanketed with snow in the winter. Bushwalking and cross-country skiing are the best ways for the adventurous to explore the remote sections of this alpine wilderness. For many visitors, however, it is the mountainous landscape's sheer beauty, and the short, quiet, secluded walks that appeal.

The cold-climate vegetation includes rare alpine bogs, tussock grasslands and low, thick heaths. On the lower slopes a variety of gum forest and woodland clings to the mountain slopes.

A rare pygmy possum

Mount Hotham was the site of an extraordinary find that ignited scientists' interest around the globe. Fossil records from the Wombeyan Caves in New South Wales revealed the existence of an unusual type of tiny possum. It was assumed to have been extinct for thousands of years but in 1966 a live specimen of the Mountain Pygmy Possum turned up in a pile of ski gear in a mountain hut.

Extraordinarily rare and endangered, the possum is now known to survive only in a small area around Mount Hotham and a similar small area around Mount Kosciuszko. It is active under the snow in winter and is the world's only alpine marsupial.

WILLY WAGTAIL

The Willy Wagtail is one of Australia's most ubiquitous birds. Whether you are camping in a gorge in the Kimberleys, watching Uluru's sunset or taking a photo of the Opera House from Sydney's Royal Botanic Gardens, there is almost always a chirpy little wagtail about. Tasmania and the tip of Cape York are the only spots where you are unlikely to see one. Australia has few birds that are at home in the high alpine country but the Willy Wagtail is an exception. Feeding on a variety of insects, worms and spiders this bird can usually find something to eat even amongst the thawing snowfields.

Willy Wagtails are black on the head, back and tail and white on the throat, chest and undertail. The black head has a slight white eyebrow. Their call is a sweet chattering sound sometimes likened to the phrase 'sweet pretty creature', and they are often heard calling at night.

Wagtails are so-named as they constantly swing their tail from left to right. In a perpetual state of motion, they dart restlessly out from a low tree perch, grab an insect on the wing and swoop back to their perch to consume the prey. The birds frequently use domestic animals or humans to help them in their search for food. Sheep and cattle stir up insects as they graze and wagtails perched near the animals catch the insects as they are disturbed. Sometimes cows or sheep even become a convenient perch. People moving through the bush can perform the same function as stock. Aborigines at Uluru have a story claiming that Willy Wagtails are the camp gossips. As the birds constantly move back and forward between the groups of people in camp, it is claimed that they listen and chatter to each human group in turn.

LEFT *Tall eucalypt forests near Falls Creek are typical of much of the vegetation that cloaks the Great Dividing Range from Victoria to north Queensland.*

BELOW *Lake Hume on the upper Murray River is a large, permanent waterway, ideal for boating and wildlife observation.*

Area. West of Omeo is the Victoria Falls Historic Area with waterfalls and a camping ground. Both these sites, rich in reminders of a gold-seeking past, are worth exploring.

Four-wheel-drive adventure trails

Running from Omeo to Thredbo, a distance of 153km is a four-wheel-drive adventure trail linking Kosciuszko with the Victorian Alps. The route from Omeo winds through Benambra to Sassafras Gap, Wheelers Creek Hut, Tom Groggin and finally Thredbo. Many sections of the road are tricky and the Murray River ford crossing is at times difficult. There are several remote camping spots and stunning views of the Snowy Mountains. This trip is best in spring and summer. Preparations should be thorough, and should include a supply of good maps and the use of a reliable vehicle.

State parks in the upper Murray River

The upper Murray River Valley between Wodonga and Cooryong has a number of parks which are a bit off the beaten track but worth a visit. There are no visitor centres but there is an up-to-date park information board beside the Murray Valley Highway 15km east of Tallangatta.

Newly declared Mount Granya State Park, between the arms of Lake Hume, has basic camping facilities. Lawson State Park has picnic areas and lookout tracks. Burrowa Pine National Park has marked nature trails and two basic camping areas. The main one is at Bluff Creek.

Bluff Creek with its granite peaks and many waterfalls is the pick of the upper Murray parks. A wilderness walk to the top of Pine Mountain provides a panorama of the Snowy Mountains to the east and the Murray River to the north and west. The northern area of these parks contains stretches of the Murray which are excellent for canoeing, with the most accessible parts lying downstream of Biggara.

Lofty walking trails

There are many marked walking trails, especially from the Alpine Tourist and Bogong High Plains roads. The Alpine Walking Track meanders across the spectacular high plains. The start can be reached 4km east of Falls Creek.

Accommodation and camping facilities

For those wishing to spend a few nights in the region, the Bogong section of the Alpine National Park has three main camping areas with basic facilities. These are located at Mountain Creek near Mount Beauty and on the Bogong High Plains Road at Langford Gap and Raspberry Hill. There are many other camping areas for walkers. On the Alpine Tourist Road, east of Mount Hotham, the JB Plain camping area has modest facilities. The Dartmouth section has five camping areas with basic facilities. Several more remote camp sites at Dart Arm and Eustaces are on four-wheel-drive tracks with access from the Benambra to Cooryong Road. Resorts are located at Mount Hotham and Falls Creek.

Historical lake shores

The northern Dartmouth section of the park is at a lower altitude and activities focus on the lake's forested shores. East of Falls Creek on the Omeo Highway is Mount Willis Historic

How to get there

The Bogong region includes the Mount Hotham and Falls Creek resorts, and Bogong High Plains in Alpine National Park. The main access by vehicle is from Bright on the Ovens Highway. In summer you can also reach the Bogong from Dargo. The three sub-alpine parks between Wodonga and Cooryong can be reached from the Murray Valley Highway.
Bright NR and Environment tel: (03) 5755–1577
Cooryong tel: (03) 5776–1655

Camping and picnic walking areas are located at Jacksons Crossing and near Raymond Falls, with the best access from the eastern side of the river. These sections of the river flow through temperate rainforests, which to some resemble the thicker tropical forests found elsewhere in the world. Sections of this river valley are called New Guinea and the Bengal Jungle.

Buchan limestone caves
The Buchan area is well known for its limestone caves, some of which are open for guided tours. A few of the closed caves have large bat roosts and others contain rare Aboriginal paintings and occupation sites. These caves have archaeological material similar to that found in caves on the Nullarbor Plain. Camping facilities are available at the Buchan Caves Reserve and marked walking trails leave from the picnic area.

SNOWY RIVER

The Snowy River, subject of Australian bush legends, starts as a brook at Mount Kosciuszko in New South Wales and cuts great valleys through the geologically young Snowy Mountain Ranges as it sweeps south into Victoria. The Snowy River National Park is noted for its magnificent riverine scenery, deep gorges and wild walking country.

North of the river
McKillop Bridge, which crosses the Snowy River in the north of the park, has a delightful camping area with basic facilities. Nearby walking trails and a picnic area are popular, especially in the summer months when swimming in the numerous rock pools is a delight. Above the Snowy River at Little River Lookout are marked walking trails. Further south, four-wheel-drive tracks to the lower river from the Mount Tabby–Orbost Road provide access to some of the best canoeing sections of the river.

Mount Cobberas
To the north of the Snowy Mountains National Park is the Mount Cobberas section of the Alpine National Park. The Gelantipy–Benambra Road cuts through this wilderness. Basic camping facilities are provided along the route at Native Dog Flat, which is the end of the Victorian section of the Alpine Walking Track. Other camping grounds are located at Willis, close to the Victoria–New South Wales border and Limestone Creek.

West of the Snowy River
West of the Snowy River National Park and on either side of the Omeo Highway is an extensive area of state forests dotted with small reserves, beautiful waterfalls and historic mining areas. There are many camp sites, lookouts and hundreds of kilometres of rough unsealed roads. These areas are well worth investigating with the aid of detailed up-to-date maps.

Errinundra: temperate rainforest

A wild remote park, Errinundra is located east of the Snowy River National Park. Protected within its confines are the largest stands of cool temperate rainforest to be found in Victoria. There are a number of walking trails at the foot of Mount Ellery leading to several fine lookouts.

The park can be reached from the Bonang Highway near the Bendoc Road turn-off or via an additional access road from Bendoc Road. Both these roads join at the park and then run 53km south to Club Terrace and the Princes Highway. There are two basic camping areas, one a delightful spot near Goongerah on the Brodribb River, the other 31km north of Club Terrace. North of the park on the banks of the Delegate River and south of Bendoc is another basic camp area which lies within the state forest.

Retracing botanist Baldwin Spencer's steps

In 1889, one of Australia's most famous botanists, Baldwin Spencer, undertook a difficult expedition from the coast near Orbost into what is now the Errinundra National Park, returning to Orbost via Lind National Park and the coastal parks at Cape Conran and Marlo. Today there is an excellent driving trail that retraces his steps. A park map, available at park offices in Orbost, Bendoc, Cape Conran and the store in Club Terrace, details the 262-km Baldwin Spencer Trail, which can be completed in a day. With stops and overnight camps the trail can be a good two- or three-day trip. There are great overnight cabins available at Cape Conran where the full botanical richness of the region, from alpine forest to coastal sand palms, can be experienced. The coastal camps provide an opportunity for a swim and some beachcombing at the end of the trek.

How to get there

The main access is from the Princes Highway at Nowa Nowa via Buchan Road to Suggan Buggan, or from Orbost via the Bonang Highway to Bonang. Access is also via Barry Way to Suggan Buggan from Jindabyne in New South Wales or via Bendoc from Bombala in New South Wales.

Orbost NR and Environment tel: (03) 5161–1222
Cape Conran cabins tel: (03) 5154–8438

DON'T MISS...

ADVENTURE EXPERIENCES

The Alpine Walking Track, 765km from Walhalla, on the edge of Mount Baw Baw National Park, to Canberra, features spectacular high-country scenery. It takes about three to four weeks to complete and hikers need to be completely self-sufficient. Sections of the track are accessible by vehicle and the walk can be done in short sections. Maps are available at national park offices and the Melbourne Map Centre.

Snowy, Mitta Mitta and other eastern rivers are suitable for whitewater canoeing expeditions organised year-round by adventure companies in Melbourne.

Rock climbing at Mount Buffalo is renowned as some of the best in southern Australia. Apart from huge granite tors and cliffs, there is an internationally rated climb on the north wall of The Gorge.

Mount Buffalo is one of the world's best hang-gliding sites and was used for the 1986 World Championships. Launch sites include Bents Lookout.

Throughout the high country there are thousands of kilometres of four-wheel-drive tracks which explore parks and state forests. Detailed park and forestry maps can be obtained from the NR (Natural Resources) and Environment Department in Melbourne or from a regional office.

Wangaratta NR and Environment tel: (03) 5721–5022
Peregrine Tours tel: (03) 9663–8611
Climb Australia tel: (03) 9387–9620

The Horn at Mount Buffalo provides a scenic viewing platform.

OTHER INTERESTING AREAS

Mount Baw Baw National Park is a small park on the southern edge of the Great Dividing Range. Located only 200km east of Melbourne the park offers a large range of cross-country skiing, camping facilities and walking options in a relatively small but very diverse area.

Mount Baw Baw National Park tel: (03) 5174–6166

GIPPSLAND

Croajingolong • The Lakes •

Wilsons Promontory

The Gippsland encompasses the Australian mainland's most southerly point, a major inland waterway and a magnificent coastline of unspoilt beaches and headlands. It is easy to link the eastern area of Victoria with a tour of New South Wales's high country. In addition to the parks detailed here, there are a number of smaller parks and state forests with scenic areas and good facilities. The advantage is that these areas often attract fewer people than the better-known spots.

Travel Tips

The nearest major airport is Melbourne with regional airfields at Bairnsdale and Eden in New South Wales. Interstate coaches serve the region but public transport is infrequent. Organised tours are available so check with tourist centres for details of any new operations.

The Gippsland is well serviced with good roads to major scenic places such as lookouts, lakes and beaches. The Princes and South Gippsland highways link Melbourne with Wilsons Promontory. The Princes Highway also links the Lakes, Croajingolong and Mallacoota before heading on to Canberra and Sydney. Most conventional vehicles are suitable with four-wheel-drive necessary only in state forests and perhaps at Croajingolong.

This area is situated between the country's two most populous cities (Sydney and Melbourne), so try to avoid school holiday periods, especially December and January. Winters are cold and wet. Summers can be hot, but there is no shortage of fresh drinking water, and all other supplies are readily available.

ABOVE *Squeaky Beach on the western side of Wilsons Promontory is easily accessed and is an ideal location at which to relax after a day's walking to the nearby peaks of mounts Bishop and Oberon.*

OPPOSITE *The Genoa River flows into Mallacoota Inlet, a delightful waterway which provides secluded boat access to many parts of Croajingolong National Park. The park is situated in Victoria's eastern corner.*

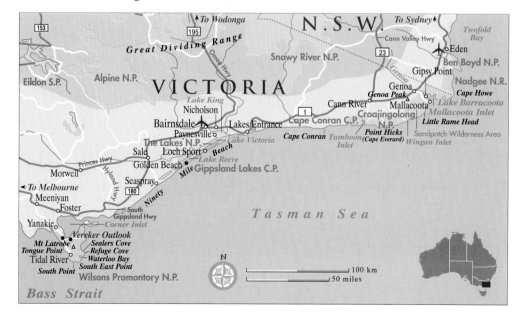

174

CROAJINGOLONG NATIONAL PARK

Croajingolong is characterised by granite headlands, long white beaches and tall wet forests clinging to a storm-drenched coast 100km long. Located on the highway between Australia's two largest cities, it is surprising that a sense of coastal wilderness can still be found so easily amongst so much urbanisation. The area has a special historical European significance as Point Hicks was named in 1770 after one of Captain James Cook's crew members, the first one to sight the continent on the *Endeavour* expedition.

Croajingolong National Park's remoteness is enhanced by state forests and Cape Conran Coastal Park to the west, while Nadgee Nature Reserve and Ben Boyd National Park in New South Wales conserve another 50km of wild coastline to the north. All these parks help to protect the Croajingolong from the urban and agricultural encroachment which is typical all along the east coast of Australia.

Pockets of subtropical rainforest can be discovered in the deepest, most protected gullies, but tall gum forests typically dominate the park's interior. The wind-buffeted headlands and coastal plains are covered in heathland plants that colour the landscape with blooms in spring. Water dragon lizards, over 1m in length, live along the freshwater creeks. Many birds are found in the forests but it is perhaps the shore birds that leave the strongest impression. Sea eagles scouring the ocean edge and penguins yapping in the surf are characteristic sights and sounds of the park.

Overnight coastal walks

The park has a variety of overnight walking experiences. The best option is to take the coastal walk from Wingan Inlet to Mallacoota. This ever-changing route passes through the Sandpatch Wilderness and follows the coastline along the path of the old coast road.

Wide white beaches and vegetated headlands beckon the walker onto the next section. The views from the headlands at Sandpatch Point and Little Rame Head are well worth the detour, but the base of these cliffs is difficult to negotiate so it is best to stay on the inland route.

Croajingolong's 10-day trail

Those with time should take the 150-km coastal walk from Cape Conran to Eden in New South Wales. This encompasses the whole of the Croajingolong coastline and is one of the country's best and most enjoyable coastal walks. Most of the 10- to 12-day walk is spent on beaches and rocky foreshores. There are plenty of camp sites and fresh water is available from creeks.

Nature day-walks

The Dunes and Lighthouse walks at Point Hicks are two of many short, marked nature day-walks. Another, leading to the top of Genoa Peak, the highest point in the park, includes a steep climb, with steel ladders in some sections. The walk starts at the end of a track 5km south of Genoa.

A freshwater drink from Lake Barracoota in the park's Cape Howe wilderness area is worth the day's walk. This walking trail leaves the Lake View Track on the northern side of Mallacoota Inlet where 30-m-high sand dunes separate the lake from the sea.

Canoeing on the lakes

Quiet inlets perfect for canoeing are another feature of the region. Croajingolong surrounds Mallacoota Inlet, which has a series of interconnecting small lakes and allows the lower reaches of the Genoa and Wallagaraugh rivers to be explored. Genoa, Gipsy Point and Mallacoota are the easiest launching places, while Tamboon Inlet is also ideal for lake and estuary canoeing. Many areas around Mallacoota are particularly suitable for mountain bike riding. Bush tracks in the parks and forest provide access to lakes, creeks and beaches.

Camping facilities

Both Mallacoota and Cann River have basic camping areas near the visitor centres. Tracks from the highway lead to camping grounds at Swan Lake, Tamboon Inlet, Point Hicks, Wingan Inlet and Shipwreck Creek. Popular camping sites are booked in advance for the Christmas and Easter holidays.

Four-wheel-drive vehicles are required on some access tracks, especially after frequent rains. In particular, the track from Point Hicks to Wingan Inlet is four-wheel-drive only.

How to get there

Located halfway between Sydney and Melbourne and south of the Princes Highway, the Croajingolong region constitutes an easy drive. Hop on an interstate coach or bus tour from either city. Conventional vehicles are usually satisfactory to gain access to this national park.

A four-wheel-drive is useful in wet weather and on some forestry tracks. There are visitor centres at Mallacoota and Cann River with a service centre at Mallacoota.
Croajingolong National Park
tel: (03) 5158–6351

KOALA

Despite an international reputation as an endearing ambassador for the country, koalas can in fact be pugnacious to one another and to human handlers. Their long powerful claws are designed to enable them to climb smooth gum tree-trunks but are equally adept at digging deep into a careless handler's hand.

Prior to European settlement, Aborigines and dingoes preyed on koalas, which were then thinly distributed across the eastern third of the country. As Aboriginal hunting declined and dingoes were controlled, koala numbers increased. At the end of last century there was a large trade in koala skins. As large areas of forested land were cleared, koala numbers again declined. Today, colonies of these creatures can be found scattered throughout their previous range, although many of the now isolated colonies are at risk. Loss of habitat is a major problem while other colonies suffer through over-population since there are no natural control measures. These koalas now die only from disease, food shortages or old age.

It is curious that koalas are Australia's only tree-dwelling mammal with no tail. Like other marsupials they have a pouch in which to rear the young, however the koala's pouch opens backwards. The lack of a tail and the rear-opening pouch suggest that the koala evolved from a ground-dwelling animal such as the wombat, yet a close link has not yet been established.

Koalas are very particular about their diet. They prefer to eat only the leaves of certain trees and their preferences may vary with the time of year or locality. Most of the time, koalas eat only the leaves of a few species of gum tree such as river red and manna gums. Koalas do occasionally eat the leaves from a variety of other plants such as wattle trees. Because of the high water content of the leaves, koalas rarely need to drink.

THE LAKES

Between the towns of Seaspray and Lakes Entrance, the Tasman Sea washes onto the shores of Ninety Mile Beach. This long shoreline is squeezed between the ocean and the four main Gippsland Lakes, and comprises several long strips of land and islands that make up a coastal wilderness and wildlife paradise. Immediately behind the beach is the long finger-shaped Lake Reeve. A wider peninsula of sand dunes, up to 40m high, separates this lake from the three larger, more rounded lakes further inland. Various sections of these two sandy peninsulas form the Gippsland Lakes Coastal Park and The Lakes National Park.

Lakes Entrance is an artificial ocean canal, dug in 1889 to connect the Gippsland Lakes to the sea. Previously the lakes had been sealed off from the ocean by sand dunes and had contained fresh water. After the canal was dug the water levels in the lakes dropped and sea water entered the system. Today the lakes are saline or brackish.

Coastal vegetation
The sand spits that make up the parks are covered with fragile dunes and sparse coastal vegetation. Salt marshes fringe the lakes' edges. Where underground fresh water is accessible, woodland dominated by banksias and gum trees clings to the dunes. Low shrubs and bracken cover the ground. These coastal forests protect a number of very rare heath plants, including orchids. Grey kangaroos and swamp wallabies find their way onto the wooded sand spits.

Wildlife research and bird studies
Over 200 bird species have been recorded in the 2000-ha national park. Shorebirds, waterfowl, parrots, honeyeaters, king-fishers, owls and eagles are all present. The proximity of ocean, lake, salt marsh, woodland and heath partially explains this extraordinary bird diversity. The area is well studied and on Rotamah Island there is a Bird Observatory operated by the Royal Australasian Ornithological Union. Resident naturalists run wildlife research programs and environmental courses, which may last for up to a week. Many courses on bird study are offered but other courses may cover orchids, wildlife photography, woodland mammals or plant pollination. Accommodation is

available and visitors can participate in formal courses or research projects. A very modest fee is requested as well as help with domestic duties around the observatory. A boat from Paynesville transports visitors to the island. For those with an interest in wildlife, a few nights at the observatory is highly recommended.

Nature walks at the lakes

Loch Spot is at the entrance to the national park. The visitor centre and picnic area are located nearby at Dolomite Swamp. All the walks are short since the whole park is only 12km long. Self-guided nature walks loop to the Lookout Tower and Pelican Point. A circular park road runs close to the peninsula edge and there is a spur track to a jetty and picnic area at Point Wilson. Several sandy loop tracks explore the swamps and heaths behind Point Wilson.

Footbridges cross Lake Reeve, which is little more than a canal at this point, linking Rotamah Island to Ninety Mile Beach. This dramatic region with its windswept dunes has many short interconnecting walking trails and some elevated points from which to view the lakes.

Exploring by water

Canoeing and power boating are popular ways to explore the parks and lakes. Jetties are provided at many points, with some camping areas accessible only by water. Canoes are an excellent way to observe the wildlife, however the lakes are subject to sudden coastal squalls and dangerous surface conditions can develop quickly.

RIGHT *Deep in the gullies of the Strzelecki Range, tracks have been constructed so that the old rainforests of the Bulga National Park can be explored with minimal harm to the environment.*

BELOW *Lakes Entrance is the central town from where boats and houseboats can be hired to explore the vast network of Gippsland's coastal waterways.*

Camping facilities

The Lakes National Park has a camp site with basic facilities on Rotamah Island with access only by boat. Another camp site is at Emu Bight. The coastal park has a number of camping facilities. At Paradise Beach north of Golden Beach is a camp site with basic facilities. Another is located at Bunga Arm in the park's north, with access only by boat. Between Golden Beach and Seaspray, camping is permitted behind the beach dunes but no facilities are provided. South of Loch Sport at Red Bluff, camping is also permitted, but again there are no facilities.

How to get there

Located 320km east of Melbourne, road access to The Lakes National Park is via Princes Highway to Sale and then 54km to Loch Sport. Gippsland Lakes Coastal Park's Golden Beach is also reached 40km from Sale. To get to both areas by boat, board at Paynesville and Hollands Landing and head for Lake Victoria or Lake King.
The Lakes National Park Phone tel: (03) 5146–0278

WILSONS PROMONTORY

Mountain peaks, steep granite headlands and desolate white sand beaches are the hallmarks of the 'Prom'. Wilsons Promontory National Park encompasses the whole of the peninsula and 13 adjacent islands. Most of the rainfall at Wilsons Promontory is during winter. It is often bitterly cold and windy. The best times to visit are in November or between March and April as the region is popular during the summer holidays.

The exposed, rounded granite boulders and cliffs of the area are the visible parts of deep lava beds over 300 million years old. These lava flows once formed a high range that was part of a continuous chain of mainland ranges. Millions of years ago, rises in sea level made what is now Wilsons Promontory a Bass Strait island. Recent sand accumulations at Yanakie reconnected the island to the mainland. South Point at the peninsula tip is the most southerly place on the Australian mainland. Roaring Meg camp site is located near this spot.

Sheltered forests

This mountainous wedge of land protrudes into Bass Strait and bears the brunt of Southern Ocean storms – the western side is drenched with cold rains. On the sheltered eastern side of mounts Bishop and Latrobe, however, temperate rainforests occur deep in the park gullies. Tropical lilly pillys, Antarctic beech and aerial gardens of tree ferns grow here. Some huge lilly pillys with trunks in excess of 6m in circumference were recorded behind Sealers Cove. More

typically the park's vegetation consists of dry gum forests, heathland, coastal scrub and grassland. Along the shore is a variety of marine habitats, mangroves and extensive mudflats.

Aborigine shell middens

An interesting range of wildlife occurs in the park, from koalas and wombats to black cockatoos. The moist park soils are home to a curious burrowing yabbie, an aquatic creature normally found in ponds and rivers.

Evidence of human activity goes back at least 6500 years. The promontory's western shore is a huge Aboriginal site. Piles of shells from countless meals make up the middens along the foreshore. With European arrival, human activity turned to whaling, sealing, tin mining and timber cutting. A lighthouse was built on South East Point in 1859, while parts of the promontory were first declared a national park in 1905.

Walking and swimming on the Promontory

About 100km of walking trails cross the park, many of them for short day-walks. Quite near the park's visitor centre, a short steep track climbs to the summit of Mount Oberon. From here a wide panorama can be viewed over Norman Bay, Anser Islands and the west of the park.

ABOVE *From Whisky Bay sea kayaks can be launched so that Norman Island, just offshore, can be explored.*

The Lillypilly Nature Walk at the foot of Mount Bishop is a delightful 5-km trail revealing specimens of all the park's main plant communities. For a full-day's walk the climb to the summit could be added. Millers Landing walk is a 3-km-loop walk from the end of Five Mile Road. A short spur track leads down to the mangrove-lined water's edge of Corner Inlet. A modest view is possible from Vereker Outlook on the return walk.

The most easily accessed swimming beaches are along the western shore off the Wilsons Promontory Road. There are short tracks that lead down to beaches at Whisky, Picnic and Darby bays.

Overnight trekking

Highly recommended for their scenic beauty and isolation, are overnight hikes into the park's remote corners. The most notable areas are in the south and east. One good plan is a quick two-day walk, camping overnight at Refuge Cove. For a longer, more leisurely trip, a three-day circuit walk, camping at Sealers Cove and Little Waterloo Bay, allows time for a swim at each of the main southern beaches. The distance covered on this walk is about 40km.

Accommodation and camping facilities

The visitor centre and the only car-based camping sites are at Tidal River. Generally, facilities are extensive and include lodges, cabins and shops. Scattered throughout the park are about a dozen walkers' camp sites. Limited camping and walking permits are issued at the park visitor centre. Sometimes demand for permits exceeds the capacity of the camp sites, so book ahead.

How to get there

Wilsons Promontory National Park is located 230km southeast of Melbourne. To get there, take the South Gippsland Highway. At Meeniyan or Foster, 170km from Melbourne, turn south onto Wilsons Promontory Road. There are sealed roads into the park.

The main centre for the 'Prom' is at Tidal River, 32km inside the park. Tours for speciality adventure activities such as sea kayaking are sometimes arranged by clubs and tour organisers to Wilsons Promontory. Check with your travel agent for the latest information.

Wilsons Promontory National Park tel: (03) 5680–8538

DON'T MISS…

ADVENTURE EXPERIENCES

The excitement of swimming or diving around fur seals at The Skerries, a wild place that forms part of the Croajingolong National Park, is hard to beat. However be warned: people swimming amongst seals can be attacked by white pointer sharks in southern Australian waters.

Wilderness rock-climbing areas exist throughout the far western Alps, north of Cann River. Sea kayaking around Wilsons Promontory is highly recommended; there are one- to 10-day trips. Tours are available – contact clubs in New South Wales and Victoria.

White-water canoeing on the Snowy River is possible through organised tours or as part of a club or a private trip. Wilderness walking in Nadgee Nature Reserve in New South Wales, especially to Cape Howe and Disaster Bay, is not to be missed. Another walking highlight is the trail through the Genoa River Gorge in Coopracambra National Park.

Tourism Victoria tel: (03) 9790–2121
Spindrift Kayaking tel: (03) 5966–5110
River Runners tel: (06) 6288–5610
Climb Australia tel: (03) 9387–9620
Bairnsdale Visitor Centre tel: (03) 5152–3444
Mallacoota Visitor Centre tel: (03) 5144–1108
Eden NSW National Park and Wildlife Service tel: (02) 6496–1434

Rock climbing can be arranged through clubs or tour organisers.

OTHER INTERESTING AREAS

West of **Bairnsdale** are many state forests with a variety of facilities. If you are spending time in western Victoria, it's worth obtaining Gippsland state forest maps (in Melbourne or Bairnsdale). **Orbost** has a major rainforest information centre.

Rotamah Bird Observatory offers accommodation and wildlife courses and is highly recommended.

Bairnsdale Conservation and Natural Resources tel: (03) 5152–0400
Orbost Rainforest Centre tel: (03) 5161–1375
Rotamah Bird Observatory tel: (03) 5156–6398

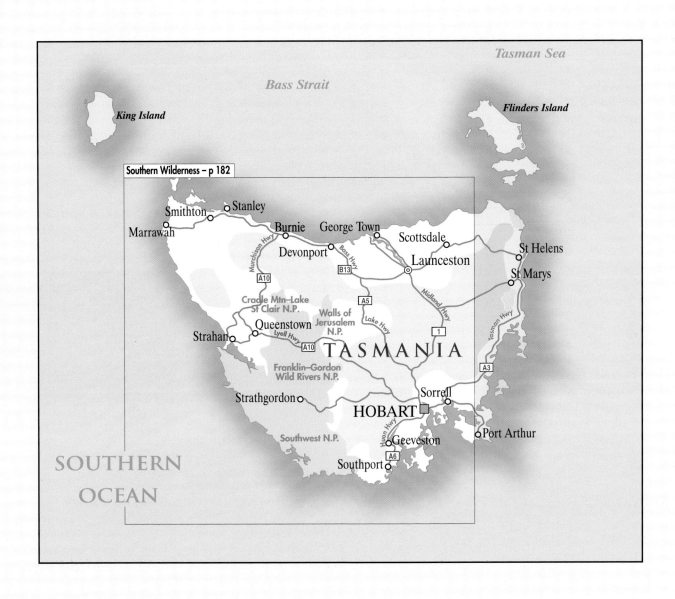

Tasman Sea

Bass Strait

King Island

Flinders Island

Southern Wilderness – p 182

Smithton
Stanley
Marrawah
Burnie
George Town
Scottsdale
Devonport
St Helens
Launceston
St Marys

Murchison Hwy
A10
Bass Hwy
B13
Midland Hwy

Cradle Mtn–Lake
St Clair N.P.
Walls of
Jerusalem
N.P.
A5
Lake Hwy
Tasman Hwy

Queenstown
1
Strahan
Lyell Hwy
A10
TASMANIA
A3

Franklin–Gordon
Wild Rivers N.P.
Sorrell

Strathgordon
HOBART
Port Arthur

Southwest N.P.
Huon Hwy
Geeveston

SOUTHERN
Southport
A6

OCEAN

TASMANIA

SOUTHERN WILDERNESS

Cradle Mountain • Lake Pedder • Huon

*T*asmania has a vast World Heritage wilderness region. There are six major national parks, edged by state forests and various conservation zones. The area is very popular in summer, so avoid December and January. Although it is a great place to tour by car, the best way to experience Tasmania's natural wilds is on foot, on water or from the air. Australia's island state is recognised around the world as one of the world's great multiple-day walking and rafting wildernesses.

Travel Tips

The nearest airports are located at Hobart and Launceston. Many organised bus, walking, caving, cycling and rafting tours depart from these two towns. Highly recommended are the scenic flights from Hobart or Strahan, and flights to the remote south-west walks. Tasmania can be very cold and foggy, and can snow in both summer or winter. It is always wet and visitors should prepare both physically and mentally for the conditons.

Overnight ferries for passengers and cars sail from Melbourne to Devonport. Conventional vehicles will get you to most parks although some forestry areas need a four-wheel-drive. Tasmania is well serviced with roads to major scenic places. Road access from Hobart is via Huon, the Gordon River or the Lyell Highway. From Launceston, travel via the Murchison Highway or Cradle Mountain Road.

PREVIOUS PAGE *Dove Lake creates a serene vista in the rugged Cradle Mountain region.*

ABOVE RIGHT *Near Strahan, seaplanes and ferries are considered to be essential transport.*

OPPOSITE TOP *Cradle Mountain offers one of the world's greatest wilderness treks.*

OPPOSITE BOTTOM *Bennett's wallaby makes its home on Cradle Mountain.*

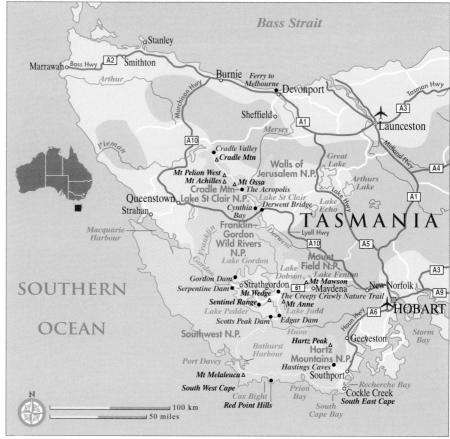

CRADLE MOUNTAIN

This region contains some of the wildest mountain and river landscapes in Australia. It includes the Cradle Mountain–Lake St Clair and Walls of Jerusalem national parks and the northern end of the Franklin–Gordon Wild Rivers National Park. The Cradle Mountain region also includes parts of western Tasmanian accessible from Devonport and from the Lyell Highway.

Greek-inspired Mount Ossa

Mount Ossa, a craggy dolerite peak and Tasmania's highest, is one of many high points in Cradle Mountain–Lake St Clair National Park. Its name is sourced from ancient Greek and means 'a lookout post'. Many features in the region possess classical names, including mounts Pelion West and East (after a mountain in Greece that was home to the centaurs), The Acropolis, Mount Achilles and Mount Olympus.

Forged by glaciers

Unlike much of the ancient Australian mainland, the rugged forms of Cradle Mountain–Lake St Clair evoke reflections of another place and time but are geologically young. The high plateau was created as recently as 20 000 years ago during the last ice age. The sharp peaks and cliffs are the result of ice mountains shearing away at the plateau, and a myriad alpine lakes today occupy the hollows left by the retreating glaciers.

The national park takes its two-part name from Cradle Mountain, a strikingly shaped feature that rises to 1545m, and Lake St Clair, a deep glacial lake. They are separated by a

40-km-high glacial plateau. The Overland Track that winds between them across the mountain moorlands has become Australia's most famous and popular walking adventure and the image of Cradle Mountain reflected in the waters of Lake Dove is an icon of the Australian wilderness.

The Overland Track

From Cradle Valley, south of the main visitor centre, the track heads south for 80km and finishes at Cynthia Bay on the southern end of Lake St Clair, near the Derwent Bridge.

Normally the walk takes about five to six days and huts are positioned along the way at appropriate locations. Other than bush camping at the walk's well-equipped camp grounds or staying in the cabins provided at Cradle Valley and Cynthia Bay, luxury accommodation and cabins are available at Cradle Mountain Lodge on the northern edge of the park. The popularity of this route, however, means that huts are often full and tents are essential back-up equipment. Escorted walking tours can be arranged and private huts are provided for these groups.

The Overland Track and others that connect with it traverse an extremely varied landscape of heathland, woodland and cool temperate rainforest. King Billy pines, Antarctic beech and the deciduous fagus beech are a few of the distinctive trees of this high plateau. Possums and wallabies, looking for food handouts, are frequently encountered by bushwalkers.

Franklin–Gordon Wild Rivers

To the west of the Derwent Bridge the Lyell Highway heads south-west and enters the northern end of the famous Franklin–Gordon Wild Rivers National Park. Back-country walks and bush camping are possible from several points along the highway. A trail of around 20km starting south of the highway (and about 40km from Derwent Bridge) climbs to Frenchmans Cap, the source of the Franklin River. The easiest access to the park, however, is from the water at Strahan, located at the end of the Lyell Highway.

Strahan: exploring the waterways

At Strahan rafting trips, cruises and seaplanes allow visitors to explore the Macquarie Harbour and lower reaches of the Gordon and Franklin rivers. In the early 1980s these impressive stretches of river were the scene of Australia's most significant conservation battles. Centred on Warners Landing, protesters successfully stopped a major hydro-dam project that would have flooded both the Gordon and Franklin rivers. Thousand-year-old, giant Huon pines were also saved in the process.

The spectacular river gorges are now protected. The 1981 victory was a major turning point in the conservation of the Tasmanian wilderness and a catalyst for similar actions in other parts of Australia throughout the 1980s. The Franklin–Gordon Wild Rivers National Park was declared in 1981 and the 1 380 000-ha Tasmanian World Heritage area in 1989.

How to get there

Cradle Mountain National Park is reached by vehicle from Devonport through Sheffield, from Launceston through Deloraine and Sheffield, or from Hobart via the Lyell Highway to Derwent Bridge. There are coaches from Launceston and Devonport. The journey from Hobart to Strahan, which is four hours by vehicle, allows access to one point on the lower Franklin River.

Cradle Mountain National Park tel: (03) 6492–1133
Cabins tel: (03) 6289–1137

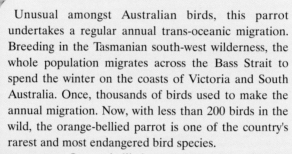

ORANGE-BELLIED PARROT

Unusual amongst Australian birds, this parrot undertakes a regular annual trans-oceanic migration. Breeding in the Tasmanian south-west wilderness, the whole population migrates across the Bass Strait to spend the winter on the coasts of Victoria and South Australia. Once, thousands of birds used to make the annual migration. Now, with less than 200 birds in the wild, the orange-bellied parrot is one of the country's rarest and most endangered bird species.

Orange-bellied parrots are about the size of a large budgerigar and are delicately plumaged. They are yellow on the underneath of their body and green above, and have bright blue wings and forehead. Ironically, the orange belly is not obvious in wild birds. Their call sounds like a strange buzzing chatter and is very distinctive.

The wild sedgelands of the western coastal plains, wedged between the Tasmanian mountain massifs and shores pounded by the Southern Ocean, are the only known breeding grounds for this parrot. In little tree hollows protected from the summer storms, pairs raise one or two chicks which are fed a mixture of grass and boronia seeds. The youngsters join the adults in April for what may be a 1000-km flight to wintering grounds along the Coorong on the coast south of Adelaide. Some take the shorter but equally dangerous journey to the coasts of Port Phillip Bay around Melbourne. During the winter the birds live on low-growing plants occurring close to the ocean's edge. Here they are subject to a range of threats including coastal developments, feral animals and constant human disturbance.

Measures in the last two decades to protect the birds have included protecting their wintering grounds. In addition, the breeding areas in Tasmania's south-west are being managed to increase the abundance of preferred seed plants. This is achieved by careful patch-burning of the sedgelands. Such precise targeting and control of the environment has apparently halted the decline of wild birds.

LAKE PEDDER

East of Hobart the Gordon River Road cuts through the centre of the western wilderness to Strathgordon and the flooded Lake Pedder. For most of its length the road passes through or beside World Heritage national parks. The first of these is Mount Field.

Rugged Mount Field
The rugged beauty of Mount Field was recognised in 1916 when it became one of Tasmania's first national parks. An hour's drive west of Hobart, this mountainous region is suitable for a range of winter pursuits, including down-hill and cross-country skiing and mountaineering. Summer activities include bushwalking and wildlife watching.

The park contains a wide range of vegetation, from the high-altitude alpine heaths to protected, lowland temperate rainforests. The Lake Dobson Road, as it winds up from the Tyenna River floor to the highest peaks around Mount Mawson, reveals to visitors a dramatic cross-section of the habitats to be experienced.

Walking at Lake Dobson
At the park's entrance is a basic camp ground and visitor centre, and Lake Dobson offers a number of small huts, to be booked in advance, accessible by vehicle. A number of other huts are accessible to walkers. Short marked walks encompass Russell Falls and Lady Barron Falls. The Lyrebird Loop Walk is located at a point 7km up the Lake Dobson Road. Longer walks start at Lake Fenton and Lake Dobson.

Two recommended round-trip walks are the four-hour walk to Mount Field East and the two-day Lake Dobson–Twilight Tarn–Lake Fenton walk, which circles the Rodway Range. The latter reveals great scenery and allows one to take in the region's diversity. Vehicles require tyre chains for traction in winter on Lake Dobson Road and freezing, wet conditions can be expected at any time of the year.

ABOVE *Still dramatic, Lake Pedder today comprises a large hydro-electric water-storage area that covers the original lake and sparked the campaigns to prevent further loss of Tasmania's wilderness.*

was a unique, strikingly beautiful place, unlike the deep hydro-dam that replaced it. The conservation defeat ignited the determination to stop further hydro projects and started a movement, which in the 1980s, had success in protecting other areas of the south-west. Pressure is building to have the new dam drained in order to resurrect the original Lake Pedder. Ecological surveys reveal the new dam is now home to hundreds of platypus, so the conflict over Lake Pedder remains.

Day and wilderness walks

Many short nature walks are located at the picnic areas along Scotts Peak Road. The Creepy Crawly Walk leaves the road close to where it intersects with the Gordon Dam Road. This 20-minute track twists and turns through the rainforest and its intricate world of invertebrates. Longer, more challenging day walks lead to Lake Judd and Mount Anne. The final ascent to the summit of Mount Anne is a breathtaking challenge.

Wilderness walkers can take the Scotts Peak Road south to the southern edge of Lake Pedder and the beginning of the Port Davey Track. This 60-km, four-day track leads down to Melaleuca on Bathurst Harbour in the heart of the Southwest National Park. Cruise boats operate on these waters. From Melaleuca walkers can fly to Hobart or connect with other wilderness walks. The wild, wet weather of this region is legendary and walkers must be well prepared and take all necessary precautions.

Sentinel Range: heading west

Further west along the Gordon River Road the Southwest National Park boundary is approached at Tim Shee Lookout, about 15km from Maydena. About the same distance further on is the Scotts Peak Dam Road, which heads south. A little further along are excellent views to Sentinel Range and down to Wedges Creek.

For those keen to conquer craggy peaks, the Sentinel Range summit is a good 4km with a climb that is ideal for the fit and adventurous. From the picnic area at Wedge Creek the track heads directly towards the peak but gradually veers to the left as it climbs. Once on the ridge the climb to the top is not so apparent in places.

Lake Pedder: a fight to conserve

Once back on the road it is a half-hour drive to the Gordon and Serpentine dams. A battle to save the original Lake Pedder was lost in 1972 and the Gordon and Upper Huon rivers were dammed. This created two huge hydro-dams, Lake Gordon and Lake Pedder. The original Lake Pedder

How to get there

Mount Field National Park can be reached by vehicle from Hobart through New Norfolk. From here, access to Lake Pedder and Gordon River is via Maydena and Strathgordon. Access to the northern parts of Southwest National Park is south of Junction Hill at Scotts Peak Dam. Coach tours go to Strathgordon and Scotts Peak.
Southwest National Park tel: (03) 6288–1283
Mount Field National Park tel: (03) 6288–1149

HUON

The Huon is a region of forests and caves and the step-off point for intrepid wilderness walks or sea kayak adventures into the wild and largely inaccessible Southwest National Park. The original rare natural resources of the area were minerals, whales and Huon pine. Today, equally rare in the modern world, wilderness adventure touring is the attraction. Lieutenant Colonel Collins, a 19th-century visitor, said that this coast 'ranks amongst the foremost of the grand and wildly magnificent scenes of nature'. Its raw remoteness, exposure to the elements and compelling beauty are almost incomparable in the rest of the world.

Hartz Mountains: dramatic heights
Heading south from Hobart, through the gentle countryside and apple orchards of the Huon Valley, the Hartz Mountains loom on the horizon. Hartz Mountains National Park is the closest World Heritage area to any of Australia's capital cities.

The entrance road to the park passes through state forests before the steep, winding climb to the top of the range. This high mountainous park is subject to the full force of the furious storms from the roaring forties. Bitterly cold snow storms can hit suddenly and at any time of the year so be prepared. Hartz Mountains is an awe-inspiringly powerful and dramatic place.

Walks to Hartz Peak
Short walks are marked to Arve Falls (20 minutes) and Lake Osborne (40 minutes), a serene and picturesque glacial tarn. The dramatic walk to the park's highest point, Hartz Peak, is highly recommended. This walk, exposed to nature's powerful forces, takes about three to five hours return to the car park. The adventurous are rewarded with spectacular scenes of glacial lakes, dolerite peaks and distant wilderness landscapes from the summit. There are simple facilities, including toilets and a shelter shed. Bush camping is allowed on extended walks.

Impressive dolomite caves
Further south Hastings Caves, near Lune River, are the only dolomite caves open to visitors in Australia. One of a group of three, Newdegate Cave was opened in 1939 and is often said to be one of the most impressive caves in the country. The nearby public thermal pools are located by a streamside reserve, which includes picnic sheds and change rooms. The Exit Caves close by have some of the longest systems in Australia and are not open for general public viewing. Private operators do conduct adventure cave expeditions.

ABOVE *The Huon River cuts through the remote Southwest wilderness and opens out onto the D'Entrecasteaux Channel.*

Tasmania's southernmost point

At the end of the road that runs off the Huon Highway towards the Southwest National Park lies Recherche Bay State Recreation Area, a delightful seaside camping spot tucked away from the wet forests and exposed mountain tops. A number of little white beaches line the bay out to the headland ruins and lighthouse.

The beautiful South Cape Bay Walking Track begins at Cockle Creek and leads out to the southernmost point of mainland Tasmania. Here, steps lead down to the beach at South Cape Bay. The walk takes about five hours return. It is a great day's outing into the outskirts of the spectacular Southwest wilderness.

Southwest Track: facing the elements

From Cockle Creek the serious business of wilderness walking begins. The track heads for the famous Southwest Track are at Cockle Creek in the east and at Melaleuca over on the edge of Bathurst Harbour in the west of the park. This five-day, 75-km hike passes through bogs, mud, rain and some of the most untamed wilderness areas left on the globe. With no protection from the fury of the roaring forties, the rugged coastline is battered by wild storms year-round. Melaleuca's annual rainfall averages 2250mm.

The track frequently crosses kilometres of buttongrass swamps as it winds along the coast. It runs over Ironbound Range and Red Point Hills and skirts the desolate beauty of Prion Bay and Cox Bight. There are many side-trips to extend the length of the trek over the five days. Once in the heart of the wilderness at Melaleuca, the return options are varied. The journey can be repeated in reverse or there is a walk up onto the Lost World Plateau, across Arthurs Range and onto Scotts Peak Dam. Road transport can be organised from there. Alternatively the spectacular and more relaxed return route is by light aircraft from Melaleuca to Hobart.

How to get there

Hartz Mountains National Park can be reached by vehicle from Hobart through Geeveston on the Huon Highway. A half-hour further to the south is Hastings Caves and still another half-hour southwards is Cockle Creek, one of the Southwest National Park Track heads. Coaches travel to Cockle Creek. Flights to the area leave from Hobart to Cox Bight and Melaleuca.

Hartz Mountains National Park tel: (03) 6298–1577
Hastings Caves National Park and Wildlife Service tel: (03) 6298–3209

DON'T MISS...

ADVENTURE EXPERIENCES

Many adventure experiences are possible in Tasmania. Bushwalking highlights are the 60-km Overland Track in Cradle Mountain (on your own or on a guided tour with fully equipped Cradle Mountain Huts available), or the 75-km South Coast Track in Southwest National Park.

Whitewater canoeing and rafting trips are available as part of organised trips for a day or for up to 11 days on the Franklin, Cataract and Huon rivers. Organised sea kayaking is conducted on the quiet Derwent estuary near Hobart or on the dramatic waters of the Tasman Peninsula.

Adventure caving can be arranged at Mole Creek (near Launceston in the north), Hastings Caves and Exit Caves (both in the south, off the Huon Highway from Hobart).

Organised cycling tours in the northern regions, down the east coast including Maria Island, and along the Huon are possible along scenic routes and accompanied by support vehicles.

In addition, cross-country skiing, cliff-top hang-gliding, scuba diving and sail charters are available. Rock climbing on classified climbs is possible within an hour of either Launceston or Hobart. Many major climbing sites are found at Cradle Mountain–Lake St Clair National Park and on Flinders Island.
Cradle Huts tel: (03) 6331–2006

Whitewater rafting on the Huon River.

Rafting Tasmania tel: (03) 6227–9516
Wild Cave Tours tel: (03) 6367–8142
Exit Cave Adventure Tours tel: (03) 6243–8546
Brake Out Cycling tel: (03) 6228–5022

OTHER INTERESTING AREAS

Otherwise difficult to visit, there are seaplane flights and cruises from Strahan to Macquarie Harbour and into or over the lower reaches of the Franklin–Gordon Wild Rivers National Park.
Strahan Wharf Centre tel: (03) 6471–7488

Contact Numbers

Every effort has been made to ensure these phone numbers are correct at the time of publishing. Should you have difficulties, please check the local telephone directories or contact regional directory assistance on 0175.

Australian Tourist Commission
Level 3, 80 William Street
Woolloomooloo NSW 2011
Ph: (02) 9360-1111; Fx: 9331-6469

TOUR OPERATORS
Aircruising Australia
Ross Smith Avenue
Mascot NSW 2020
Ph: (02) 9693-2233; Fx: 9669-6064

World Expeditions
3rd Floor, 441 Kent Street
Sydney NSW 2000
Ph: (02) 9264-3366; Fx: 9261-1974
Toll free: 1 800 803 688

Peregrine Tours
Level 5, 38 York Street
Sydney NSW 2000
Ph: (02) 9290-2770; Fx: 9290-2155

Echo Experience
22 Bennett Street
Marylands SA 5000
Ph: (08) 8363-4234

Ecotour Travel Agency
Level 1, 99 Elizabeth Street
Sydney NSW 2000
Ph: (02) 9223-2811; Fx: 9223-2260

Australian Ecotours
2 Drysdale Place
Mooroolbark VIC 3138
Ph: (03) 9726-8471; Fx: 9727-1545

Auswalk
(accommodated, escorted & self-guided walking tours in Victoria, NSW and Queensland)
GPO Box 13
Northcote VIC 3070
Ph: (03) 9482-1206; Fx: 9482-6844

Great Australian Walks
(accommodated, escorted & self-guided national walking tours)
Suite 2, 637 Darling Street
Rozelle NSW 2039
Ph: (02) 9555-7580; Fx: 9810-6429

Australian Eco Adventures
(wholesale tour operator)
PO Box 297
Newport NSW 2106
Ph: (02) 9979-5850; Fx: 9979-5743

Australian Wilderness Expeditions
(specialises in cultural & natural tours of northern Australia)
GPO Box 1221
Darwin NT 0801
Ph: (08) 8981-0888; Fx: 8941-3881

Willis Walkabouts
(two- to three-week bushwalks in northern Australia)
12 Carrington Street
Millner NT 0810
Ph: (08) 8985-2134; Fx: 8985-2355

National Transport Operators
Greyhound Pioneer
(national scheduled coach travel)
Reservations Ph: 13-20-30

MAPS
Australian Surveying and Land Information Group
(for detailed topographic maps & specialist maps covering Australia)
PO Box 2
Belconnen ACT 2616
Ph: (02) 6201-4201; Fx: 6201-4366

Westprint Maps and Travel Guides
(for detailed maps & guides to wilderness & remote regions)
RMB 33
Nhill VIC 3418
Ph: (03) 5391-5233

Hema Maps
(national, regional & national park maps & atlas)
24 Allgas Street
Slacks Creek QLD 4127
Ph: (07) 3290-0322; Fx: 3290–0478

ASSOCIATIONS
Australian Canoe Federation
PO Box 666
Glebe NSW 2037
Ph: (02) 9552-4500; Fx: 9552-4457

Australian Sport Climbing Federation
(affiliated with UIAA)
GPO Box 3786
Sydney NSW 2001
Ph: (02) 9264-2908; Fx: 9264-2035

Australian and New Zealand Scientific Exploration Society
PO Box 174
Albert Park VIC 3206
Ph: (03) 9866-8699

Ecotourism Association of Australia
PO Box 26
Red Hill QLD 4059
Ph: (07) 3352-7220

GOVERNMENT
NSW Travel Centre
11–31 York Street
(GPO Box 11)
Sydney NSW 2000
Ph: 13-20-77; Fx: (02) 9224-4411

Canberra Tourism
Level 13, CBS Tower
Bunda Street
Canberra ACT 2601
Ph: (02) 6205-0044; Fx: 6205-0629

NSW National Parks and Wildlife Service
43 Bridge Street
Hurstville NSW 2220
Ph: (02) 9585-6444; Fx: 9585-6555
State-wide Information (02) 9585-6333

ACT Parks and Conservation Service
(park information, maps & brochures)
PO Box 1119
Tuggeranong ACT 2901
Ph: (02) 6207-2334; Fx: 6207-2335

NSW State Forests
Locked Bag 23
Pennant Hills NSW 2120
Ph: (02) 9980-4100; Fx: 9481-8510

MAPS
Land Information Centre
Panorama Avenue
(PO Box 1557)
Bathurst NSW 2795
Ph: (02) 6332-8200; Fx: 6331-8095

Map World
338 Pacific Highway
Lane Cove NSW 2066
Ph: (02) 9428-3566; Fx: 9428-4602

Traveller Maps and Guides
65 Northbourne Avenue
Canberra City ACT 2601
Ph: (02) 6249-6006; Fx: 6257-4446

TOUR OPERATORS
World Expeditions
(rafting, sailing, bushwalking & cycling tours)
3rd Floor, 441 Kent Street
Sydney NSW 2000
Ph: (02) 9264-3366; Fx: (02) 9261-1974
Toll free: 1 800 803 688

Peregrine Tours
(rafting & canoeing)
Level 5, 38 York Street
Sydney NSW 2000
Ph: (02) 9290-2770; Fx: 9290-2155

Country Walks
(guided bushwalking in the Blue Mountains)

PO Box 65
Leura NSW 2780
Ph: (02) 4784-3266; Fx: 4731-7759

Wander Round Nature Tours
(small group four-wheel-drive tours of northern NSW rainforests)
PO Box 325
Kingscliff NSW 2487
Ph: (02) 6674-0909; Fx: 6674-4211

Wildframe Ecotours
(day tours of Blue Mountains & other regions near Sydney)
720A Anzac Parade
Kingsford NSW 2032
Ph: (02) 9314-0658; Fx: 9344-5691

High Adventure
(Blue Mountains rock climbing)
182 Katoomba Street
Katoomba NSW 2780
Ph: (02) 4782-2014; Fx: 4782-5787

TRANSPORT
Countrylink Railway Travel
Bookings Ph: 13-22-32
Information ph: (02) 9224-4744
Fx: (02) 9224-4513

NRMA
(details on road conditions & maps)
151 Clarence Street
Sydney NSW 2000
Ph: (02) 9260-9222; Fx: 9292-8786
Emergency help ph: 13-21-32

ACCOMMODATION
Youth Hostels Association
422 Kent Street
Sydney NSW 2000
Ph: (02) 9261-1111; Fx: 9261-1969

Crystal Creek Rainforest Retreat
(cabin accommodation on large private rainforest reserve)
PO Box 69
Murwillumbah NSW 2484
Ph: (02) 6679-1591; Fx: 6679-1596

Jemby–Rinjah Lodge
(environmentally friendly cabin-style lodge)
336 Evans Head Lookout Road
Blackheath NSW 2785
Ph: (02) 4787-7622; Fx: 4787-6230

GOVERNMENT
Queensland Government Travel Centre
196 Adelaide Street
Brisbane QLD 4000
Ph: 13-18-01

Queensland National Parks and Wildlife Service

160 Ann Street
(PO Box 150)
Brisbane QLD 4002
Ph: (07) 3227-7801
Fx: 3227-6534/7676

DPI Queensland Forestry Service
160 Mary Street
(GPO Box 944)
Brisbane QLD 4001
Ph: (07) 3234-0159

Natural Water Resources
Cnr George and Margaret streets
(GPO Box 2454)
Brisbane QLD 4001
Ph: (07) 3224-8884; Fx: 3224-8922

Aboriginal Land
(for permits to enter Aboriginal land
write to individual councils via the
Aboriginal Coordinating Council)
North Queensland Land Council
GPO Box 679
Cairns QLD 4870
Ph: (07) 4031-4843; Fx: 4031-7414

MAPS
Sunmap
Locked Bag 40
Coorparoo Street
Coorparoo QLD 4151
Ph: (07) 3896-3333

World Wide Maps and Guides
187 George Street
Brisbane QLD 4000
Ph: (07) 3221-4330; Fx: 3211-3684

TOUR OPERATORS
Peregrine Tours
(rafting, canoeing, sea kayaking,
four-wheel-drive safaris from Cairns)
258 Lonsdale Street
Melbourne VIC 3000
Ph: (03) 9663-8611; Fx: 9662-2422

Down Under Tours
(luxury coach tours of north
Queensland)
26 Redden Street
Portsmouth, Cairns QLD 4870
Ph: 008-079-119; Fx: 4035-5588

Far Horizons Nature Tours
(small group nature tours in
southern Queensland)
PO Box 49
Woody Point QLD 4019
Ph: (07) 3284-5475; Fx: 3883-1399

Discover Fraser Island Tours
(All inclusive four-wheel-drive tours
of Fraser Island)
PO Box 771
Cleveland QLD 4163
Ph/Fx: (07) 3821-1694

Wait-a-while Rainforest Tours
PO Box 6647
Cairns QLD 4870
Ph: (07) 4033-1153; Fx: (07) 4031-3783

TRANSPORT
Queensland Rail
Info Line ph: 13-22-32

Flight West Airlines
GPO Box 1126
Eagle Farm QLD 4008
Toll free: 1 800 777 879
Fx: (07) 3212-1297

Jolly Frog
(four-wheel-drive & minibus rentals,
including one-way Gold Coast–Cairns)
147 Sharon Street
Cairns Qld 4870
Ph: (07) 4031-2379; Fx: 4031-1452

Royal Automobile Club of
Queensland (RACQ)
(details on road conditions & maps)
300 St Pauls Terrace
Fortitude Valley QLD 4006
Ph: (07) 3361-2444
Recorded road information: (07) 11655

ACCOMMODATION
Youth Hostels Association
GPO Box 1128
Brisbane QLD 4001
Ph: (07) 3236-1680; Fx: 3236-1702

Heron Island Resort
GPO Box 5287
Sydney NSW 2001
Ph: 13-24-69; Fx: (02) 9299-2477

Kingfisher Bay Resort, Fraser Island
GPO Box 1122
Brisbane QLD 4001
Toll free: 1 800 072 555
Fx: (07) 3221-3270

Daintree Wilderness Lodge
PO Box 532
Mossman QLD 4873
Ph: (07) 4098-6125
Fx: 4098-6192

Pajinka Wilderness Lodge
PO Box 7757
Cairns QLD 4870
Ph: (07) 4069-2100
Fx: (07) 4031-3966

| NT STATE CONTACTS |
GOVERNMENT
Northern Territory Tourist
Commission
GPO Box 2532
Alice Springs NT 0871
Toll free: 1 800 621 336
Toll free fx: 1 800 808 666

Australian Nature Conservation Agency
(Kakadu & Uluru national parks)
PO Box 1260
Darwin NT 0800
Ph: (08) 8946-4300; Fx: 8981-3497

Parks and Wildlife Commission of
the Northern Territory
(for Darwin & Top End)
PO Box 496
Palmerston NT 0831
Ph: (08) 8999-4555; Fx: 8999-4558

(for Alice Springs and the Centre)
PO Box 1046
Alice Springs NT 0871
Ph: (08) 8951-8211; Fx: 8951-8268

Aboriginal Land Council
Pitjantjatjara Land Council
(for permits to cross Aboriginal land
in central Australia – most major
towns & tourist destinations, eg
Uluru, can be visited by road
without permits)
PO Box 3321
Alice Springs NT 0871
Ph: (08) 8953-4400

Northern Land Council
(for permits to cross Aboriginal land
in the Top End. Most major towns &
tourist destinations, eg Kakadu, can be
visited by road without permits)
PO Box 42921
Casuarina NT 0811
Ph: (08) 8920-5178; Fx: 8945-2633

Tiwi Land Council
(for details on Melville and
Bathurst islands)
Wingate Centre
(PO Box 38545)
Winnellie NT 0821
Ph: (08) 8978-3755

MAPS
Maps Northern Territory
(for speciality maps of places within
the Northern Territory; Map Sales,
Land Planning and Environment)
PO Box 1680
Darwin NT 0801
Ph: (08) 8999-7032; Fx: 8999-7750

TOUR OPERATORS
World Expeditions
(safaris, bushwalking & cycling tours)
3rd Floor, 441 Kent Street
Sydney NSW 2000
Ph: 1 800 803 688; Fx: (02) 9261-1974

Kakadu Parklink
(tours of Kakadu National Park)
PO Box 95
Jabiru NT 0866
Ph: 008-088-9113; Fx: 8979-2303

Uluru Experience
(tours of Central Australia)
PO Box 188
Yulara NT 0872
Ph: (08) 8956-2563; Fx: 8956-2711

TRANSPORT
Automobile Association of the
Northern Territory (AANT)
(for road condition details, emergency
assistance & maps)
Shop 4, 105 Gregory Terrace
(PO Box 3353)
Alice Springs NT 0871
Ph: (08) 8953-1322; Fx: 8952-3716
For Darwin ph: (08) 8981-3837

ACCOMMODATION
Yulara (Ayers Rock) Resort
GPO Box 3589
Sydney NSW 2000
Ph: (02) 9360-9099; Fx: 9332-4555

Ayers Rock Campground
GPO Box 96
Yulara NT 0872
Ph: (08) 8956-2055; Fx: 8956-2260

Kings Canyon Resort, Watarrka
(deluxe motel, cabin & camping)
Lurilka Road
Watarrka NT 0872
Ph: (08) 8956-7442
Fx: 8956-7410

MacDonnell Ranges
(Deluxe lodge or camp in the park;
modern camping facilities at Ross
River in the East MacDonnells)
Ph: (08) 8956-8711

Glen Helen, West MacDonnells
Ph: (08) 8956-7489

All Seasons Frontier Oasis
(deluxe motel, cabin & camping)
10 Gap Road
(GPO Box 161)
Alice Springs NT 0871
Ph: 1 800 815 658
Fx: (08) 8952-3776

Australia/Asia Pacific Hotel
GPO Box 465
Darwin NT 0801
Ph: (08) 8946-3740
Fx: 8941-3763

Toddy's Backpacker
41 Gap Road
Alice Spring NT 0871
Ph: (08) 8952-1322; Fx: 8952-1767

YHA, Alice Springs
GPO 1019
Alice Springs NT 0871
Ph: (08) 8952-8855; Fx: 8952-1767

YHA, Darwin
GPO Box 2556
Darwin NT 0801
Ph: (08) 8981-3995; Fx: 8981-6674

Frontier Kakadu Village
GPO Box 721
Jabiru NT 721
Toll free: 1 800 811 154
Fx: (08) 8979-2254

Frontier Katherine
Stuart Highway
Katherine NT 0850
Toll free: 1 800 812 443
Fx: (08) 8972-2790

Backpacker Palm Court
Parkway Motel
(GPO Box 1452)
Kalbarri NT 0851
Ph: (08) 8972-2644; Fx: 8972-2720

WA STATE CONTACTS

GOVERNMENT
Western Australian Tourist Centre
Forest Place
(GPO Box W2081)
Perth WA 6001
Ph: (08) 9483-1111
Fx: 9481-0190
Toll free: 1 800 812 808

Department of Conservation and
Land Management (CALM)
(park & forestry information, maps
& brochures)
50 Hayman Road
Como WA 6152
Ph: (08) 9334-0333; Fx: 9334-0498

Aboriginal Affairs Planning Authority
(for permits to cross or enter
Aboriginal land)
Cloisters Square
(PO Box 7770)
Perth WA 6850
Ph: (08) 9235-8000; Fx: 9235-8088

MAPS
Perth Map Centre
1st Floor, 894 Hay Street
Perth WA 6850
Ph: (08) 9322-5733; Fx: 9322-5673

TOUR OPERATORS
Dirk Hartog Island Tours
GPO Box 81
Applecross WA 6153
Ph: (08) 9316-2971
Fx: 9316–2959

Eremia Camel Treks
(remote week-long camping treks)
Lot 117 Hopetoun Road
Ravensthorpe WA 6346
Ph: (08) 9838-1092

Nangar Wilderness Backpacking
Expeditions
GPO Box 1209
East Victoria Park WA 6101
Ph: (08) 9458-9738

Perth and Beyond
GPO Box 705
Mount Claremont WA 6010
Ph: (08) 9389-8601
Fx: 9389-8773

Sail Training Ship Leeuwin
Leeuwin Sail Training Foundation
PO Box 1100
Fremantle WA 6160
Ph: (08) 9430-4105
Fx: 9430-4494

Design A Tour
(small group four-wheel-drive tours
to Karijini & Pilbara region)
PO Box 155
Port Hedland WA 6721
Ph: (08) 9144-1460
Fx: 9144-2397

Pinnacle Tours
(coach & four-wheel-drive tours
from Perth north to Exmouth)
533 Hay Street
Perth WA 6000
Ph: (08) 9221-5411; Fx: 9221-5477

Footprints Expeditions
(camping safaris in Western
Australia & Northern Territory)
15 Bentley Close
Mount Claremont WA 6010
Ph: (08) 9385-2534; Fx: 9385-2534

Ningaloo Safari Tours
(natural history tours of the Cape
Range National Park)
PO Box 203
Exmouth WA 6707
Ph/Fx: (08) 9949-1550

Discover West Holidays
(extended four-wheel-drive tours
throughout the state)
PO Box 8451
Perth WA 6849
Ph: (08) 9328-4277
Fx: 9227-5867

Western Geographic Eco Tours
31 Marmion Street
Fremantle WA 6160
Ph: (08) 9336-4992; Fx: 9336-4485

TRANSPORT
Royal Automobile Club of Western
Australia (RACWA)
228 Adelaide Terrace
Perth WA 6000
Ph: (08) 9421-4000

ACCOMMODATION
Youth Hostels Association WA
286 William Street
Northbridge WA 6003
Ph: (08) 9227-5122; Fx: 9227-5123

El Questro Station
(luxury & camping accommodation
on a remote cattle station)
GPO Box 909
Kununurra WA 6743
Ph: (08) 9161-4318; Fx: 9161-4355

SA STATE CONTACTS

GOVERNMENT
South Australia Travel Centre
(tour information &bookings)
1 King William Street
(GPO Box 1972)
Adelaide SA 5000
Ph: (08) 8212-1505; Fx: 8430-3223

Department of Environment
and Natural Resources
(park information, maps & brochures)
77 Grenfell Street
(GPO Box 1047)
Adelaide SA 5000
Ph: (08) 8204-1910; Fx: 8204-1919

Aboriginal Land Councils
(for permits to enter & cross
Aboriginal land)
Pitjantjatjara Land Council
PO Box 2189
Alice Springs NT 0871
Ph: (08) 8950-5411; Fx: 8952-6371

Maralinga Tjaruta Tribal Council
PO Box 435
Ceduna SA 5690
Ph: (08) 8625-2946; Fx: 8625-3076

MAPS
The Map Shop, Adelaide
16A Peel Street
Adelaide SA 5000
Ph: (08) 8231-2033; Fx: 8231-2373

TOUR OPERATORS
Ecotrek
(walking & canoeing tours in SA,
particularly Flinders Ranges &
Kangaroo Island)
PO Box 4
Kangarilla SA 5157
Ph: (08) 8383-7198
Fx: 8383-7377

Exploranges
(hiking tours of South Australia,
particularly Flinders & Gawler
ranges & Kangaroo Island)
Glenelg Street
(GPO Box 1100)
Somerton Park SA 5044
Ph/Fx: (08) 8294-6530

Chris Paines Outback Australia
(small group four-wheel-drive travel
to remote inland locations)
James Road
Clare SA 5453
Ph: (08) 8842-3469; Fx: 8842-2586

Peregrine Travel
Scout Outdoor Centre
192 Rundle Street
Adelaide SA 5000
Ph: (08) 8223-5905; Fx: 8223-5347

Outback Camel Co
(extended camel safaris in the
central deserts)
PMB 53
Waikerie SA 5330
Ph/Fx: (08) 8543-2280
Toll free: 1 800 625 556

Blackwater rafting
(rafting in the caves of the
Nullarbor Plain)
Ph: (08) 8388-2552
Fx: 8388-2552

Wildlife Experience Tours
(walking & kayaking – day &
overnight tours)
GPO Box 912
Victor Harbour SA 5071
Ph: (08) 8554-6555
Fx: 8552-5722

Wilderness Escape Outdoor
Adventures
(adventure tours & hikes
throughout South Australia)
PO Box 639
Kent Town SA 5071
Ph: (08) 8414 5813
Fx: 8331-0148

FreeWheeling Australia
(4- 10-day mountain bike
tours departing Adelaide)
235 Pirie Street
Adelaide SA 5000
Ph: (08) 8359-3344
Fx: 8359-3355

TRANSPORT
Royal Automobile Association
of South Australia (RAASA)
(details on road conditions & maps)
41 Hindmarsh Square
Adelaide SA 5000
Ph: (08) 8202-4500
Recorded road information (08) 11633

ACCOMMODATION
Youth Hostels Association
38 Sturt Street
Adelaide SA 5000
Ph: (08) 8231-5583
Fx 8231-4219

Arkaroola Resort and Wildlife
Sanctuary
via Port Augusta SA 5700
Ph: (08) 8648-4848; Fx: 8648-4846

Meranwyney Farmstay Homestead
(commercial cereal farm & wildlife
sanctuary adjacent to mallee
conservation park)
PO Box 51
Lameroo SA 5302
Ph: (08) 8576-5215

GOVERNMENT
Tourism Victoria
(tour information & bookings)
403 George Street
Sydney NSW 2000
Ph: (02) 9299-2288; Fx: 9299-2425

Natural Resources and Environment
Department (NR and Environment)
(details, maps & brochures on national
parks & state forests)
Outdoor Information Centre
240/250 Victoria Parade
East Melbourne VIC 3002
Ph: (03) 9412-4795; Fx: 9412-4835

Alpine Resorts Commission
(all state alpine resorts except
Mount Buffalo)
36 Rutland Road
Boxhill VIC 3128
Ph: (03) 9895-6900; Fx: 9899-3410

MAPS
Melbourne Map Centre
740 Waverley Road
Chadstone Vic 3148
Ph: (03) 9569-5472; Fx: 9569-8000

TOUR OPERATORS
World Expeditions
(rafting, bushwalking &
cycling tours)
1st Floor, 393 Little Bourke Street
Melbourne VIC 3000
Ph: (03) 9670-8400
Fx: 9670-8474
Toll free: 1 800 803 688

Peregrine Tours
(rafting & canoeing tours)
258 Lonsdale Street
Melbourne VIC 3000
Ph: (03) 9663-8611
Fx: 9662-2422

Bogong Jack Adventures
(cycling, walking & canoeing tours
in the Victorian Alps)
PO Box 221
Oxley VIC 3678
Ph: (03) 5727-3382
Fx: 5727-3559

Grampian National Park Tours
C/- GPO Box
Halls Gap VIC 3381
Ph: (03) 5356-6221; Fx: 5356-6330

Adventure and Climbing Expeditions
247 East Boundary Road
East Bentleigh VIC 3165
Ph: (03) 9570-1651; Fx: 9570-3810

Snowy River Expeditions
Karoonda Park
Gelanteipy VIC 3005
Ph: (03) 5155-9353

Ricks Rambles
(day walks & longer bushwalks in
central Victoria)
PO Box 616
Ballarat VIC 3353
Ph: (03) 5339-5256

Journey Beyond Eco Adventures
PO Box 177
Mallacoota VIC 3892
Ph: (03) 5158-0166
Fx: 5158-0909

Gippsland High Country Tours
(nature-based walking tours in the
eastern alpine parks)
PO Box 69
Bruthen VIC 3885
Ph: (03) 5157-5556; Fx: 5158-6866

Walkabout Gourmet Adventures
(summer walking tours in the
Victorian alps)
Big Muster Drive
(GPO Box 52)
Dinner Plain VIC 3898
Ph: (03) 5159-6556
Fx: 5159-6508

TRANSPORT
Peninsula Searoad Transport
(daily passenger & car ferry to
Queenscliffe & Sorrento)
GPO Box 204
Queenscliffe VIC 3225
Ph: (03) 5258-3244; Fx: 5258-1877

Royal Automobile Club of
Victoria (RACV)
(details on road conditions & maps)
550 Princes Highway
Noble Park VIC 3174
Ph: (03) 9790-2755
Emergency help ph: 13-11-11
Fx: (03) 9790-2628

ACCOMMODATION
Youth Hostels Association, Victoria
205 King Street
Melbourne VIC 3000
Ph: (03) 9670-9611
Fx: 9670-9840

Mount Buffalo Chalet
Mount Buffalo VIC 3745
Ph: (03) 5755-1500; Fx: 5755-1892
Gipsy Point Lodge
Gipsy Point VIC 3891
Ph: (03) 5158-8205; Fx: 5158-8225

Coolart Wetlands and Homestead
PO Box 84
Balnarring VIC 3926
Ph: (03) 5983-1333; Fx: 5983-1644

Victorian Host Farms Association
(private residences, cabins on
farms, historic homes)
332 Banyule Road
View Bank VIC 3084
Ph: (03) 9457-5413; Fx: 9457-6725

GOVERNMENT
Tasmanian Government Travel
Information Service
20 Davey Street
Hobart TAS 7001
Toll free: 008-068-900
Fx: (03) 6230-8233

Forestry Tasmania
199 Macquarie Street
(GPO Box 270B)
Hobart TAS 7000
Ph: (03) 6233-8203
Fx: 6334-3463

Parks and Wildlife Service
GPO Box 44A
Hobart TAS 7001
Ph: (03) 6233-6191

TOUR OPERATORS
World Expeditions
see Australia General

Tasmanian Expeditions
(cycling, walking, rafting & climbing)
110 George Street
Launceston TAS 7250
Toll free 1 800 030 230
Fx: (03) 6231-7759

Rafting Tasmania
(rafting & canoeing trips)
GPO Box 403
Sandy Bay TAS 7006
Ph: (03) 6227-9516; Fx: 6227-9679

Tasmanian Highland Tours
PO Box 168
La Trobe TAS 7307
Ph: (03) 6426-9312
Fx 6426-9350

Tasmanian Wilderness Travel
(tours, bus passes & wilderness
transport)
Ph: (03) 6234-4442

TRANSPORT
Bass Strait Line
(ferry between Tasmania & Victoria)
TT Line Reservations
Ph: 13-20-10

Tasair
(wilderness flights & bushwalker
drops & pickups)
GPO Box 415E
Hobart TAS 7000
Ph: (03) 6248-5088; Fx: 6248-5528

Wilderness Air
(seaplane tours to Gordon River)
GPO Box 92
Strahan TAS 7468
Ph: (03) 6271-7280; Fx: 6271-7317

Gordon River Cruises
Strahan TAS 7468
Ph: (03) 6271-7187; Fx: 6271-7317

Royal Automobile Club of Tasmania
(RACT)
Cnr Murray and Patrick streets
(GPO Box 1292)
Hobart TAS 7000
Ph: (03) 6232-6300; 6234-8784
Emergency ph: 13-11-11

ACCOMMODATION
Youth Hostels Association
GPO Box 174
Hobart TAS 7001
Ph: (03) 6234-9617; Fx: 6234-7422

Cradle Mountain Lodge
GPO Box 5287
Sydney NSW 2001
Ph: 13-24-69; Fx: (02) 9299-2477

Cradle Huts Pty Ltd
PO Box 1879
Launceston TAS 7250
Ph: (03) 6231-2006; Fx: 6231-5525

Tasvillas and Innkeepers Hotels
and Apartments
147 Patterson Street
Launceston TAS 7250
Ph: (03) 6331-6699
Fx: 6231-2168
Toll free: 1 800 030 111

Home Host and Heritage Tasmania
(private residences, cabins on farms,
historic homes)
PO Box 780
Sandy Bay TAS 7005
Ph: (03) 6224-1612
Fx: 6224-0472

Tasmanian Campervan Hire
PO Box 1129
Cremorne TAS 7001
Ph: (03) 6248-9623; Fx: 6248-9525

INDEX